GV
365
.N48
1999

SO-AHA-888

The New Leadership Paradigm for Physical Education

What We Really Need to Lead

Editor/Author
Bonnie Mohnsen

Co-Authors
Jayne Greenberg
Bobbie Harris
Dorri Hawkes
Betty Hennessy
Karen Mendon
Rita Mercier
Spencer Sartorius
Carolyn Thompson
Kathy Ermler

WITHDRAWN

Published by the
National Association for Sport and Physical Education (NASPE)
an association of the
American Association for Health, Physical Education, Recreation and Dance

NASPE Publications
1900 Association Drive
Reston, VA 20191-1599
(703)476-3410
naspe@aahperd.org

GOSHEN COLLEGE LIBRARY
GOSHEN, INDIANA

Copyright © 1999
National Association for Sport and Physical Education, an association of the American Alliance for
Health, Physical Education, Recreation and Dance.

All rights reserved.
Reproduction of this work in any form or by any electronic, mechanical, or other means, including photo-
copying or storage in any information retrieval system is expressly forbidden without the written permission of the publisher. Requests for permission to make copies of any part of the work should be mailed
to: NASPE Publications, 1900 Association Drive, Reston, VA 20191-1599.

Address orders to: AAHPERD Publications, P.O. Box 385, Oxon Hill, MD 20750-0385, or call 1-800-
321-0789. Order Stock No. 304-10176.

Printed in the United States of America.

ISBN: 0-88314-706-8

Copy Editing: Carol A. Bruce
Graphic and Cover Design: Carole A. Thieme

Dedication

To the leaders of today and tomorrow—may they lead by positive example

4/5/99   PHEIBKR

So, you want to be a leader. Do you know yourself? Are you open to feedback? Are you eager to learn and to improve? Are you curious? Do you take risks? Do you concentrate at work? Do you learn from adversity? Can you balance tradition and change? Do you have open communication channels? Do you work well within the system? Do you serve as a model or mentor? If so, this book is for you!

There are currently several management books on the market that target physical education and athletics. However, these books focus on the theory of management and assume that the individuals leading our field are in "official" administrative positions.

This is not the case in today's world. In many school districts today, there are no physical education supervisors, directors, or coordinators. This begs the question, "Who is minding the store, and what skills and knowledge do these individuals have to lead the field of physical education through the twenty-first century?"

This book acknowledges the current state of affairs and provides a practical approach to current leadership theories as applied to the many duties of a physical education leader. In addition, it takes into consideration the various individuals who currently assume leadership roles in our profession.

This book is definitely timely, since it is closely linked to the recent publication by NASPE of *Moving into the Future: National Physical Education Standards: A Guide to Content Assessment, Concepts for Physical Education: What Every Student Needs to Know, National Standards for Beginning Physical Education Teachers, Developmentally Appropriate Practice in Movement Programs for Young Children: Ages 3–5, Developmentally Appropriate Physical Education Practices for Children, Appropriate Practices for Middle School Physical Education, Appropriate Practices for High School Physical Education, Physical Education Program Improvement and Self Study Guides: Middle School, Physical Education Program Improvement and Self Study Guides: High School, Physical Education Program Improvement and Appraisal Checklist for Elementary School, Shape of the Nation,* and *Including Students with Disabilities in Regular Physical Education.* It provides important information for the leaders who will chart the course of physical education in this era of educational reform, standards and assessment, and accountability.

The first part of the book looks at the changing role of leadership and the leadership skills required for success in the next decade. Part 2 delves into the various tasks required of a leader, including dealing with change, developing curricula, creating assessment and accountability tools, planning professional development opportunities, finding financial assistance, and applying and promoting the use of technology. Part 2 provides all physical educators, regardless of their current roles, with the knowledge and skills necessary to become a leader.

The third part of this book looks at the position of leadership from a variety of perspectives, including state director of physical education, regional coordinator of physical education, district director of physical education, high school physical education teacher and department chairperson, middle school physical education teacher and team leader, and elementary school teacher. Part 4 turns an eye on the future and looks at how current trends in education may affect physical education and the role of leadership.

Each chapter in this book is organized around seven key points. The latest in brain-based learning research suggests that seven is the maximum number of items that an individual can retain in short-term memory at one time. Therefore, each author has selected the seven most significant points related to the chapter topic, so that you—the leader—can focus on the most critical information as you lead the way for your fellow physical educators.

TABLE OF CONTENTS

Part 1. Where To Start

Leaders take initiative, make things happen, dream dreams, and then translate them into reality. Leaders attract the commitment of followers, energize them, and transform programs and organizations into new entities with greater potential for survival, growth, and excellence. Effective leadership empowers a program or organization to maximize its contribution to the well being of its constituents and the larger society of which it is a part. If managers are known for their skill in solving problems, then leaders are known for being masters in designing and building institutions; they are the architects of the organization's future.

–Adapted from Burt Nanus
The Leader's Edge: The Seven Keys to Leadership in a Turbulent World

Leadership— a behavioral process in which one person attempts to influence other people's behavior toward the accomplishment of goals.

Wanted: Leaders for the Twenty-First Century

Bonnie Mohnsen

Research demonstrates that leadership is essential to substantive and enduring progress in business and education (Schmoker 1996, p. 67). Teachers, principals, and central office administrators all acknowledge that physical education leaders play a key role in the success of the physical education program (Evaul 1995). Physical education leaders range from teachers, to mentor teachers, to department chairpersons, to school district administrators, to regional administrators, to state-level administrators. And, while each person and each position is unique, each also must blend the art and science of leadership to ensure continued progress toward the vision of quality physical education.

FIGURE 1.1: Leaders versus Managers

MANAGER	LEADER
Administers	Innovates
Maintains	Develops
Controls	Empowers
Short-term views	Long-range perspectives
Accepts status quo	Challenges status quo
Focuses on structure	Focuses on people
Commands	Communicates
Imitates	Originates
Reacts to change	Initiates change
Fixes the blame	Fixes the problem
Takes credit	Gives acknowledgment
Manages today's crisis	Creates tomorrow's opportunities
Does things right	Does the right things

Although the terms "leader" and "manager" may be thought of as synonymous, writers in the field of leadership have begun to delineate the differences between the two (see Figure 1.1). I believe it is clear—after looking at the characteristics of each—that we need leadership, not management, in physical education for the twenty-first century. Think about the roots for both of these words: leadership comes from "guide," and management

comes from "hand." Both in terms of teaching and leadership, the future needs the "guide on the side" (the facilitator), not the "sage on the stage" (the commander).

Leadership in the twenty-first century will require **strength** of character and conviction, **endurance** for advocacy, and **flexibility** for changing the immediate objective without compromising the long-range plan. The leader also must possess the **cognitive skills** for planning, organizing, staffing, directing, coordinating, and reporting, while at the same time remaining sensitive to those who are responsible for delivering the vision—the physical educators. An individual with these skills will be physically and mentally fit and able to perform the many tasks required of a physical education leader.

The seven major points to be made in this chapter are:

1. Wanted: Passionate Leader

2. Wanted: Visionary

3. Wanted: Life Long Learner

4. Wanted: Risk Taker

5. Wanted: Moral and Ethical Character

6. Wanted: Efficient Worker

7. Wanted: Adaptable Style.

Wanted: Passionate Leader

One of the easiest ways to determine the type of leader you want to be is to look at the type of leader you want to follow. What makes this physical educator unique and different from others? No doubt this individual models leadership through personal example and dedication. He or she creates standards of excellence and sets high expectations for all to achieve.

During the early 1900s, leadership was defined by the "great man theory." This theory held that by identifying and adopting the characteristics or traits of great leaders, anyone could become one. While we now know that the ability to lead is far more complex than a series of characteristics or traits, researchers still search for those traits that separate great leaders from others in their fields.

Great leaders tend to possess vision, compassion, courage, conviction, competence, integrity, character, energy, persistence, self-confidence, composure, humor, knowledge, and, above all, respect for others (Zand 1997, Waitley 1995, Senge 1990,

Kouzes & Posner 1995). These leaders also tend to be effective communicators, decision makers, planners, and risk takers. When leaders are at their best, they challenge the process, inspire a shared vision, enable others to act, model the way, and encourage the heart (Kouzes & Posner 1995).

When I look at the type of physical educators whom I want to follow, I find they have many, but perhaps not all, of the characteristics outlined in the previous paragraph. But, one characteristic that they all seem to possess is a sense of passion. Many people go to work in order to earn a living to pay for food and other basic necessities; great leaders seem to work because they "must." They are compelled to create quality physical education programs not only because they want to, but also because they need to. There exists in each of them a desire, love, and enthusiasm for performing the task at hand.

Passionate leaders are committed to quality physical education—not an elusive goal, but a measurable outcome. They have accepted the obligation to lead, guide, and facilitate. These leaders have found the purpose in their lives. They possess a harmony that comes from their ability to blend and integrate their personal and professional needs and desires.

Wanted: Visionary

What is a compelling idea or purpose; what is a vision? A vision is the picture we carry around of what we want to create. It defines the ideal physical education program. It is one part insight and one part foresight, along with plenty of imagination and creativity. A vision must be ambitious; it must set standards of excellence and reflect high ideals. It must clarify both purpose and direction. In order to be effective, a vision must be well articulated and easily understood by those who will turn the vision into reality. A vision answers the questions:

- Where are we going?

- Why are we going there?

- How will we get there?

- What will we do once we get there?

Visionary leaders spark others' imaginations with compelling ideas that extend beyond what is known today. They can translate the ideas into reality. Visionary leaders passionately believe they can make a difference. They envision the future, creating an ideal and unique image of what physical education can become. They ensure that amid the daily crises, the dream remains at the center of all work.

A shared vision must be cultivated in order to secure and maintain the involvement of others. A shared vision connects with the personal visions of each person involved with its implementation. People want to be a part of something greater than themselves; something where they can contribute their energy, skills, and abilities.

Visionary leaders provide that "something." Through their strong appeal and persuasion, they enlist others in the dream of quality physical education for all students. They breathe life into the shared vision and get people to see the exciting future possibilities (Kouzes & Posner 1995). Visionary leaders nourish the dream by keeping all participants fully aware of the progress and by letting them know how their individual efforts are contributing to its success.

Vision formation is not a task for those who like to avoid complexity or who are uncomfortable with ambiguity. It can be a messy, introspective process that is difficult to explain, even by the person who conceives the vision. However, visionary leaders are able to solve day-to-day crises while continuing to focus on their vision: They have a special sense of purpose. For these leaders, a vision is a calling rather than simply a good idea. They feel as if they are part of a larger creative process that they can influence but cannot unilaterally control. Visions occur to individuals with well-informed open minds, minds prepared by a lifetime of learning and experience. Their minds are sharply attuned to emerging trends and developments in the world—both inside and outside the arena of physical education.

Wanted: Life Long Learner

In order to create a vision of quality physical education based on the constant changes that are the norm in today's world, physical education leaders also must be life long learners. They must constantly seek out growth and learning opportunities. Being a learner means living in a learning mode. There is never a finish line, only a life long pursuit. Life long learners are acutely aware of their ignorance, and this awareness motivates them to learn more.

Life long learners ingest and digest large quantities of information. They collect and analyze the same data that everyone else has in ways that allow them to conceive of new and unseen ideas. If you want to be a learning leader, you must be inspired to learn as much as you can, to know as much as you can, and to gain as many skills as you can. The ability and desire to grow constantly will help you to develop relevant information bases. As Senge states, "Personal mastery is a special level of proficiency… discipline of continually clarifying and deepening our personal vision, of focusing our energies, of developing patience, and of seeing reality objectively" (Senge 1990, p. 7).

The amount of information available today is overwhelming. Therefore, leaders must select the most relevant information on which to focus their attention. Leaders must be aware of general trends both in and out of the field of education. (*The Futurist, Learning and Leading with Technology,* and *Educational Leadership* are excellent information sources.) Leaders also must be knowledgeable about physical education. (*Journal of Physical Education, Recreation & Dance, Strategies, Journal of Teaching Physical Education,* and *Research Quarterly for Exercise and Sport* are excellent resources for this category.) The information needs of each leader will vary according to past learning and experiences.

To begin the information selection process, create a list of skills that you desire to attain. Next, list the information you need in order to competently demonstrate the skills. Then, find the necessary resources (i.e., books, training, experts) that will provide you with the information and skills you wish to acquire. If your list of desirable skills is substantial, then take the time to make a plan, set goals, prioritize the skills, and schedule the time to implement your plan.

Once your personal learning is progressing, the next step is to help others in your organization become learners—to create a learning environment or community of physical education learners. In learning communities, leaders become designers, teachers, and stewards. They are responsible for helping their followers expand their capabilities to shape their own futures.

School agencies should be places where adults and children learn simultaneously to think critically and analytically and to solve problems. Leaders help their organizations to become learning communities by modeling their own life long learning habits, acknowledging their own inadequacies, collaborating with other learners, and creating learning situations.

Learning situations are created when the taboo that prevents the sharing and discussing of physical education teaching ideas among teachers is overcome. Creating learning situations involves making discussions about teaching effectiveness as commonplace as discussions about discipline problems, getting students dressed for physical education, and weekend adventures. They are initiated by bringing physical educators together and providing them with the time and motivation to discuss instructional problems and solutions.

Wanted: Risk Taker

This book isn't about being in a leadership position; it is about being a leader regardless of the position you're in. It is about having the courage and spirit to make a significant difference in the field of physical education. It's about leadership, how ordinary physical educators exercise it, and how—in the process—they become physical education leaders. It is, in fact, about taking risks.

A sure sign that a leader is stale is when he or she becomes complacent or finds decision making difficult. Such static behavior—as compared to the proactive behavior of a leader—is a virus for which effective leaders must be inoculated.

Leaders look for innovative ways to improve a situation. They experiment and take risks. Effective leaders use the vast amount of information they have collected to minimize failure while encouraging risk taking. However, since risk taking often involves mistakes and failures, leaders prepare themselves to accept the inevitable disappointments by viewing them as learning opportunities.

Leaders who are new to risk taking should begin by taking small steps. They should experiment with actions that require only a small risk, and work up from there. The more you experience risk, the more comfortable you will become with taking risks. Keep in mind, however, that effective leaders take only calculated risks. Situations where there is little chance of succeeding are considered frivolity, not risks. So, when taking a risk be sure to weigh the odds of success against failure, and the benefits against the liabilities.

Wanted: Moral and Ethical Character

All great leaders have wrestled with their souls—it is inherent to the role of leadership. In fact, it is essential in the development of great leaders, since leaders can't elevate others to higher purposes until they have elevated themselves. I have a colleague who says that making decisions is never difficult; staying in tune with your values and beliefs is difficult. Once you know your values and beliefs the answers are easy.

As we enter the twenty-first century, it is imperative that we have physical education leaders with high moral and ethical

convictions, so that their values are exemplary. Leadership must be based on moral authority. Moral authority comes from the duties leaders accept and the obligations they feel toward others and toward their work. Leaders must hold the highest of values and beliefs, and they must demonstrate integrity by being direct and honest.

Leaders must be willing to take a stand on important issues and principles. They should focus on the identified ends, ensuring that the ends and the means to achieving those ends are consistent with shared purposes, values, and commitments.

In becoming a moral and ethical leader, it is important to identify your priorities. The following priorities have served me well in numerous physical education leadership roles:

1. Student safety

2. Student learning

3. Teacher needs

4. Site administrator needs

5. District administrator needs

6. My personal needs.

Knowing these priorities—along with my purposes, values, and commitments—makes it much easier to act when dealing with important issues and situations.

Wanted: Efficient Worker

How do you spend your time? Are you accomplishing the most important things, or the things that are easy to check off your "to do" list? Do you allow crises to eat up your time, so that you are constantly putting out fires rather than moving forward?

The first step in managing your time is to identify the tasks you must accomplish. Then, place them in priority order and assign deadlines. The next step is to repeat the prioritizing on a daily basis, assigning each task to a particular time slot.

Stephen Covey (1990) defines a four-quadrant time management matrix to assist with prioritizing tasks. Quadrant I defines its activities as urgent and important (e.g., crises, pressing problems, and deadline-driven projects). Quadrant II defines its activities as not urgent and important (e.g., prevention, relationship building, recognizing new opportunities, and planning). Quadrant III defines its activities as urgent and not important (e.g., interruptions, some calls, some mail, some reports, some meetings, and pressing matters). Finally, Quadrant IV defines its activities as not urgent and not important (e.g., busy work, some mail, some phone calls, and time wasters).

Covey suggests that "effective people stay out of Quadrants III and IV because, urgent or not, they aren't important. They also shrink Quadrant I down to size by spending more time in Quadrant II" (Covey 1990, p. 153). Quadrant II represents organizing and executing activities around priorities. Learning to focus on Quadrant II activities requires the leader to:

1. Identify significant projects related to the vision of quality physical education.

2. Separate the projects into manageable pieces.

FIGURE 1.2:
Situational Leadership Model: Matching Readiness and Style

Follower readiness	Leadership style
Unable and unwilling or insecure:	Provide specific instructions and closely supervise performance
Unable but willing or confident:	Explain decisions and provide opportunity for clarification
Able but unwilling or insecure:	Share ideas and facilitate followers in decision making
Able and willing or confident:	Turn over responsibility for decisions and implementation
(Hersey 1992, p. 71)	

3. Assign a portion of the project to different days.

4. Schedule time on these days to work on the project.

5. Honor the commitment to work on the project as if it were a required meeting.

Time-wasters eat up our day because we aren't aware that we are wasting time. Here are seven time wasters to watch for:

■ Chasing trivial data after the facts have been identified.

■ Socializing at great length between and during tasks.

■ Starting a job before thinking it through, or leaving a job before it is completed.

■ Doing things that can be delegated to another person or piece of equipment.

■ Doing unproductive things from sheer habit.

■ Paying too much attention to low-yield projects.

■ Handling too wide a variety of duties.

In order to maintain a high level of efficiency and to stay in Quadrant II, it is important to keep interruptions to a minimum. Here are six suggestions:

■ Group your return telephone calls and e-mail messages.

■ Plan for activities in advance to minimize crises.

■ Call meetings only when necessary, and request the presence of only the people necessary.

■ Attend meetings only if you have something valuable to offer or learn.

■ Be sure there is a clear purpose and agenda for every meeting you call or attend and stick to it.

■ When visitors linger, edge them toward the door by your actions in order to terminate the visit.

Wanted: Adaptable Style

Leadership style refers to the patterns of behavior (words and actions) of the physical education leader as perceived by others. It is defined in terms of how leaders appear to others whom they're trying to influence. Leadership style is typically defined in terms of both task behavior and relationship behavior. Task behavior refers to telling people what to do, how to do it, when to do it, where to do it, and who's to do it. Relationship behavior refers to listening, encouraging, facilitating, providing clarification, and giving support. The physical education leader with the widest range of appropriate responses will be most successful.

The specific response to any situation depends upon the interaction between the leader, the follower, the organization, the job demands, and the time constraints. The most important of these variables is the readiness of the follower to assume responsibility for a specific task. Readiness is the extent to which the follower has the ability (knowledge, experience, skill and willingness, confidence, commitment, and motivation) to accomplish the task.

Hersey's (1992) Situational Leadership Model associates four basic leadership styles with four different levels of follower readiness (see Figure 1.2). When followers have low levels of readiness, the physical education leader must take responsibility for the "traditional" management functions such as planning, organizing, motivating, and controlling. The leader's role is that of supervisor of the group. However, when leaders have spent time helping their followers evolve to high levels of readiness, the followers can assume much of the responsibility for step-by-step management functions. Again, the key is flexibility or adaptability—understanding that one style will not work in every situation.

Chapter Summary

Leadership can't be taught, but it can be learned. Learning to deal effectively and efficiently with crisis, adapting to different situations, making tough decisions while maintaining one's moral convictions, taking acceptable risks and handling the stress, and rebounding from failures will help you to become a physical education leader for the twenty-first century.

Part two of this book will provide you with the necessary cognitive skills and abilities to put your vision into practice.

References

Bernhardt, V. (1994). *The school portfolio: A comprehensive framework for school improvement.* Princeton Junction, NJ: Eye on Education.

Covey, S. R. (1990). *The seven habits of highly effective people: Restoring the character ethic.* New York: A Fireside Book.

Davis, S. & Botkin, J. (1994). *The Monster under the bed.* New York: Simon and Schuster.

Evaul, T. (1995). *Characteristics of quality physical education programs.* Paper presented at the national convention of the American Alliance for Health, Physical Education, Recreation and Dance Portland, OR.

Helgesen, S. (1995). *The web of inclusion.* New York: Doubleday.

Hersey, P. (1992). *The situational leader.* Escondido, CA: Center for Leadership Studies.

Hesselbein, F., Goldsmith, M., & Beckhard, R. (Eds.). (1996). *The leader of the future: New visions, strategies, and practices for the next era.* San Francisco: Jossey-Bass.

Kouzes, J. M, & Posner, B. Z. (1995). *The leadership challenge: How to keep getting extraordinary things done in organizations.* San Francisco: Jossey-Bass.

Lambert, L., Walker, D., Zimmerman, D. P., Cooper, J. E., Lambert, M. D., Gardner, M. E., & Slack, P.J. F. (1996). *The constructivist leader.* New York: The Teachers College Press.

Prestwood, D. C. L., & Schumann, P. A., Jr (1997). Seven new principles of leadership. *The Futurist, 31*(1), 68.

Schmoker, M. (1996). *Results: The key to continuous school improvement.* Alexandria, VA: Association for Supervision and Curriculum Development.

Senge, P. M. (1990). *The fifth discipline: The art and practice of learning organization.* New York: Doubleday.

Sergiovanni, T. J. (1996). *Leadership for the schoolhouse: How is it different? Why is it important?* San Francisco: Jossey-Bass.

Waitley, D. (1995). *Empires of the mind: Lessons to lead and succeed in a knowledge-based world.* New York: William Morrow.

Zand, D. E. (1997). *The leadership triad.* New York: Oxford University Press.

Journal References

Educational Leadership, Association for Supervision and Curriculum Development, Alexandria, Virginia

Journal of Teaching Physical Education, Human Kinetics, Champaign, Illinois

Journal of Physical Education, Recreation & Dance, American Alliance for Health, Physical Education, Recreation and Dance, Reston, Virginia

Learning and Leading with Technology, International Society for Technology in Education, Eugene, Oregon

Research Quarterly for Exercise and Sport, American Alliance for Health, Physical Education, Recreation and Dance, Reston, Virginia

Strategies: A Journal for Physical and Sport Educators, American Alliance for Health, Physical Education, Recreation and Dance, Reston, Virginia

The Futurist, World Future Society, Bethesda, Maryland

Part 2. Becoming a Leader

Finding the leader within begins with the belief that you possess the foundation on which to build leadership. Remember: Leadership can be learned. Learners are totally committed. Leaders are super listeners and excellent communicators. Leaders are students of their respective industry, company, and its people. Leaders have "the authority of knowledge."

—Adapted from Howard G. Haas, *The Leader Within*

CHAPTER 2

The Dynamics of Successful Change Efforts

Rita Mercier

Autopoiesis (from the Greek for self-production): A natural process that supports the quest for structure, process, renewal, integrity. This process in not limited to one type of organism—it describes life itself. Every living thing that expends energy will do whatever is needed to preserve itself, including changing. (Wheatley 1992, p. 18)

Why is it important for educational leaders to study the nature of change? According to Wheatley (1992, p. 8), "We inhabit a world that is always subjective and shaped by our interactions with it. Our world is impossible to pin down, constantly changing and infinitely more interesting than we ever imagined."

Based on this perspective, it appears that our world continues to change regardless of our individual willingness to change with it. It is the nature of all living things to constantly renew themselves. Living things are compelled to continuously improve. Even individuals who resist change are swept up in it. Therefore, the question that each of us answers—consciously or unconsciously—is, "what will my role be in this change?"

Responses can vary from actively leading the effort, to passive acceptance, to resistance, and many more. Strong physical education leaders have typically found themselves compelled to action. But over-aggressive or inappropriate action may actually inhibit change efforts. There are times that we may not even be aware of the decisions we make. For example, doing nothing is the result of a decision.

Change will occur regardless of the stance we take. But understanding the nature of change can provide some advantage in dealing with this inevitable reality. The most important step in a successful change effort is recognizing the need to understand the process of change. "No change would be more fundamental than a dramatic expansion of the capacity of individuals and organizations to understand and deal with change" (Fullan & Miles 1992, p. 745).

You will notice that "educational" leadership/leader often is used to describe the physical educator's role in leadership. This is a purposeful attempt to depict physical educators as "educators" first, who also are primarily responsible for the content of physical education. Physical educators can most effectively influence change in the system when they perceive themselves primarily as educational leaders. From an educational leadership perspective, they demonstrate how physical education concepts, knowledge, and skills are integral to student attainment of a wide breadth of general educational concepts, goals, and outcomes.

The intent of this chapter is to assist physical educators with their leadership efforts through the understanding of the nature of change. This understanding includes personal, interpersonal, and systemic change. A deeper knowledge of the change process can help leaders direct their energy in efforts that will be most likely to produce desired results. Change will be explored through seven areas. They are:

1. The Leader's Role in Change
2. Developing a Common Vision and Shared Goals
3. Systemic Components and Systemic Thinking
4. Appropriate Resources and Support for Change
5. Creating a Risk Taking Environment for Change
6. Resistance to Change
7. Assessing the Effectiveness of the Change Effort.

The Leader's Role in Change

What does understanding individual and organizational change mean to me as an educational leader? What can I do to build upon my personal power to effect meaningful change?

The first step in understanding how to effect change is recognizing the fallacy of "cause and effect." Sir Isaac Newton promoted the machine model of comprehending the world: reducing everything to its parts, examining them, dissecting them and then putting them back together. His premise was that one had control over the parts and their effect on the machine (Cause and effect).

New Science suggests that to understand systems we must first give primary value to the relationships among seemingly discrete parts. Seemingly discrete parts that can be viewed through the dynamic of how they relate might include departmentalizing curricular areas, teacher autonomy, student behavior and meaningful work, parent/teacher roles, and administrative and teacher leadership. This theory presents an entirely new perspective for explaining phenomena that cannot be reduced to simple cause and effect, but are rather a continuous flux of Dynamic processes (Wheatley 1992, p. 9). In practical terms this means that people cannot cause a particular outcome in change. What we can do is influence how the change process occurs. However, we must first understand as much as we can about various models of change and change facilitation strategies.

Gene Hall's research on change led to the development of the "Concerns Based Adoption Model" (CBAM). This is a personal change process that focuses on the individual's expressions of concern throughout the various stages of an innovation. The model makes several assumptions regarding the adoption of innovations. These include:

1. Viewing change not as an event, but as process, which takes a lot of time and goes through many stages

2. Focusing on the needs of the individuals first in relationship to their roles in the change process

3. Understanding change as a highly personal experience, involving the frustrations, perceptions, concerns, satisfactions, motivations, etc. of each person involved in the change

4. Completing several predictable stages in individuals' perceptions and skill levels regarding any innovation

5. Using a teacher-centered diagnostic/prescriptive model of staff development for facilitating effective change

6. Being adaptive to individual needs relative to total organizational needs.

These assumptions provide the framework from which the individual's personal response to change is examined.

Although there are people who are exceptions to every model, and progress through the stages will not always be as linear as the model would suggest, it does provide a framework from which leaders can offer support for individuals involved in change.

The typical pattern of individual responses through the process of changing, or adapting to a new innovation, involves seven stages:

- ▓ **Level 0—Awareness:** The individual has little concern about or involvement in the innovation. This stage might be illustrated by the physical educator who handles new curriculum guides, instructional strategies, policy issues, etc. with indifference, apathy, and indulgent smiles—a "this too shall pass" attitude. It also could be illustrated by the physical educator who believes that the new information and innovations don't have anything to do with teaching, therefore it is not necessary to pursue them further.

- ▓ **Level 1—Information:** The individual has a general awareness of the innovation and wants to learn more about it. This might be demonstrated by a staff meeting in which several ideas/ resources are mentioned. The individual finds something interesting and requests more information about it. This is a stage that is usually nonthreatening to teachers because they are exploring, gathering knowledge, deciding how or if they will use the information.

- ▓ **Level 2—Personal:** In this stage the individual begins to be concerned with how the innovation will affect his or her work, potential role in the reward structure of the school, and decision making ability. Financial or status implications of the program are considered. This stage can produce feelings of inadequacy and uncertainty. Physical educators in Level 2 may be heard saying things such as: "I'm not sure I want all the extra work it will take to implement the tenets of the new state framework." "I probably won't be able to decide how it will affect my budget." "How much am I going to be expected to change?" "Will I have the time I need to learn to do this?"

- ▓ **Level 3—Management:** At this level, individuals focus their attention on the tasks involved in using the innovation. Their concerns are largely related to efficiency, organizing, managing, scheduling, and handling time demands. A physical educator in Level 3 wants to know how to organize the lesson for tomorrow. What materials will be needed? Where can the resources needed to plan be found? How can equipment set up time be reduced? Problems be anticipated?

- ▓ **Level 4—Consequence:** The attention in this level is focused on how the innovation affects students. What is the relevance of the innovation to students? Emphasis is on evaluation of student outcomes and how to best use new innovations to maximize student outcomes. Teachers in this level might say things such as, "This strategy worked really well for some of my students, but not for others. I wonder what I have to do to modify it so more students will benefit."

- ▓ **Level 5—Collaboration:** The main focus of this level is coordinating and cooperating with others to maximize use of the innovation. Individuals in this level are very comfortable with the innovation, have probably used it successfully for a long time, and want to share ideas with other knowledgeable teachers. Physical educators in this stage of the change continuum are usually strong advocates for the innovation. They want to affect change and are anxious to gain new knowledge.

- ▓ **Level 6—Refocusing:** The focus of this level is exploration beyond the current understanding of the innovation. Individuals want to find new ways, more powerful alternatives, and major adaptations to the existing form of the innovation. A physical educator in this stage has an in-depth knowledge of the strategy and can adapt it for use within his or her own situation. The educator may have done extensive Action Research on the implementation of the strategy in working with eighth grade coed classes, for example, and shared the results at professional meetings or in papers. Educators at this level are usually innovators and leaders.

A depth of understanding about how people change characterizes effective leadership at all levels. Innovative actions require a number of varied support systems, access to information, facilitative abilities, resources, communication skills, and insights that directly correlate to an understanding of change. An example of the need to understand the levels of change would be that of a school administrator who assigns teachers in Level 2 to collaborate to create a new curriculum based on the state framework.

This kind of error is made frequently, and is often the result of fiscal needs/time constraints. Whether we are leaders at the instructional level, within a department, a school, or at the district level, knowledge of how to respond appropriately for different stages of change is critical. This knowledge can provide each type of leader with the ability to determine the direction, methods, and kinds of support systems that are required. It can offer lower level leaders current and compelling research on effective change strategies to challenge policy and higher level decisions that are not in the best interest of the change effort.

The CBAM model of change is a practical approach to self-examination in relationship to the continuum of stages. Individuals can ask themselves a number of questions to determine their level of concern in any given change effort. These include:

- Am I aware of the innovation?
- Am I using it?
- What can I share about the innovation?
- How do I feel about it?
- What problems or concerns do I have about it?
- What do I think of it?
- How does it affect me? How does it affect others I am involved with?
- Is there anything I have a question or wonder about?
- What is my reaction to it?
- What is my attitude toward it?
- Do I have any reservations about it?
- Would I like any information about it?

(Hall & Hord 1987.)

It may be useful to consider such self-examination as a pliable, flexible self-description rather than a definitive self-depiction. For example, you are not a "Level 3" simply because you have some concerns regarding organizational tasks in an innovation you are currently trying to apply. It is more accurate to examine the strongest prevailing feelings, issues, and concerns when trying to understand your personal relationship to any given change effort/innovation. The goal of understanding your own level of concern is being able to participate in selecting appropriate interventions as well as personal and professional growth experiences. This understanding also can provide valuable insight into your leadership readiness and the types of leadership tasks that are best suited to your abilities and levels of concern.

Developing a Common Vision and Shared Goals

Change is a continuous process of improving. To accomplish this, Fullan and Miles (1992) suggest creating accurate maps of change. Each person involved in the change—from teachers, to the principal, to parents, to board members—has a perception of what the reform means. When everyone involved creates a different "map" or way of approaching the change, there is no direction, no clarity in the map.

This affects physical educators in at least two ways: We cannot possibly begin to implement profound changes in content and process unless we are an integral part of the system—the "map" of the school site plan—and in a larger context, the district map. Physical educators must be as knowledgeable and involved with the formulation of a schoolwide vision, of general goals, policy, reform measures, instructional uses of technology, interdisciplinary connections, and powerful

teaching and learning strategies as every other teacher and administrative leader on staff.

A microcosmic example of the urgent need to function using the same map can be illustrated in the diversity of perceptions regarding purpose, instruction, and content of teachers within many physical education departments. What efforts are made to assure that everyone in the department agrees on a Common vision, purpose, educational objectives and strategies to achieve those objectives? The largely autonomous nature of our profession over the years has greatly inhibited our ability to cooperate and collaborate—an essential if we are to create valid maps for change.

Physical educators have, by and large, been able to select the games and sports they want to teach or that they know best as their physical education "curriculum." They may collaborate to share equipment and space, but are more often likely to pursue their interests instructionally. In cases where staff members do cooperate and collaborate on curriculum decisions and instructional strategies aligned with current research and National Guidelines, much more Common visioning occurs, thereby stimulating the effectiveness of the change process.

Change is a journey, not a blueprint (Fullan & Miles 1992). Rather than try to account for the overwhelming complexity of change with an implementation plan, Louis and Miles (1990) suggest a "guided journey" approach, based on the assumption that Organizational elements are by nature chaotic. These structures can't be controlled in the sense that any specific plan can account for the variabilities that abound. Gaining consensus for incremental strategies, decentralizing experimental applications of ideas (allowing teachers more freedom to experiment by themselves versus administrators forcing experimental strategies on them), harnessing creativity in all staff members, and focusing the resulting energy on the change are more compatible ways to address the nature of change.

Continuously identifying and considering the sense of purpose of the people involved in the change also helps to shape and reshape a shared vision. Louis and Miles (1990) refer to this process as, "Do... Plan...Do...and plan some more." Rather than attempting to have a philosophy and vision statement drive program implementation, physical educators would have an ongoing dialogue as they begin to implement predetermined curricular objectives. They would discuss the effectiveness of the implementation, make adjustments, and carry it out while continuing the cycle of reflection. As the process evolves, a Common vision is formed and reformed.

People often talk about visioning, establishing a vision, and a leader with a vision as critical to organizational leadership. Wheatley (1992, p. 53) defines vision as, "the need for organizational clarity about purpose and direction." Thus, creating a vision most often occurs in a linear fashion with the belief that the clearer the image of the destination, the more likely it is that people will achieve it.

In New Science theory, vision is thought of as a "field" that permeates organizational space rather than a linear destination. This profound shift in thought has tremendous implications for the way we view vision in relationship to understanding change. Traditionally, a small group of elite individuals determine the vision of the organization, which is then given to the employees to embrace as their own. In a field theory model, every individual involved in the success of the system would be a part of the formation, shaping and reshaping of the vision throughout time. Actions such as leaders being present and accessible, modeling, stating the vision continuously, clarifying and discussing the vision, and filling every space with messages about the purpose and direction of the organization would characterize vision creation. The energy of all of the individuals in the organization would be linked to form behavior congruent to the organizational goals. Peter Senge (1990, p. 212), an authoritative organizational consultant believes, "that an organization's vision grows as a by-product of individual visions, a by-product of ongoing conversations."

Formulating a vision can occur on many levels. Within a school system, all subdivisions, schools, departments, classes, teachers, etc. develop their purposes and goals based on the permeation of the larger vision throughout the organization. One definition of a vision is "a type of propagation of characteristics... ." This definition is compatible with effective vision transformation. If the vision is clear and easy to understand, and if ownership occurs, every subdivision should reflect the larger vision. Physical education leaders who have contributed to and are committed to the larger vision of the school/district are much more likely to be regarded by others in the learning organization as viable, important contributors in decision making. They are in a strong position to gain support for their physical education program goals.

What power do physical educators have to influence organizational visioning? Is it something that emanates from on high, leaving those in its wake at the mercy of the wisdom of those above? The New Science model of change clearly supports the idea that change can occur from anywhere in the organization, at any time, by any individual or group of individuals. It is not enough for teacher leaders to wait until higher level decisions are made. True leadership is self-initiated. Any effort made to move the system toward authentic Participatory management will ultimately result in moving the whole system to adapt to the increasing Self-empowerment of the individuals comprising the system. A physical educator who successfully leads a schoolwide interdisciplinary connection effort will be viewed as a respected decision maker in the future. The action by the physical educator to initiate a leadership effort automatically shifts future decision making power to him or her.

Self-empowerment is necessary for contributing to visioning. Although I have seen many books and theories on empowering others, it seems to me to be a contradiction in terms. The notion that one person can "give" another empowerment indicates that the person doing the giving has the control to do so. Although the control might be positional power, it still is incompatible with the ultimate goal of accessing and recognizing one's own personal power.

Accessing personal power means just that. Be willing to take risks. Gain access to the people who can influence the changes in your school or district. Learn everything you can about the needs and wants of those individuals. Negotiate for the needs of your students with informed confidence and a willingness to take responsibility for the vision you helped to create.

Physical education leaders have a tremendous opportunity to shape the vision of their programs relative to the larger organizational vision. Rather than focus on how we have in a sense become stepchildren of a monolithic educational system, I will focus on the things physical educators can do to become an integral component of the educational vision for all students.

This is by no means an exhaustive list. It is a starting place for physical educators who want to play a part in shaping the vision in an organization that rarely recognizes or appreciates the worth of their content area:

- Crave, seek out, and acquire knowledge in all areas of the curriculum and in every instructional process. Know as much as you possibly can about the goals, needs, and wants of others in the system. This would include policy issues, budgeting, scheduling, special projects, political issues, legislation, major educational trends and reform movements.

- Develop the five traits of holonomy described later in this chapter.

- Be a life long learner—as a teacher, colleague, leader, student of life, and researcher.

- Understand the change process and use it to your advantage.

- Continuously develop your professionalism for yourself and in relationship to colleagues.

- Be aware of how to negotiate for what your program and students need. The more physical educators know about schoolwide programs and content issues, the more connections they can make and the more resources they can share.

- Always negotiate to a win-win outcome. Winning at the expense of other programs or individuals can backfire.

To create a vision for physical education programs aligned with the larger educational vision, we need to know much more about how others in the system operate than we generally realize. We need to share common language and understandings among all of the individuals that operate in the school or district. How much of the terminology used by educators in other subjects, the staff development personnel, and administrators do you understand? What do you do if you don't understand?

To gain access to the world of general education, physical education leaders must be willing to ask a lot of questions. They have to admit that they don't know but are extremely interested in knowing in order to contribute to the success of the effort. The more physical educators know about the issues, the "educationese," the content of other curriculum areas, the greater access they will have to the source of power. It is in the center of power that they will become players in the intricate web of connections required to effectively address the learning needs of all students. They also will be able to share knowledge about physical education content and instruction that others may know little about. Shared knowledge is essential to creating a shared vision. Physical educators need to get off the bench and enter the game!

Physical educators also must learn to understand one another and make time to discuss philosophical differences regarding the content and instructional processes used in our programs.

Because change doesn't occur in a vacuum, they also should network with action-oriented individuals throughout the school to discuss their educational values, beliefs, and understandings. As people share, listen, and seek new learning, commonalties are formed. These evolve into a Common vision. And a common school vision provides impetus for a common physical education department vision.

Systemic Components and Systemic Thinking

For change to succeed, it must be systemic (Fullan & Miles 1992). Systemic change means addressing the impact of change on every part of the organization (school/district) at the same time. When episodic innovations and segmented and disjointed answers are steadily imposed on teachers, they become cynical and unresponsive to the "next, newest right answer." Systemic change must be focused on the interrelationships of all of the main components of the system at the same time; and it must pay attention to the culture of the system. For physical education leaders, this might include paying attention to enabling other physical educators to perform the functions that are set in place by the leader's efforts. It might mean helping others to take ownership responsibility for enough of the program that it can sustain itself without the enthusiastic innovator. Shared knowledge and skills can be the key to sustaining powerful change efforts.

If systemic efforts are to be successful, they must combine knowledge and all components of change. Unfortunately, many physical educators neglect to notice opportunities for systemic change. For example, physical educators cannot continue to change half of a department, or remain isolated from the larger site or district systems and expect to achieve any lasting reform. One of the most widespread and self-defeating practices impeding successful change is that of segregating into "men's" and "women's" domains. This practice has serious implications for continuous growth and renewal as a content area.

Some physical educators also remain isolated from the larger school site and district program, either by self-segregating or by perceiving that the larger school community does not value them. This practice also is singularly self-defeating. In cases where the physical education department of a school has immersed itself in every aspect of the larger school community, it has emerged as integral to the school. To participate as an equal is clearly a choice that every physical educator makes.

Physical educators have the power and the ability to determine how influential and integral they are to the whole system. The more knowledge and understanding any one part of the system has regarding the remaining parts of the system, the more effective that part will be in contributing to the whole. If physical educators are to be integral to the system, they need to risk learning more, being involved in more, contributing in more ways, and networking more to create meaningful interdisciplinary connections.

> Dissipative structures in chemistry also teach a paradoxical truth, that disorder can be the source of new order.... Dissipation didn't lead to the demise of a system. It was part of the process by which the system let go of its present form so that it could reemerge in a form better suited to the demands of the present environment. (Prigogine 1983.)

Physical education leaders are responding to the professed need of twenty-first century students to be Self-directed, life long learners. Examples include a shift in emphasis from students knowing sports and sports skills to knowing exercise physiology, biomechanics, motor learning, sociology, etc. Physical activity choices have the potential to be profoundly different 20 years from now. Evolving physical education programs prepare students for the future by teaching them how to learn and by giving them the skills they need to teach themselves. The program changes and subsequent teacher skills, abilities, and philosophies needed to implement those changes are many and complex. Simplistic solutions—such as adopting a new curriculum, teaching new games, giving homework or more written tests—often are employed in disjointed change efforts.

Applying simplistic solutions to complex problems undermines change efforts in many ways (Fullan & Miles 1992). The interaction of needs and wants between the multitude of discrete segments that exist in any educational structure are staggering. To suggest that we have answers given the current quick fix, reactive mode of many educational organizations is a gross mistake. As physical education leaders, our course should include understanding and communicating the role of physical education as it relates to all other programs and content areas.

A good example of applying simplistic solutions to complex problems is the practice of mandating that physical educators make interdisciplinary/thematic connections. In attempting to implement this mandate, many physical educators find that they are making superficial connections, which can result in frustration and undue anxiety for both students and teachers. Meaningful interdisciplinary connections are not made easily or quickly. Physical educators, like all educators, need time and access to learn about each other's content areas as well as about general teaching/learning strategies designed to meet the diverse and increasingly complex needs of students.

Systems thinking is perhaps the most challenging facet of change dynamics. Variables can be almost imperceptible, yet all of the interactions in an organization are shaped—either directly or indirectly—by systems thinking. When one part is affected, the entire system is affected. Traditional systems thinking is based on order and assumed predictability. New Science—Quantum physics, Chaos theory, and Fractal geometry—all suggest that viewing systems this way is inaccurate.

> We may harbor the hope we will regain predictability as soon as we can learn to account for all variables, but in fact no level of detail can ever satisfy this desire.... In complex ways that no system will ever capture, the system feeds back on itself, enfolding all that has happened, magnifying slight variances, encoding it in the system's memory—and prohibiting prediction, ever...Chaos theory and quantum science share the uncertainty that arises from the wholeness of the universe to resist being studied in pieces. (Wheatley 1992, p. 127.)

By this definition, the minutest details shape the whole, but they cannot be studied in isolation from the whole. Physical education leaders who try to understand every aspect of the system and how the multitude of pieces affect their program goals may find themselves more confused than comforted. The real value of a "quantum" view of organizations for physical education leaders is that it provides a strong argument for Self-empowerment.

What physical educators do matters to the system. Decisions made regarding curriculum, assessment, and instructional strategies within the physical education department can dramatically affect the whole system in ways that may not even be attributed to them. A department that teaches students to interact positively by using Cooperative learning and social skills instruction will be contributing not only to its students' ability to acquire and value movement skills, but also should produce a positive learning environment throughout the school. Physical education leaders can make these connections apparent to others in the system by first recognizing their contributions themselves, offering to share innovations at staff and other leadership meetings, inviting others to observe their teaching, collaborating on student projects, and making meaningful interdisciplinary connections.

> Quantum matter is influenced by the very act of observation. If the investigator chooses to study wave properties, matter appears in wave forms. The act of observation joins in the greater process, removing the ideal of pure, objective science. To observe and measure is to make a choice. In such choice making the observer joins the system being observed. Each act of observation is also an act of influence. (Wheatley 1992.)

This powerful statement is evident in schooling/planning/problem solving in the way that schools, departments, and teams selectively examine issues. Even when multiple measures are used to collect data, the lack of depth and breadth in identifying the problem has a decidedly prejudicial effect on the outcome.

For example, consider the practice of grading on dressing out. If the problem is examined in terms of student resistance to authority, willful acts of rebellion, laziness, or even irresponsibility, the solutions will reflect the original assumptions—harsher dressing out grading systems, harsher follow-through with parents to force submission, etc. If the problem is viewed in terms of student needs, the teacher's thinking may lead to assessing instructional strategies, content, rapport with students, etc. to determine the factors that may be inhibiting student enjoyment and participation. Solutions may include surveying students to gather information regarding likes, wants, and needs. Teachers might apply Peer coaching, Cooperative learning, Self-directed Meaning centered projects, and other strategies to involve students.

Some educational systems are plagued by segmenting planning processes into departments, projects, school programs, extracurricular activities, student support strategies, etc. While they can have a profound effect on the system, physical education programs are usually so far out of the system's thinking that they are barely included in the system thought process. An unfortunate consequence of a systemic error such as this is that physical educators often don't realize what is happening and don't take appropriate action to become viable, active participants in the system. All it takes to change this dynamic is to become visible and involved in school meetings, decision making, policy, reform measures, innovations, and schoolwide program implementations. Don't give people the opportunity to think that you are any less important to the success of the school than teachers in any of the other content areas.

Although there is no one "right answer" in interpreting all of the implications of the New Science Theories relative to system components and culture, some suggestions for ways to align applied practice with these theories include:

- Ensure that educational organizations (such as physical education departments) continually ask themselves two vital questions: "Who are we?" and, "What is our purpose?" Basing every decision on these questions while filtering responses through agreed-upon core values will increase the likelihood of an evolving system (Garmston 1994).

- Focus efforts on building effective relationships among everyone in the educational organization.

- Approach problems differently: step back from the problem to gain enough perspective to recognize the myriad of variables that shape it, while looking for themes and patterns rather than isolated causes.

- Help people to know, understand, and appreciate the multiple components that comprise the learning organization. The more people know about the roles that each individual plays in the system, the greater and stronger those connections can be.

Some major implications for physical educators in understanding system components and culture are:

- Everything matters. This includes the way we interact with students; the way we participate in the structure of the school; the way we interact with parents, community members, and peers; and how well we understand ourselves. In a quantum system, every action produces a reaction that can have an unpredictable effect on the system. If we are consciously aware that every action we take can contribute to the vision of the system (to extent this is possible), we are more likely to contribute positively to that vision.

- Adaptability is paramount to survival. The system's desire to continuously renew itself into new and improved states of efficiency will cause disintegration in those components that are not contributing to the maintenance of the system. Those physical educators who continue to remain impervious to change or who continue to find no relevance in reform efforts and trends in education will eventually be eliminated by the system.

- Relationships between the individuals involved in the success of the system must be supported, nurtured, and given time to develop. Physical educators need to talk to one another continuously, offering and being open to professional feedback. The single most likely cause of a dissipative structure is the alienation of forces in the system working toward the same goal.

- Decisions must be based on criteria developed from what students need to know and be able to do. Make sure that every action, strategy, program component, curriculum item, and manner of interaction with students supports the attainment of those criteria.

Appropriate Resources and Support for Change

By avoiding the impulse to adopt impatient and superficial solutions, one can increase the possibility that the application of more time, energy, and resources eventually will contribute to successful change (Fullan & Miles 1992). When we do not allow ourselves the time and energy to engage in in-depth, long-term planning processes, we perpetuate the conditions that cause crisis. Superficial solutions usually make matters worse.

The change effort would benefit from consideration of the way in which the change affects the culture of the system, and of the personal responses of each individual. Neglecting behavior patterns that accompany structural changes is a sure-fire recipe for failure. A excellent example of this tenet is the way that many physical educators have responded to Title IX legislation. For more than 20 years, they largely avoided, often undermined, and even more often ignored the intent of the legislation. A monumental change effort was needed to produce real, substantive change relative to gender equity. What happened instead, in many instances, was a series of crisis or quick fix kinds of interventions designed to force the mandates of the new legislation on predominately uncooperative teachers.

When problems are embraced as opportunities to learn, deeper change and deeper satisfaction in the outcome results. Immersion in problems that evolve as a natural consequence of change enables people to develop creative solutions. If problems are used to blame and defend positions, successful change is inhibited.

If we were to apply this approach to Title IX implementation it might look something like this:

1. Teachers are given the opportunity to meet together to discuss the pros and cons of coed physical education.

2. They implement coed physical education in stages, with those teachers most willing and knowledgeable taking the lead.

3. Teachers self-monitor and peer coach over a period of time as all teachers receive staff development in gender equity and instructional strategies along with ongoing technical and moral support.

4. Teachers begin to conduct Action Research by observing successes and failures, maximizing successes and learning how to make program/teaching modifications as a result of failures.

There are legitimate, sometimes profound, philosophical differences among physical educators. It may not be possible to reconcile those differences into a common belief system. What change theory tells us, however, is that systems will continue to evolve as necessary in order to survive or they will perish. Reforms are not merely an inconvenience; they are an evolutionary necessity.

Reforms and innovations are often symbolically implemented rather than substantively implemented (Fullan & Miles 1992). Common symbols include slogans, district or schoolwide kickoff events, media fanfare, speeches, and new equipment or instructional materials. Some new curriculum or innovation may be adopted, but no follow-up staff development, support, program evaluation or accountability is ever carried out. This happens most often because change is also a political process. Many times, decisions are made that have more to do with satisfying a current agenda item than creating a long-term, effective reform.

Symbols in and of themselves are not necessarily negative. Symbols can provide personal and collective meaning and inspire confidence and faith, but only if they are used in conjunction with substantive, concerted action. An example of symbolic support is the practice of having a state or district-sponsored kickoff event to showcase the new state physical education framework/ curriculum guide/course of study. This "symbolically" represents support of the framework/guidelines. Substantive support would be demonstrated by providing adequate professional development offerings, resources, and support structures, such as Peer coaching, department and inter-disciplinary planning time, instructional material development time, mentor teacher support, visitations to successful programs in other schools, etc.

Change requires resources to support and sustain it. Resources are needed for inservices, instructional materials, substitutes, space, equipment, planning time, etc. Time for learning, planning, and sharing is especially crucial. Louis and Miles (1990) found that at least 30 days a year of external professional assistance—i.e., university classes, consultants, seminars, conferences, etc.—was essential for success. They also recommended several more days a year to allow for developing a Common vision, shared goals, instructional support, and program planning, and for sharing individual expertise.

Louis and Miles (1990) encourage leaders to be creative with existing resources. They describe "resourcing" as the ability to scan resources that already exist and adapt them to meet the current needs. Examples include flexible scheduling, block scheduling, sharing space/equipment, innovative use of personnel, volunteerism, student projects, and teaming.

Change also requires the power to manage it (Fullan & Miles 1992). Change efforts necessitate monitoring, information sharing, linking multiple change projects, identifying unsolved problems, and applying clear coping actions. This requires legitimate Shared leadership, ownership of the problems by all parties involved, cooperation with others, trust, open communication, and conflict resolution.

Personality Styles workshops, diversity trainings, trained group facilitators, Conflict Mediation, and more have been employed extensively in an effort to help physical educators develop collaborative, cooperative interactions. Shared leadership is a learned process. Physical educators need access to these skills and abilities in order to carry out successful change efforts.

There are pockets of success where physical education programs have achieved recognition and acclaim. However, these pockets often face attrition: There is little evidence that they can remain successful over time. They seem to rely on the energy and skills of one or more individuals. When lost, the progress made while those individuals were there disintegrates. This occurs because the innovation is not institutionalized into the normative structure of the educational organization.

A physical educator's experience with this phenomenon might look something like this: You are hired as the only physical educator for a large elementary school. For the next five years, you develop an amazing awareness and advocacy among the staff for daily, quality physical education for all students. You have a model program, multiple interdisciplinary connections, a fitness lab, running clubs, parent/student "play" nights, extracurricular activities, etc. Then, you leave.

What happens to the program? Although there are a range of possible outcomes, we can conclude, with some certainty, that widespread commitment, more than one person trained to do the program, and appropriate resources are critical to maintaining the change effort.

Creating a Risk Taking Environment for Change

Change is learning loaded with uncertainty (Fullan & Miles 1992). It is disrespectful to believe that others are ignorant or prejudiced when they don't immediately embrace a new idea or innovation. It takes months or years to assimilate change.

The changes that are being proposed for the field of physical education constitute a dramatic change for some physical educators from what they believed when they decided to enter the field. The shift from an activity based curriculum to a conceptual based curriculum requires an enormous philosophical shift in thinking.

Everyone deserves the chance to go through this process. Everyone must be allowed to go through the process, or the change effort will be impeded. If people view change as a learning process, one of coming to grips with personal meaning, a sense of shared ownership occurs. Mutual understanding evolves. This can only happen when the needs of others are considered in a climate of support, a climate where risk taking is valued by all. For physical educators, this means accepting that others in the department may not be as enthusiastic about a new idea while at the same time inviting them to read, visit other programs, and try something new with support and encouragement. Risk taking and ownership of the innovation are optimized by focusing on what can be learned from mistakes as well as from successes.

Robert Garmston, nationally renowned for his research in whole school reform, has created a theory he calls "Holonomy—The Five States of Mind." Garmston maintains that these five states are the foundation of a person's ability to adapt to an ever changing environment; that they are necessary attributes for facilitating a risk taking environment. Change, he contends, demands adaptability. Holonomy is a way to describe a balance between autonomy—an individual's desire for independence—and community—the welfare of the whole.

The five states of mind necessary to achieve this balance are:

▓ Efficacy. An efficacious person regards events as opportunities for learning, believes that personal action produces outcomes, is resourceful, recognizes and proactively pursues what is not known, and initiates visions of desired states with feedback systems that allow for course of action modifications.

▓ Flexibility. A flexible person sets aside his or her own views and opinions to seek to understand others, searches for possibilities and generates novel connections, adjusts cognitive style and perceptual position to the situation, and considers data from a kaleidoscope of perspectives.

▓ Consciousness. A conscious person selectively attends to one's own style and other's styles, modalities, beliefs, values, and behaviors; monitors and directs attention from external to internal stimuli; generates, holds, and applies criteria for decision making; is aware of intentions and outcomes; and mentally rehearses before, monitors during, and reflects on experiences.

▓ Craftsmanship. An individual who has mastered craftsmanship creates, holds, calibrates, and refines outcomes; monitors and manages refinements in thought/language; perseveres to resolve disequilibrium between present and desired states; predicts, monitors, and manages time well; and creates and refines standards of excellence.

▓ Interdependence. An interdependent person values and draws upon the resources of others, reframes events and communications in the pursuit of the common good, defers his or her own needs and desires, believes that conflict is an opportunity for growth, and envisions expanding the capacity of the group and its members (Garmston 1994, pp. 18-23).

Garmston's five states of mind, or holonomy, can be particularly useful when examining interactive processes—how we work together toward successful change. Physical educators who reflect regularly about their own teaching, personal, and collaborative skills are most likely to regard change positively and to operate successfully within change initiatives. "Power in organizations is the capacity generated by relationships" (Garmston 1994, p.17).

After developing an understanding of his or her personal change paradigm, with the realization that change is a dynamic process, the physical education leader can work on fostering professional relationships with others. Everything that occurs in change happens in response to the ways that individuals in the system respond to the innovation relative to each other (Wheatley 1992). Although it is impossible to predict or even plan for exactly the kinds of interactions that will best facilitate each innovation, there are some strategies that are more likely to produce successful change efforts:

▓ Developing supportive organizational arrangements— actions taken to develop policies, plan, manage, staff, fund, structure roles, provide space, equipment, and resources that establish and maintain the innovation.

▓ Training—actions that develop individuals' knowledge about and skills in using the innovation. Workshops, modeling, and discussion sessions for users are examples of training.

▓ Providing consultation and reinforcement—actions taken to assist individuals in problem solving, peer support groups, and support for using the innovation.

▓ Monitoring and evaluation—actions taken to gather, analyze, or report data about the outcomes of the change effort. Examples include ongoing discussions, surveys, assessments of individual concerns, pre and post-analysis of learner outcomes, and personal goals assessment.

- External Communication—actions taken to gain support from individuals or groups external to the users. Examples for physical educators include board reports, open houses, publications and events for parents and the community, involvement on schoolwide committees and organizations, interdisciplinary knowledge, and applications

- Dissemination—actions that inform others and encourage adoption of the change or innovation (Hall & Hord 1987).

If the ability to nurture relationships is the single most critical element in successful change efforts, how is it accomplished? A genuine concern for the feelings and needs of others in their efforts to align past practices and beliefs with new information and expectations is beneficial. People need the opportunity to share their fears and discuss their losses. One way of determining the kind of intervention most appropriate for another person would be to ask the questions listed in the section on the CBAM model. The person asking the questions could lead the interviewee to understand the level of his or her concern in relationship to the change.

Once an understanding is developed, suggestions can be made for appropriate interventions. It is common for individuals to enter the change process in the lower levels. Some may act as if they are uninterested, or even somewhat hostile. Avoid assuming another's motives, feelings, or beliefs regarding a change. Such labeling can result in polarization and can breed miscommunication that becomes systemic and inhibits future change efforts.

Stallings (1991) suggests that there are nine conditions under which teachers are most likely to change and use new ideas. Teachers are more likely to change if they:

1. Become aware of a need for improvement through their own analysis or observation profile

2. Make a written commitment to try new ideas in their class the next day

3. Modify workshop ideas for their own situation

4. Try new ideas and evaluate the effect

5. Observe in each other's classes and analyze their own data

6. Report their successes and failures to their group

7. Discuss problems and solutions regarding individual students, teaching, and subject matter

8. Use a wide variety of approaches such as modeling, simulations, observation, critiquing videotapes, presenting at professional meetings, conferences, workshops, and Peer coaching

9. Learn to set personal goals for professional growth.

Another strategy that may be useful in working with others in an effort to support the adoption of a specific innovation is called Reflective Interviewing. This process is a component of Richard Sagor's Collaborative Action Research model (Sagor 1992). Staff members select a partner and decide who will ask questions and who will answer questions first. They each select an issue to discuss that meets the following criteria: the issue is directly related to the new innovation, the issue is something

that the person being interviewed can influence, and the issue is of deep concern to the person being interviewed. Issues for physical educators might include: "How will my most gifted athletes be challenged if I teach boys and girls together?" or, "This new curriculum includes a lot of concepts and skills I don't know anything about."

In step two, one partner interviews the other for approximately 20 minutes. The facilitator stops the interview and the partners switch roles. The purpose of the interview is to help teachers surface the concerns regarding an innovation that matter most to them.

Here are some interview guidelines:

1. Make the interview comfortable but challenging.

2. Keep it challenging but not threatening.

3. Try to elicit both deep and broad responses.

4. Keep the interview structured, but allow for flexibility and spontaneity.

5. Consider the rights and feelings of the respondent.

After teachers develop an understanding of their own issues and concerns, they are ready for a process of Analytic discourse. This technique helps them to more deeply explore their current understanding of a phenomena and enhances collegiality. Analytic discourse begins with groups of approximately six people sitting in a circle. Each group member takes several minutes to share the issues that surfaced in the reflective interview. If one particular issue is raised repeatedly, it becomes the focus of the Analytic discourse. A volunteer is then asked to be the subject of a group interview. A leader usually explains the purpose of the interview (to help the volunteer come to a full understanding of a troubling issue or concern). The interview ends when the volunteer states that everything known and understood about the issue has been explained to the best of his or her ability, and each interviewer can accurately paraphrase the volunteer's problem.

Interviewers must follow a strict set of rules if Analytic discourse is to be effective. Interviewers can only ask questions, make no critical comments, and offer no solutions.

After the interview, the interviewees should be asked how it felt to be interviewed, and how it felt to have the undivided attention of their colleagues on a topic they were concerned about. Interviewers should be asked what it was like to be an interviewer, and what it was like to refrain from offering suggestions and to focus on understanding the complexity of the issue.

Analytic discourse allows several things to occur that facilitate change: teachers discover common issues and concerns; they have the opportunity to develop a deep understanding of their issues which increases the possibility of working through them; and they develop a sense of community along with the ability to communicate and be heard (Sagor 1992, pp. 12-15).

Resistance to Change

Resistance to change does not have to be considered a threat to the survival of the system. People often misunderstand resistance; understanding individual attitudes and behaviors is essential to transitioning. It is not surprising that people seem resistant, when in fact any number of issues could be affecting their behaviors. These include lack of technical skill, lack of sufficient resources to change, and lack of clarity for the innovation goals and outcomes. The propensity for humans to want to label individuals as "resistant" probably causes more damage to the change process than do those who are resistant.

Change involves periods of intense personal and structural learning and problem solving. People need to feel supported during this time, not blamed or met with impatience. Self-interest is an important component of furthering change. It helps people consider appropriate support structures for the innovation, such as computer networking, rescheduling, planning time, student grouping strategies, and teacher teaming and sharing options.

Some physical educators have mentally divided themselves into "teachers who teach" and "teachers who resist teaching" (although there are any number of variations on the descriptors of these two groups). The net outcome of such actions is that physical educators become more and more polarized and unable to understand each other's needs and wants. The same strategies that have been discussed throughout this chapter for helping all teachers deal with change can work for resistant staff. And, keep in mind that staff members are not the only people who may be resistant to the change effort. Others could include parents, community members, and even students.

It is important to consider that parents and community members also may have concerns about the innovations being proposed. The most effective means of addressing their needs is to listen with compassion and empathy. Give them access to resources and information that will enable them to make informed decisions. Provide forums for sharing their concerns with others. Invite them to see the change in action. Make them a part of the culture of the learning community.

I have heard parents and community members described as obstacles, as if their very involvement impaired the implementation of change. We need to remember that they are part of the change process. They are just as integral to the process as any educator. If they are not allowed to participate in the initial stages of change (either by design or neglect), and if they are not valued for their contributions, they will very likely become detriments to implementation. The physical educator's role in relationship to parents and community members is to provide them with multiple opportunities—on an ongoing basis—to see, hear, read about, and become involved with change.

What about students? Most students demonstrate amazing adaptability, as evidenced by their ability to function in disparate learning environments, alternating from class to class, with 12 or more teachers a year from the time they are 12 or 13 years old. To develop the capacity of students to deal with change, teachers need to provide constructs for students that enhance adaptability.

Some structures and strategies that can help students deal effectively with change are:

- Using thinking/meaning teaching strategies and allowing the students to develop projects in which they construct their own meaning

- Employing Cooperative learning strategies that emphasize social skills and self-assessment

- Making "goal setting" and "achieving" a priority

- Providing a leaning environment that is physically and emotionally safe and that allows for positive student risk taking

- Using positive versus punitive discipline; positive discipline teaches responsible behavior, while punitive discipline inhibits the student's ability to internalize positive decision making skills

- Having routine forums for students to share feelings and concerns; e.g., class meetings, journals, peer feedback, peer discussions, and small-group processing

- Modeling critical thinking skills within teaching and learning

- Encouraging students to problem solve and share problem solving processes

- Having daily rituals that students can count on

- Providing grieving ceremonies and transition periods when students are getting used to a new way of doing something and saying goodbye to the old.

Students are constantly bombarded with changes, and they will be exposed to changes at an exponential rate compared to that of past generations. The best we can offer them is our appreciation and wonder at the ability of the world to continually adapt for renewal.

Assessing the Effectiveness of the Change Effort

How do you measure the success of the implementation of your innovation—whether it is a new direction in curriculum content, implementing student-centered instructional strategies, a new approach to discipline, authentic assessment, or any other new idea, strategy, or program? You may choose any number of methods from informal (Does this seem to be working for us?) to formal (complex data collection strategies, surveys, student assessments).

I will suggest some possible ideas for measuring the effectiveness of change with the reminder that not all variables can or should be isolated for observation. The nature of change is seldom linear. It may take years to notice the impact of a single innovation. There are, however, some indicators that the change is leading you in the right direction. These include:

- Answering questions such as: "Are we taking incremental steps?" "Are we getting consensus on the change from all personnel affected by the change?" "Are we collaborating and cooperating on goals of the change?" "Have we been willing and open to share successes and failures?" "Do we feel free to take risks and value mistakes for what they can teach us?" "Do the individuals involved in the change feel a profound personal and professional connection to the change effort?" "Is the staff involved in the change continually and actively seeking and participating in professional growth activities related to the change?" "Is there a noticeable increase in the valuing of physical education by school site peers and administrators?" "Are we able to access greater financial support, resources, materials, etc. as a result of the change effort?"

- Gathering data: Use of authentic student projects that demonstrate the effectiveness of the new strategy, curriculum, etc.; surveys of students, staff, parents, and department personnel involved in the change; and statistics on increases in student participation, attendance, and assessment scores.

* Using the characteristics of holonomy to continuously self-assess personal and professional skills relative to implementing the change.

* Conducting individual self-monitoring using the CBAM model, periodically throughout the change.

* Using professional journals to record the successes, obstacles, and solutions to obstacles over time.

* Using collaborative Action Research projects (described earlier in this chapter) that are aimed at key issues in the change.

* Demonstrating patience, mutual respect and understanding; an openness to accept both successes and failures in the change effort; and a willingness to discuss the results of the effort and make ongoing modifications as needed to maximize the accuracy of the assessment of the change. Assessing the change over time, rather than considering it a one-time event also will increase the validity of the assessment.

Chapter Summary

The work of Edward Lorenz led to the butterfly metaphor popularized in the movie, Jurassic Park. The theory states that the wings of a butterfly in Peking generate tiny currents of air that can influence a storm system over New York City some time in the future (Garmston 1994). Educators have the capacity to generate enormous amounts of changes by taking deliberate, seemingly tiny steps in the right directions. Connecting with the web of values, visions, and culture reverberating through the system creates pathways of energy. They feed on themselves and grow into a living, dynamic whole. Educators who have experienced this feeling describe it as exciting, energizing, empowering, and immensely satisfying.

Dynamic change occurs in an environment that fosters communication and shares common goals and values; an environment where people plan and problem solve together, propagating a Common vision. Margaret Wheatley notes a general movement in all organizations toward expanded participation. This is not a fad that will pass away and be gone. This tendency for participation is rooted, "...perhaps, subconsciously, in our changing conception of the organizational principals of the universe" (Wheatley 1992, p. 143).

References

Fullan, M. G., & Miles, M. B. (June 1992). Getting reform right: What works and what doesn't, *Phi Delta Kappan*, 745-752.

Garmston, R. (1994). *Strengthening school restructuring through effective, site-based decision making*. Bellevue, WA: Bureau of Education & Research.

Hall, G. E., Newlove, B. W., Rutherford, W. L., & Horder, S. M. (1990). *Measuring change facilitator stages of concern: A manual for use of the CFSoC questionnaire*. Greely, CO: Center for Research on Teaching and Learning, The University of Northern Colorado.

Hall, G. E., & Hord, S. M. (1987). *Change in schools, facilitating the process*. Albany, NY: State University of New York Press.

Jantsch, E. (1980). *The self-organizing universe*. Oxford: Pergamon Press.

Louis, K. S., & Miles, M. B. (1990). *Improving the urban high school: What works and why*. New York: Teachers College Press.

Prigogine, I. (May 1983). Omni, 85-121.

Sagor, R. (1992). *How to conduct collaborative action research*. Alexandria, VA: Association for Supervision and Curriculum Development.

Senge, P. (1990). *The fifth discipline*. New York: Doubleday.

Stallings, J. & Freiber, H. J. (1991). *Observation for the improvement of teaching*. Publication Series 91-3. Philadelphia, PA: Temple University Center for Research in Human Development and Education.

Wheatley, M. J. (1992). *Leadership and the new science*. San Francisco, CA: Berrett-Koehler.

CHAPTER 3

Curriculum, Assessment, and Accountability

Bobbie Harris and Kathy Ermler

An integrated and comprehensive physical education program requires the leadership of many different individuals. A single individual cannot simply write the program and "give" it to teachers. The input of all physical educators who will be using the curriculum is required.

A curriculum should clearly define the skills, knowledge, and values students should acquire at various levels. Physical educators must develop and use authentic assessment tools and techniques to obtain feedback about their program and the progress of the students. If physical educators are to be truly accountable, they must be able to clearly state what the student should learn, offer activities to help the student learn, and assess whether the student has actually acquired the knowledge.

This chapter will examine the leadership factors associated with the curriculum process, assessment procedures, and the issue of accountability. The seven major points it will cover are:

1. The Need for a New Direction
2. Developing Standards
3. Creating Curriculum
4. Implementing the Curriculum
5. Creating Assessment
6. Implementing Assessment
7. Accountability.

The Need for a New Direction

Historically, some physical education programs were designed to meet the needs of athletically gifted individuals with little, if any, consideration for the needs of individuals with minimal athletic talent. This focus led many to experience the type of horror stories Passero (1995) wrote about in her article, "The Agony of the Ex-P.E. Student":

Dodgeball was another nightmare. It seemed like the twentieth-century equivalent of a stoning: OK, boys and girls, let's all stand in a circle and let the bully in the center hurl the ball at us as hard as he can. Then we'll try to leap out of the way before we get beaned! Welcome to the Klaus Barbie school of phys. ed.

Choosing teams is even worse. We stand on display as if being auctioned off. Kids around me jog off cheerfully to their respective team, but I remain alone in the center of the gym until someone relents, Oh, all right. I choose Kathy."

Panic sweeps over me and suddenly I'm 12 again, facing the horror of first hour P.E. Otherwise a relatively well-accepted, if slightly chubby, preadolescent, I am reduced to a social outcast in gym class.

He's sentencing me to the worst of all possible fates: the flexed-arm hang.
My legs turn to cold spaghetti.

It appears she learned one lesson—fear. The worst part of the article reflected how common this experience can be:

Recently, I mentioned my trauma to a few friends and, to my surprise, all but one confessed to having loathed P.E. Even though many of us have lost our extra pounds and embraced exercise, we're still wary of sports.

Many principals, school board members, superintendents, and parents have had similar experiences in physical education. We must do more than prepare students for athletic pursuits; we must meet the very real health, physical activity, and fitness needs of our students.

I spent many years teaching sports skills and games. One day, as I was testing students to determine the power of their tennis serve, I suddenly realized I was spending a great deal of time doing two things:

■ Teaching content that would not affect the students' quality of life.

■ Teaching students the way to pass skill tests.

I was spending time and energy teaching "stuff" that was not very important! I asked myself, "If I went before my school board, could I justify what I was teaching?" Suddenly, the obvious questions entered my thoughts:

■ What should I be teaching these students that matters in today's world?

■ What could I give them that would affect the quality of their lives as teenagers and as adults?

■ What skills should I give them to take into the "real" world?

I decided that healthy attitudes and a lifestyle of wellness were more important than the accuracy or power of a tennis serve. Problem solving, cooperation, teamwork, and critical thinking are skills that contribute more to the personal and educational growth of young people than does winning a game of flag football.

A very practical first step in any curriculum process is for the physical educators in the school district to answer one very simple question: What would they say to their school board to justify the physical education program?

Developing Standards

Once the need for a new direction has been established, the next step is the development of standards. In 1995, NASPE published content standards and assessment material for physical education. This extraordinary document, *Moving into the Future: National Standards for Physical Education*, established seven content standards:

1. Demonstrates competence in many movement forms and proficiency in a few movement forms. (Motor Skills)

2. Applies movement concepts and principles to the learning and development of motor skills. (Concepts)

3. Exhibits a physically active lifestyle. (Active Lifestyle)

4. Achieves and maintains a health-enhancing level of physical fitness. (Physical Fitness)

5. Demonstrates responsible personal and social behavior in physical activity settings. (Personal and Social Skills)

6. Demonstrates understanding and respect for differences among people in physical activity settings. (Diversity)

7. Understands that physical activity provides opportunities for enjoyment, challenge, self-expression and social interaction. (Values Physical Activity)

These written standards provide a general description of each content standard, and are followed by delineation of the standards for grades K-12 in two-year intervals. In addition, benchmarks and assessment examples are provided for each grade level standard. These seven standards have united our profession; they provide a unified direction and focus for all physical educators.

The leader who is facilitating the physical education curriculum change can suggest that the group accept the standards with no changes, accept the standards with modifications that reflect the community philosophy, or reject the standards and develop an entirely new set of standards. If the group envisions a focus that differs from the one identified by the NASPE standards, it must solidify that vision before it can begin to develop a comprehensive physical education curriculum. A primary function of the leader during this stage is to help the group understand the standards and how they affect curriculum development. Consider the following example.

The teachers in the Wichita (Kansas) Public School District had difficulty envisioning how the seven standards provided a "pathway" to becoming a physically educated person (Hensley

1997). As a result, they decided that all seven standards should be taught, but each grade level should emphasize different ones, as illustrated below.

- Elementary Level: The elementary level should emphasize Standards 1 (Motor Skills) and 2 (Concepts). While elementary teachers want their students to be physically active and healthy and to work together and display positive sportsmanship, their main focus is teaching all the basic skills.

- Middle Level: The middle level should emphasize Standards 5 (Personal & Social Skills), 6 (Diversity), and 7 (Values Exercise). While middle school teachers want their students to be physically active and healthy and to have basic motor skills, their main focus is teaching personal and social responsibility.

- Secondary Level: The secondary level should emphasize Standards 3 (Active Lifestyle) and 4 (Physical Fitness). While secondary teachers want their students to have basic motors skills and personal and social skills, their main focus is on the development of an active and healthy lifestyle.

The teachers began to see the whole picture as they worked together, K - 12. The process can be seen in the Curriculum Flow Chart. (See Figure 3.1.)

Creating Curriculum

Standards are not meant to be curriculum, and they are not meant to dictate instruction. They are meant to provide a framework for curriculum and to guide instruction. And curriculum does not tell the teacher how to teach; it provides a map to achieve the standards. The curriculum leader needs to ensure that the planning group identifies ways to achieve the standards. This is a systematic process. First, everyone agrees on what students should know and be able to do upon exiting the program, and then activities and experiences that will assist the students in reaching those standards are created.

Creating a written curriculum takes a great deal of time and a "buy in" from all teachers in the district. Teachers are the best curriculum writers, because they know and understand the characteristics of their clients. They are aware of the students' ages and stages of development, the community norms, and their own strengths and weaknesses.

However, decisions teachers make about activities and experiences often are made without considering the big picture of the final standards. If teachers are asked how they decided to include archery, or dance, or football in the curriculum, they often respond with a teacher-centered, rather than a student centered, approach. For example they may say, those activities are being taught because "I" enjoy them, or "I" learned those activities at a conference, or "I" decided on that because of the weather conditions of the day. This approach is in direct contradiction to the emphasis on standards, and certainly leaves the most important person—the student—out of the decision-making process.

Perhaps the most difficult task the curriculum leader has is

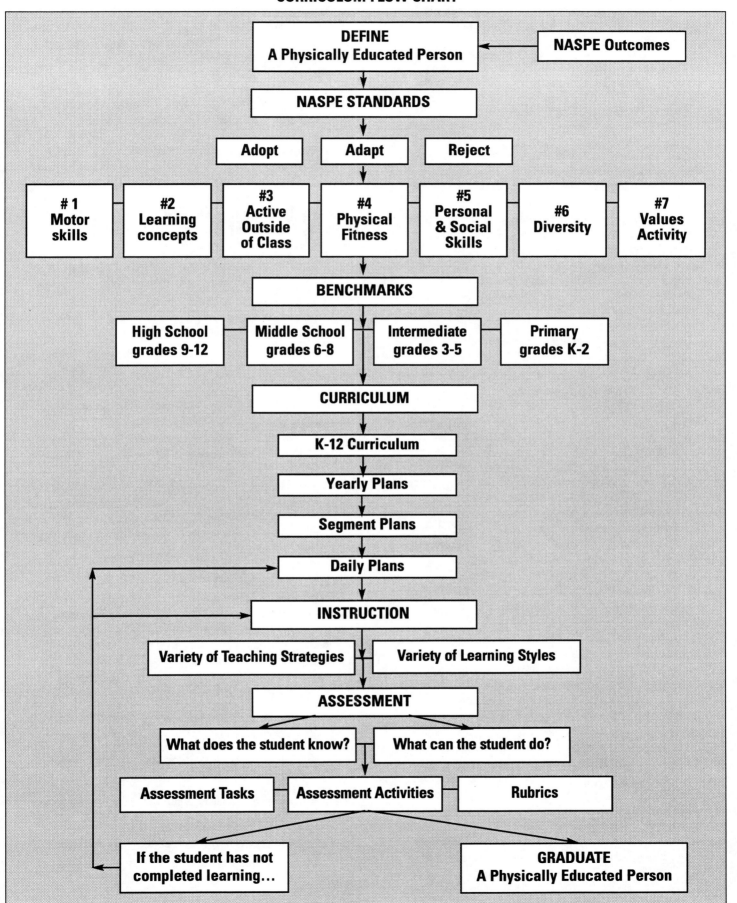

moving the group to a student-centered approach. In order to make this transition, the group needs to take the standards they are using and develop benchmarks for them. Benchmarks are competencies specific to certain grade levels. They serve two purposes:

1. They clearly define what behaviors are necessary to accomplish a specific standard.

2. They direct assessment procedures and target times for assessment.

During this stage, the leader needs to reassure the group that benchmarks are not instructional objectives, and that the decisions concerning instructional activities remain with each teacher.

At this stage, the teachers may want to break into groups with each grade level (elementary, middle, and secondary) represented in order to create appropriate benchmarks for each standard. In Wichita, the teachers took the seven NASPE standards and wrote benchmarks for each grade level. For example, for Standard 1 (Motor Skills), the teachers developed several age appropriate benchmarks for each grade. (See Figure 3.2.)

This can be a very tedious part of the curriculum process. Most teachers want to get to the "meat and potatoes" of the curriculum without examining the "nutritional needs" of the students. Once they struggle with this process, however, they will understand and be able to articulate what it means to be a physically educated person, and they will know how their programs contribute to the development of such a person.

Implementing the Curriculum

This is a critical stage: Either all the work up to this point is disregarded, or the work is actualized and put into practice. The leader's role at this point is keep the teachers focused on the benchmarks and standards, and to help them keep their instructional activities in perspective. They are no longer teaching basketball, volleyball, or football; rather, they are using these activities to achieve various benchmarks and, ultimately, to develop physically educated students who have the knowledge and skills to live a physically active, healthy life.

Teachers should be free to write yearly and unit plans that are distinctive to their educational setting. However, the plans need to be focused on the benchmarks and standards. In Wichita, as teachers developed their plans they were asked to indicate where each benchmark that had been identified for that grade level was being covered. One way to ensure the benchmarks are covered is to develop a simple check system. This check system permits a quick visual review of the integration of the plan with the benchmarks. See Figure 3.3.

This check system will enable the leader to keep the teachers focused on the benchmarks, and it may help in identifying curricular weaknesses. For example, if one of the benchmarks is not covered in any of the activities selected by the teachers, they may have to rethink what they are teaching in order to achieve that benchmark. Many teachers will try to make their current curriculum "fit" into benchmarks. Fortunately, that is like putting a square peg into a round hole—the teachers are forced

to examine the appropriateness of the activities and experiences and the focus of those activities.

At this stage, the leader also must focus on the continued growth and motivation of the staff. Teachers need time to meet, interact, and discuss problems, concerns, and successes they have had implementing the curriculum.

Wichita used district inservice days to bring all the district teachers together for this purpose. The teachers would suggest a need they had, and the leader would attempt to develop materials, resources, and presenters to meet that need.

Another way to work on professional growth is to hold monthly meetings where teachers can share new ideas or discuss new directions. A very real attempt should be made to prevent these meetings from becoming complaint sessions. The meetings should be open to all teachers, and a specific focus should be planned and conveyed to the teachers in advance.

As a result of these professional opportunities, the leader discovered that several changes had begun to occur:

▧ Many teachers who had never written yearly plans began to develop excellent yearly plans.

▧ Teachers began to communicate clearly to students, parents, and administrators about the goals and outcomes of the physical education program.

▧ Teachers began to use a common language, including terms such as physically educated person, standards, benchmarks, etc.

▧ Teachers began to network, not only with teachers at the same level, but with teachers at all levels. Teachers at the secondary level began to understand what the elementary and middle school physical educators were doing, and how those things interfaced with their programs.

▧ The physical education program in Wichita changed from a sports-oriented curriculum to a fitness/wellness curriculum. This "new curriculum" used a broad range of physical activities to teach students how to become physically educated.

Creating Assessment

Curriculum development would be incomplete without an assessment mechanism. Assessment is not an independent process; it is an integral aspect of curriculum development. This is the stage that could be considered the "glue" in the curriculum. It is a stage that allows teachers to ascertain whether the preceding stages are making a difference in their students' learning. Assessment answers the questions:

1. How do students know they have learned something in physical education?

2. How do teachers know if the students have learned the objectives of the lesson?

3. How do teachers know what to change in their learning activities?

4. How do parents know their children are making progress?

As assessment procedures are implemented, the major function of the curriculum leader will be to define and clarify terminology. Assessment terminology is confusing and the following terms frequently are used interchangeably and incorrectly.

- Assessment: Determines what students know and can do. Assessment is a developmental, ongoing process.

- Test: A series of questions or exercises or some other means of measuring the skill, knowledge, intelligence, or aptitudes of an individual or a group. Testing takes place at one moment in time. A test is a product.

- Align: To match physical education curriculum and outcomes with district mission and outcomes.

- Articulate: A physical education curriculum that is written with K–12 scope and sequence.

- Alternative assessment: Generally, any kind of assessment technique or tool other than a traditional norm-referenced or criterion-referenced pencil-and-paper test.

- Authentic assessment: A generic term for alternative assessment methods that test students' ability to solve problems or perform tasks under simulated "real life" situations.

- Formative assessment: Continuous methods of determining how students are progressing toward meeting identified outcomes at the daily lesson unit level.

- Summative assessment: Demonstrated accomplishment at the end of a given unit, course, or curriculum block that indicates students have achieved success in meeting identified outcomes at that level.

- Rubric: A set of guidelines for giving scores for student work.

- Grade: The statistical level at which a student performs on a standardized test. Often used as a tool for communicating with students and parents. At best, it is a ranking score. Grades are traditionally used by secondary teachers.

Once teachers understand the differences between these terms, the leader can facilitate the development of assessment procedures and techniques. This step can be relatively simple if the group realizes teaching is inseparable from assessment, and that assessment can enhance student learning.

In Wichita, four basic questions guided the implementation of assessment:

1. What should students know and be able to do? Can the teachers clearly identify the outcomes for their programs for the year, the unit, and the daily lesson? Can they explain what they want their students to know and be able to do at the end of a lesson?

2. How will we know if students have reached those outcomes? What evidence is there to demonstrate student accomplishments? Do students realize the connections between the objectives and their accomplishments?

3. How will we report/record student progress? What system will we use to let students, parents, administrators, and members of the community know about student progress?

4. How will assessment results be used? What will the students, parents, administrators, or community members do with this information?

Since the first question had already been addressed by the standards, benchmarks, and activity units, the leader had the assessment teams focus on the second question: What evidence should be used to determine if students had reached those outcomes? The leader should direct the group to create "evidence" for the grade levels where assessment will take place. Some districts will assess student progress at every grade level, other districts will assess every two years, and still others will have varying combinations of assessments.

While assessment procedures will vary from school to school and district to district, the principle remains the same: Identify what students should be able to do, and then develop a means to demonstrate that learning.

In Wichita, the assessment committee developed two integrated procedures:

1. The committee created a developmental rubric for each of the seven standards. (See Figure 3.4.)

2. The committee created sample assessment activities for elementary, middle, and secondary levels for each standard. (See Figure 3.5.)

Rubrics are generally used for specific tasks, but a developmental rubric will assess the level at which students perform from kindergarten through graduation. For example, catching is a basic skill that Wichita teachers want all students to demonstrate as a motor skill necessary to live a physically active life. The developmental rubric can be used by all teachers, elementary through high school, to monitor their students' catching development. A sample of a developmental rubric is seen in Figure 3.6, and a specific task rubric in Figure 3.7.

The rubrics were used to demonstrate the level of proficiency at which a student was working for each standard. The assessment activities were used to provide information to the students, the parents, and the teacher about what the students knew and could do. Students were able to use this information to set goals, recognize strengths, and correct weaknesses in their performances. Parents were able to understand the progress their children were making. Teachers were able to improve instruction and alter and supplement instructional plans when necessary.

Implementing Assessment

Initially, the Wichita teachers questioned the need for assessment. However, the paradigm shift the teachers made in the curriculum development process made it easy to overcome this resistance. Once the teachers had bought into the outcomes focused curriculum, they began to realize authentic assessment procedures were necessary to complement and improve the curriculum.

It is at this point that the leader needs to help the teachers realize that curriculum is a process, and that it takes on a life form of its own: creation, development, assessment, change, development, assessment, etc. In Wichita, the leader used the following

FIGURE 3.2: Wichita Public Schools Physical Education Program Standards

All areas of the Wichita K-12 Physical Education Curriculum are aligned with the USD 259 Curriculum and the National Standards for Physical Education developed by the National Association for Sport and Physical Education (NASPE).

Grade 1: Motor Skills/Standard 1
All students will develop the ability to control the use of fundamental motor patterns.
1. All students will demonstrate the following skills:
    Demonstrate motor patterns of running, leaping, walking, galloping, skipping, hopping, and sliding.
    Demonstrate the ability to balance on a variety of body parts.
    Demonstrate hand and foot dominance.
    Continuously self toss and catch an object at various levels.
    Negotiate a low balance beam using forward, backward and sidestep patterns.
    Dribble a ball from a seated, kneeling, or standing position.
    Demonstrate the ability to move an object with their feet.
    Run and kick a moving ball without hesitating or stopping prior to the kick.
    Demonstrate continuous striking skills using hand or other object.
    Demonstrate underhand and overhand throwing skills into or at a target.
    Jump and land safely and in control from a height of approximately 12".
    Use different locomotor skills to move at different speeds, levels, and directions while moving in relationship to others.
    Continuously jump a turned rope held by others.
    Demonstrate the correct movement patterns for self-turned rope skills.
    Travel in forwards, sideways, and backwards directions and change directions safely without falling.

Grade 2: Motor Skills/Standard 1
All students will develop the ability to control the use of fundamental motor patterns.
1. All students will demonstrate the ability to catch, dribble with hand and foot, kick, strike, throw, and volley.
2. All students will demonstrate the ability to gallop, skip, how and slide showing mature motor patterns.
3. All students can jump a long rope.
4. All students can perform the skills of rolling, balance, jumping and landing, and transfer of weight.

Grade 3: Motor Skills/Standard 1
Demonstrates competency in many and proficiency in a few movement forms. All students will develop maturity and versatility in the use of fundamental skills.
1. All students will demonstrate the following skills:
    Perform locomotor movements, starting and stopping on command and in control.
    Refine forward jump rope skills and initiate backwards skills and beginning individual tricks.
    Demonstrate agility and the ability to change directions during group activities while manipulating an object.
    Consistently demonstrate proper striking patterns when attempting to hit a thrown object.
    Negotiate medium height beam using forward, backward, and sidestep pattern and hold a steady position.
    Lift and control body weight and hold for a specified time.
    Transfer weight to a handstand position against a wall and attempt to hold that position.
    Demonstrate simple sequence patterns using combination of movements.

Grade 4: Motor Skills/Standard 1
All students will develop maturity and versatility in the use of fundamental skills.
1. All students will demonstrate the following skills:
    Escape, catch, or dodge an individual or object while traveling.
    Leap, leading with either foot.
    Jump and land, throw, catch, and kick using mature motor patterns.
    Travel into and out of a rope turned by others.
    Roll into a backwards direction without hesitating or stopping.
    Balance with obvious control on a variety of moving objects (e.g. balance boards, skates, skis).
    Transfer weight from feet to hands at fast and slow speeds using large extensions (e.g. mulekick, handstand, cartwheel).
    Strike a softly thrown, lightweight ball back to a partner using a variety of body parts and combination of body parts (e.g. the bump or volley as in volleyball; the thigh as in soccer).
    Hand and foot dribble a ball and maintain control while traveling within a group.
    Consistently strike a softly thrown ball with a bat of paddle demonstrating an appropriate grip, side to the target, and swing plane.
    Develop patterns and combinations of movements into repeatable sequences.

Grade 5: Motor Skills/Standard 1
All students will develop maturity and versatility in the use of fundamental skills.
1. All students will demonstrate the ability to catch, dribble with hand and foot, kick, strike, throw, and volley.
2. All students will demonstrate the tumbling skills of balance, rolling, jumping and landing, and transfer of weight.
3. All students will demonstrate the skill of jumping rope.

Grade 6: Motor Skills/Standard 1
All students will demonstrate motor patterns, now having evolved into specialized skills, that are used in increasingly complex movement activities.
1. All students will demonstrate the following motor skills:
   Leap, roll, balance, transfer weight, bat volley, hand and foot dribble, and strike a ball with a paddle, using mature motor pattern.
   Design and perform gymnastics and/or dance sequences that combine traveling, rolling, balancing, and weight transfer into smooth, flowing sequences with intentional changes in direction, speed, flow.
   Perform a routine combining various jump rope movements so that it can be repeated without error.
   Consistently throw and catch a ball.
   Throw a variety of objects demonstrating accuracy (e.g.frisbees, deck tennis rings, footballs).
   continuously strike a ball to a wall of a partner with a paddle or racquet using both forehand and backhand strokes.
   In a small group, keep an abject continuously in the air without catching it (e.g. ball, foot bag).
   Play small group games that involve cooperating with others to keep an object away from opponents, using basic offensive and defensive strategy (e.g. by throwing, kicking, and/or dribbling a ball).

Grade 7: Motor Skills/Standard 1
All students will demonstrate motor patterns, now having evolved into specialized skills, that are used in increasingly complex movement activities.
1. All students will demonstrate the ability to catch, dribble with hand and foot, kick, strike, throw, and volley.
2. All students will demonstrate the ability to perform a rhythmic routine.
3. All students will demonstrate the ability to perform basic gymnastics skills.

Grade 8: Motor Skills/Standard 1
All students will demonstrate motor patterns, now having evolved into specialized skills, that are used in increasingly complex movement activities.
1. All students will demonstrate the following motor skills:
   Use basic offensive and defensive strategies in modified net games (e.g. tennis, volleyball, badminton) and invasive games (e.g. soccer, basketball).
   Combine skills competently to participate in modified versions of team and individual sports (e.g. soccer, racquetball, tennis, golf).
   Demonstrate track and field skills.
   Perform a variety of simple folk, square, and/or creative dances.
   Demonstrate knowledge of offensive and defensive strategies in games and sports.

FIGURE 3.3: Sample Benchmarks and Activities

8th Grade Benchmarks	Activities/Experiences			
	Volleyball	Aerobics	Recreation Games	Lacrosse
Uses basic offensive and defensive strategies in modified net games and evasive games	✔			✔
Applies rules and courtesies in physical activities	✔		✔	✔
Analyzes and categorizes activities and exercises according to potential fitness benefits	✔	✔	✔	✔

FIGURE 3.4: Sample Developmental Rubric

Standard #5: Demonstrates responsible personal and social behavior in physical activity settings. (Social)	Standard #7: Understands that physical activity provides opportunities for enjoyment, challenge, self-expression, and social interaction. (Values Exercise)
PK-9	**PK-9**
6 Can initiate independent and responsible personal behavior, demonstrate leadership and group work, and can anticipate and plan for safety, rules, procedures, and etiquette.	6 Can share enjoyment and influence others to participate more in physicla activity.
5 Can work independent of peer pressure, make mature behavior choices (regarding safety, conflict, etiquette, etc.), work well within a coperative and competitive group, while completing goals.	5 Can identify specific reasons for participation in physical activity.
4 Can begin to positively influence others with reflections on safety, rules, procedures, and etiquette, and demonstrate problem solving techniques.	4 Can show appreciation for physical activity by identifying positive experiences outside the classroom..
3 Can work cooperatively and independently to help establish rules, make decisions about etiquette, procedures, and safety practices, and stay on task.	3 Can identify specific positive feelings about movement and activity.
2 Can work independently and with others while following rules, procedures, etiquette, and safety practices, and to complete tasks.	2 Can express positive feelings about movement while participating in a group.
1 Can work with others and follow directions, rules, and safety practices.	1 Participates in group activities.
NS No Score	NS No Score

FIGURE 3.5: Wichita Public Schools USD 259 Physical Education Standards Sample Assessment Activities

Demonstrates competency in many and proficiency in a few motor forms. (Motor Skills)

DRIBBLE/HAND

Elementary Suggestions
1. Students dribble in self and general space. Challenge the students with variations such as, one hand only, self-space for 10 times in a row.
2. Students dribble a ball with one hand while moving in empty space and maintaining control.
3. Students dribble in empty spaces and switch hands on signal, maintaining control.
4. Students take part in a game involving dribbling (i.e. dribble tag.)

Middle Level Suggestions
1. Use Elementary suggestions.
2. Students dribble around one defender to a designated finish line or goal.
3. Students dribble a ball with control through three defenders for approximately 30 feet and challenge them to use dominant and non-dominant hand.
4. Students demonstrate dribbling skills in a Keep-Away game.

5. Play Team Handball.
6. Play modified and lead-up Basketball games.

High School Suggestions
1. Use Elementary and Middle Level suggestions.
2. Using the game of Newcomb students catch an 8 inch nerf ball.
   How to Play: Newcomb is a modified catching volleyball game. Use catching instead of bumping and passing. Use a variety of objects.
3. All Star Dribble Down:
   How to Play: In groups of 4-5, students line up along one sideline. Place 5 markers in a star formation before each group, 10 feet apart. Each student dribbles a start pattern around the cones, then returns to the starting line. Require students to use the correct hand when dribbling around each cone. The drill can be made more complex by shortening the distance between cones to 5 feet.
4. Play basketball. (3 on 3)

FIGURE 3.6: Sample Developmental Rubric

	Catch PK-9	Dribble/Hand PK-9	Dribble/Foot PK-9	Kick PK-9	Strike PK-9	Throw PK-9	Volley PK-9
6	Can catch an object thrown with increased velocity or catch an object while moving	Can dribble around moving obstacles using dominant and non-dominant hands, while moving with greater speed	Can use feet to dribble with control and agility at greater speed	Performs a variety of kicks, with defenders, showing increased velocity and accuracy	Can strike a ball with increased velocity and accuracy	Can throw with increased velocity and accuracy	Can sustain a volley using hands, arms, or racket, with two people or more
5	Can transfer catching skills to a "game situation"	Can transfer dribbleing skills with either hand to a "game situation"	Can transfer dribbling skills with either foot to a "game situation"	Can transfer kicking skills to a "game situation"	Transfers kicking skills to a "game situation"	Can transfer throwing skills to a "game situation"	Can transfer volley skills to a "game situation"
4	Can catch a variety of objects at different levels with a partner	Can dribble in control with either hand while moving	Can dribble a ball around moving obsta-cles, using both feet.	Can demonstrate a variety of kicks (stationary, drop-kick, moving ball) using various types of balls	Steps toward and makes contact with a moving object	Shows trund rotation and accuracy	Self-toss or partner volley a lightweight ball using hands, arms, or racket, showing lower body flexion and proper body position
3	Can catch a variety of self-tossed objects	Can dribble in control with dominant hand while moving	Can move a ball using a variety of pathways and can dribble around or through various obstacles	Can kick a stationary or moving ball and follow through toward target	Steps toward and makes contact with a stationary object	Follows through toward target	Volley a light-weight ball tossed by a partner, using arms, hands, or racket
2	Can catch a bounced ball from a partner	Can dribble with one hand in self-space while keeping control of the ball	Can move a ball using either foot while keeping ball in control and close to the body	Moves toward a stationary ball and makes contact wioth dominant foot	Shows side orientation and proper grip	Shows opposition	Can volley an object, main-taining control, with hands, arms, or racket
1	Arms extended toward thrower, shows avoid-ance reaction	Can bounce a ball using one or two hands in self or gener-ated space	Can move a ball with feet	Limited body movement, leg dominated action	Limited body movement, arm dominated	Limited body movement, arm dominated	Can volley a balloon with hands
NS	No score	No score	No score	No score	No score	No score	No score

five steps to keep the process growing and developing:

1. Education and training of teachers in the curriculum and assessment techniques. We used district inservice days, workshops, and meetings to bring teachers together to share new ideas. We created a physical education curriculum and assessment vocabulary in order for teachers to understand the curriculum process and assess-ment procedures.

2. Collection of data from teachers on student achievement. Each physical education teacher was asked to assess one class on all seven standards. The teachers took small steps in learning how to assess. By having teachers use assess-ment techniques on a small scale, they were able to use them more effectively and efficiently.

3. Analysis of data to improve curriculum and instruction. Data collected from teachers and students was used to make revisions in the curriculum and instruction.

4. Accumulation of data from the teachers on the assessment project. The teachers were surveyed about the assessment

FIGURE 3.7: Sample Specific Task Rubric
Physical Education Motor Skills Assessment

Outcome:
Students create a game including scoring options, a penalty system, and sample offensive and defensive strategies.

Assessment Tool Options:
Students choose from three options:
1. Students create a video of their game showing all scoring options and penalties along with sample strategies.
2. Students write an essay describing all aspects of their game.
3. On a poster board, students diagram all aspects of their game.

Rubric:
6   Game includes correct application of scoring options, penalties, and strategies. Game is original.

5   Game includes correct application of scoring options, penalties, and strategies. However, it is not original.

4   Game includes scoring options, penalties, and strategies, but it does not have correct application.

3   Game includes two of the three requirements of scoring options, penalties, and strategies with minor flaws in application.

2   Plan includes the three requirements of scoring options, penalties, and strategies with major flaws in application.

1   Plan includes only one or two requirements of scoring options, penalties, and strategies with major flaws in application.

NS No Score

project the committee had created and were asked for suggestions, ideas, and new directions.

5. Updating, rewriting, and improving the assessment techniques. The information collected from the teachers was used to update, review, and rewrite the curriculum and assessment techniques on a yearly basis.

Through these five steps, the teachers had begun to understand what Wiggins (1991) meant when he said, "The goal of student assessment is not merely to measure student performance, but to improve it."

Accountability

Physical education teachers are famous for leading classes that are fun and active. Students come to class and teachers create great activities that are full of competition, aerobic activity, and cooperative and challenging games. When the teacher is asked what was accomplished that day, the answer may cover everything from having fun to completing a weight lifting routine. But, what actually was accomplished?

Consider Alice, and how she wandered around Wonderland…

"Would you tell me, please," said Alice, "which way I ought to walk from here?"

"That depends a good deal on where you want to get to," said the Cat.

"I don't much care where…" said Alice.

"Then it doesn't matter which way you walk," said the Cat.

"…as long as I get somewhere," Alice added, as an explanation.

"Oh, you're sure to do that," said the Cat, "if you only walk long enough."

(*Alice in Wonderland* – Lewis Carroll)

Most physical education teachers are enthusiastic, caring, positive people with great attitudes. Kids love them! But, are they helping our students? And if they are, can they prove it? Or, like Alice, are they just wandering from place to place, having a great time and enjoying some wonderful experiences?

If physical education teachers do not have a purpose or a plan (a curriculum), and if they cannot clearly express their goals to the students, those 180 days of fun may be difficult to justify. On the other hand, they also wouldn't want to have a clear goal and purpose and not have fun getting there; they must have both. Never give up the wonder of having fun and being active, but also be accountable and know where you are going!

Because parents and school board members want to know what teachers are doing and why they are doing it, the big question is, "Can they prove that they've done it?" The community wants all teachers to be accountable, and in order to be accountable one must write a curriculum that contains clear outcomes and then prove that students have learned and can demonstrate these outcomes. If teachers cannot show what students know and can do, they do not have an instructional program. And they must have an instructional program in order to be part of the curriculum and ensure that all students have the opportunity to become physically educated persons.

Chapter Summary

This chapter has defined the need for a new direction for physical education curricula, demonstrated how the National Standards for Physical Education can guide curriculum development, and suggested ways to create and implement curriculum and assessment procedures. Accountability is the beginning and the end for curriculum and assessment.

References

DeMoss, M. (1996). *Physical education and teaching strategies by Wichita Public Schools elementary physical education teachers.* Wichita, KS: USD 259.

DeMoss, M. (1996). *Wichita Public Schools physical education program standards.* Wichita, KS: USD 259.

DeMoss, M. (1997). *Wichita Public Schools physical education standards: Assessment rubrics, draft 3.* Wichita, KS: USD 259.

Ermler, K. (1997). *Physical dimensions. The Kansas high school physical activity and health/wellness curriculum.* Wichita, KS: Kansas Health Foundation.

Hensley, L. (1997, March). *Creating a vision and bringing it to life.* Paper presented at the AAHPERD National Convention & Exposition, St. Louis, MO.

Passero, K. (1995). The agony of the ex-P.E. student. *Weight Watchers Magazine, 5,* 74.

Rink, J., Ed. (1995). *Moving into the future. National standards for physical education: A guide to content and assessment.* Reston, VA: National Association for Sport and Physical Education.

Wiggins, G. (1991). Standards, not standardization: Evoking quality student work. *Educational Leadership, 48*(5), 18–25.

Wilson, J. (1992). *Kansas adolescent physical activity and health/fitness pilot project.* Topeka, KS: Kansas Department of Education.

CHAPTER 4

Professional Development in Physical Education: Education Never Ends

Betty Hennessy

During my years attending kindergarten through high school, I was unfamiliar with the term metacognition. Learning how to learn did not seem to be an important outcome of the school system. Although I enjoyed some teachers more than others, felt more motivated in some classes than others, and seemed to learn more in some classes than others, I never gave much thought to *how* I was learning. Rather, I focused on what I needed to learn to earn a certain grade and pass the class.

During my teacher education preservice program I was taught how to teach children in the same the way I had been taught: by focusing on duplicating skills and knowledge. Thus, when I began my teaching career as an elementary physical education specialist, I taught my students how to duplicate skills and knowledge.

Then something changed. As I began my graduate work in night school, I had the opportunity to take a physical education course taught by a teacher from England. As a student, I was asked to work with other students to solve movement problems. By experimenting with the movements and by being engaged with the movements, we solved movement problems. Then, we were asked to reflect on how we learned to solve the problems; how we learned to move.

Although many of my teacher preparation classes were excellent, to this day I remember the most about that particular class. In addition to being engaged in the learning process, I was able to apply my new skills and knowledge immediately in the physical education classes I was teaching during the day. My students reacted to the new learning process in the same way I had reacted: They were engaged, motivated, and empowered. They were no longer recipients and duplicators of skills and knowledge; they were shapers and creators of skills and knowledge. And in turn, the physical education classes I taught became more exciting for me as I participated with the students in the learning process and learned from them.

Many of the inservice programs I attended as a young teacher were of the show and tell variety. Participants were to absorb the information and knowledge presented by an "expert." But one program was different, and it remains vivid in my mind to this day. It was an in-depth multicultural workshop that engaged a wide variety of strong emotions and provided exten-

sive time for reflection and group sharing.

In the past decade, I have been fortunate to have worked with two effective in-depth professional development programs that focus on sharing knowledge among peers and using group problem-solving processes. One program is for school administrators, and the other is for teacher/leaders from kindergarten through university. Both are nonhierarchical and focus on the valuable gifts of personal knowledge and experience each participant brings to share with other participants.

The parallels among the changes in effective professional development models for adults and those in effective instructional models for students are interesting, although not surprising. The longer I am involved with professional development for adult learners, the more similarities I note regarding how young persons and adults respond to learning situations. I have seen principals throw spitballs at each other when they have been bored by a speaker; I have done off-task work when I am coerced into attending inservice sessions that have little relevance to my daily work or interests; and I have seen students quietly daydream or become disruptive during lessons they perceive to lack relevance.

Educational models that are effective for learners of all ages tend to be engaging and relevant; they require the participant to connect and apply knowledge. Such models demonstrate care for the learner by providing an appropriate learning environment. They address the diversity of participants—including language, culture, maturity, interests, and experience. Finally, such models promote interest in continued investigation and learning.

What are we talking about when we refer to adult professional development? A professional is engaged in an occupation requiring an education. Development is becoming better or more useful. Development is achieved through enhancing knowledge, skill, ability, attitude or confidence by teaching, training, study, or experience (in other words, education). Professional development in our arena is education for the educator, with a focus on improving student achievement.

There are multiple lenses through which to examine professional development in physical education. Drawing largely on the *Standards for Staff Development* published by the National Staff Development Council (1995), my choice of seven organizers for discussion purposes is as follows:

The Role of a Professional Developer

Who is the professional developer for physical education? It may be a person with this title at the school site, or the district, county or state level. Professional developers may include consultants from profit or nonprofit firms and agencies, university professors, district managers such as superintendents or directors, or site managers such as principals and physical education department chairs. Increasingly common is the physical education teacher/leader as a professional developer. The teacher/leader might hold such positions as mentor teacher, teacher on special assignment, or peer coach.

The roles of the physical education professional developer are varied. Depending on situational needs, structure, and timing, the professional developer may recommend or provide resources, design workshops and conferences, develop curriculum and courses, manage programs, write newsletters and articles, advocate change, coach peers, and serve as a group facilitator (Killion & Harrison 1997).

In our positions as county consultants for physical education, my counterparts and I have had the opportunity to serve in each of these roles, and we know numerous outstanding teachers in the field who have done the same in addition to their daily teaching responsibilities.

A professional developer locates needed resources. Resource requests I receive most often include order information for key physical education curriculum documents such as state and national standards for physical education, sample curricula and courses from other schools and districts, annotated bibliographies and order information for instructional materials and software, equipment resources and catalogs, event calendars and workshop schedules, funding sources, and technical references for specific education codes and regulations. To be effective at providing resources, it is critical to be an active participant in professional associations and networks that share such information. It also is important to use technology to access and provide current resources through e-mail, the Internet, and web pages. Resource and media specialists in professional libraries are wonderful friends who possess skills to shortcut searches and save valuable time in accessing information.

To effectively design physical education workshops and conferences, it is necessary to first assess the need for the event through observations, surveys, or evaluations from prior events. Next, identify the target participants, establish workshop or conference outcomes, and plan engaging activities and sessions to meet those outcomes. It is especially important to connect this physical education professional development opportunity to a larger professional development thrust if you are constrained by time, budget, facilities, or other resources.

For example, a few years back there was a statewide effort to promote a middle school focus across all subject areas. There also was a statewide dearth of physical education professional development opportunities that focused specifically on the needs of middle school teachers. A group of outstanding physical education teachers, realizing this need was not being met, created a week-long summer workshop specifically for middle school physical educators. Evidence of the success of this workshop lies in its expansion to additional sites statewide, its outstanding evaluations, and the positive impact it has had in connecting middle school physical educators to cross-disciplinary concepts.

The development of physical education student standards and curriculum is, in my opinion, the base on which professional development is built at the school and district level. Curriculum provides the roadmap for establishing a long-range professional development plan, ordering instructional materials and equipment, revising facilities, and establishing assessment and grading procedures. The curriculum development process is a form of professional development for physical educators and administrators, and in most cases this process is more important than the curriculum product.

Curriculum developed or adopted in isolation of those who are expected to implement the curriculum tends to provide shelf decoration at best, and engender opposition at worst. Physical education curriculum committees provide valuable opportunities to share perspectives, experiences, and ideas; to focus on student needs; and to do group problem solving. Curriculum committees are enriched by the participation of parents, students, and community members. While the actual writing committee may be small, and published curriculum documents may be helpful resources, the physical education curriculum advisory committee should represent all individuals expected to implement the document.

The schedule for curriculum development needs to provide adequate time for representatives to interact with those they represent during each stage of product development. In a small K–8 school district, for example, a classroom teacher took the lead to convene a districtwide physical education curriculum committee. He involved physical educators, classroom teacher representatives from each elementary school, parents, community members, and administrators. The committee used various published curriculum documents. They adapted materials from each to create a document that met the needs of the students in their district. The enthusiasm of the committee carried over to the school board, which provided needed funding for equipment. Numerous teachers and administrators within the district volunteered to conduct physical education workshop sessions. (For more detailed information about curriculum development, see Chapter 3.)

A professional developer often manages a program. Physical education program management requires a multitude of skills— from budgeting and scheduling, to empowering people. Examples of professional developers in this role are the two codirectors of a high school health and fitness academy. They have had to advocate for change; gain school, district, and community support; recruit staff and students; develop coursework; order equipment and instructional materials; and provide staff workshops on such things as technology and assessment. The program they manage has become a model for other high schools in the state. The co-directors provide professional development for physical educators from other schools and districts by hosting program visits and sharing information about the health and fitness academy at regional conferences.

Professional developers create newsletters, write articles, and maintain web pages. They use the pen (or keyboard) to network and share helpful ideas and practices. While we have many excellent writers in our field in peer-reviewed and other physical education journals, I am always pleased to read articles by physical educators who reach outside our field to publish physical education articles in technology journals, cross-disciplinary journals, and parent journals. Not too long ago, I noticed a wonderful, professional response by a physical educator to an Ann Landers column in which a parent had expressed concern about her child's emotional pain at not being chosen for teams in a physical education class. The physical educator's letter, printed by the national columnist, shared appropriate practices for selecting groups in physical education and helped educate the parent (and all other readers) about the resources of the Council on Physical Education for Children.

As an advocate for change, the professional developer is empowered by an understanding of the change process. (For a detailed review of the change process, see Chapter 2.) I recall an outstanding physical education teacher who participated in an in-depth professional development program that profoundly changed the way she taught. She returned to her site determined to become an advocate for change in the physical education department and better meet the needs of students. For three years, she expressed frustration at her seeming inability to change how others were teaching at the site. Finally, she accepted a position at a new school. After she left, the physical education department at the previous site instituted the changes she had been advocating. The impact of her efforts were simply delayed!

Coaching peers is another role of the professional developer. The effectiveness of such collegial support can be seen in a middle school demonstration project. Physical education department members were involved in a three-year professional development program. They then received funds to mentor and coach at other schools that requested assistance. The peer coaching support they provided greatly facilitated the efforts underway at other schools to improve their physical education programs.

The professional developer often has the role of facilitator, helping groups to complete a task or achieve a desired outcome. For this role, understanding the stages of group development and the processes for establishing group norms is helpful. How many of us have been in meetings where a few persons dominated the conversation while other members of the group were never heard from; ideas offered were met with criticism or scorn; or conversations digressed and never returned to the key issue? The importance of facilitation skills is increasing as physical education professional development programs continue to focus more on participant engagement and group problem solving. Workshops and literature to enhance facilitation skills are becoming more prevalent in the professional development arena.

The Context of Professional Development

The power of a professional developer to effect change is situational. Physical educators who have experienced powerful professional development programs often return to department environments that inhibit their efforts to apply new skills and knowledge. Frustration, rather than change, may be the result. Other professional development efforts are focused at the physical education department level, and many have had great success in creating change at that level. Yet, these departments may be working in isolation or at odds with the norms of the school, making it difficult to maintain change.

Site-based management that affects schoolwide change is among the most powerful forms of professional development. However, even site-based efforts can be undermined by district, county, state, or national priorities that create an overlay of demands that can dilute the focus and result in teacher confusion, overload, and burn-out.

Professional developers seldom have control over all the variables that affect the quality of a professional development experience. Consider this example: Early in my career, I received great reviews at a site workshop focusing on physical education for elementary classroom teachers. A short time later, another principal called and asked me to present a physical education workshop at his school. I described my previous workshop, and the principal said it would be very appropriate at his school. Upon arriving at the school I met a friendly, but nervous, principal and a cold and hostile staff. The staff members reluctantly participated in activities, and the evaluations were devastating to this tenderfoot professional developer.

The principal felt the teachers needed to improve the physical education program. Due to negotiations and other school issues, however, the teachers were very angry with the principal, and program enhancement was among the least of their concerns. This situation taught me to thoroughly investigate the context of any professional development program in which I would be involved.

The context is the organization, system, or culture in which the new learnings will be implemented. Unless the professional developer is also a line administrator or program manager, this is usually the area in which he or she has the least control. This is especially true if the physical education professional developer comes from outside the system in which the development activity is to take place.

Research indicates that many of the barriers to improvement reside in the organization's structure and processes, not in the performance of individuals. Therefore, in recent years there has been a shift in focus from individual development to individual development and organization development (Sparks 1994).

The following standards reflect an increasing focus on the organizational setting. (Throughout this chapter all bulleted statements are standards directly from *Standards for Staff Development,* published by the National Staff Development Council in 1995, and shared with permission.)

Effective staff development:

▓ Requires strong leadership in order to obtain continuing support and to motivate all staff, school board members, parents, and the community to be advocates for continuous improvement

- Is aligned with the school's and the district's strategic plan and is funded by a line item in the budget
- Provides adequate time during the workday for staff members to learn and work together to accomplish the school's mission and goals
- Requires and fosters the norm of continuous improvement.

While a physical education professional developer may not have control over all of these factors, it is helpful to leverage system support when negotiating the agreements to provide professional development. Prior to designing physical education professional development programs, I try to access school and district mission and goal statements, district and school physical education grade level standards, school program reviews, school reports, and student, teacher, and community perspectives. Such information helps to best connect the physical education professional development with other school and district professional development programs. Even when no effective plan is in place at a site, information about the school culture enables the professional developer to better serve as a catalyst for change and promote continuous improvement.

The Process of Professional Development

The process describes the means for the acquisition of new knowledge and skills. It includes the length of professional development and follow-up, the methods to achieve group norms and collegial teams, the institutionalization of the change process, and the evaluation of the effectiveness of the physical education professional development program.

- Effective staff development provides for the three phases of the change process: initiation, implementation, and institutionalization.

The change process is critical to the success of professional development. However, since this topic is covered in depth in Chapter 2, the reader should refer to that chapter for further information on the change process.

- Effective staff development requires an evaluation process that is ongoing, includes multiple sources of information, and focuses on all levels of the organization.

Evaluation is a very important aspect of the professional development process, and this topic will be covered in more detail in a separate section of this chapter.

- Effective staff development provides knowledge, skills, and attitudes regarding organization development and systems thinking.

In business as well as education, knowledge—rather than skills—is the greatest resource. In *The Knowledge-Creating Company* (1995), co-authors Nonaka and Takeuchi contend that the most powerful learning comes from direct experience with the body and mind, as well as through trial and error. Innovation is a highly individual process of personal and organizational self-renewal. Creating new knowledge frequently requires intensive and laborious interactions among members of the organization.

The authors suggest that effective organizations get out of the mode of thinking that knowledge can be acquired, taught, and trained through manuals, books, or lectures, and instead focus on highly subjective insights, intuitions, and hunches. They indicate that in an effective organization, no one department or group of experts has the exclusive responsibility for creating new knowledge. Rather, the creation of new knowledge is the product of dynamic interaction among differentiated groups. A key recommendation of the authors is to treat every employee as a member of the "knowledge crew."

Similarities among effective business organizations, effective schools, and effective physical education classrooms are striking. As in the business organization model described by Nonaka and Takeuchi, effective schools and classrooms build learning communities with genuine sharing of experience and insight in order to solve problems and enhance student achievement.

Consider for example the Durham, Ontario, school board, which last year was honored with the Carl Bertelsmann Prize as the world's most innovative and high-performing school system. The incentive for change was the low achievement of students in relation to surrounding school systems. Student scores that are now among the highest in the region are testimony to the effectiveness of the change process. The committee bestowing the award noted: "It is particularly impressive to see how the commitment of all—teachers, parents, students, and other community members—is being encouraged.... The fostering of a vast number of bottom-up initiatives guarantees permanence and self-renovation of the process" (Richardson 1997).

Another example of "the knowledge crew" is the College of Education and Social Services at the University of Vermont. A professor of education, John Clarke, has moved virtually all of the professional preparation work into the K-12 school system. Classroom teachers serve as mentors for preservice students. Classroom teachers also serve as adjunct university faculty. Students, teachers, preservice students, and university faculty members work together on collaborative action research in the classroom. "In a professional development school, teaching, research, and service become one act, inseparable in the surging flow between classrooms and hallways" (Clarke 1997). A number of university professional preparation programs in physical education follow aspects of this model.

The need to work collegially requires that professional development address team building skills. Effective staff development:

- Requires staff members to learn and apply collaborative skills to conduct meetings, make shared decisions, solve problems, and work collegially
- Requires knowledge and use of the stages of group development to build effective productive collegial teams.

Adult learners are a diverse group, and individuals participating in physical education professional development programs have varied experiences in social skills. An important difference between group work and cooperative learning is that in the latter, social skills are specifically taught. Skills such as active listening, creating group norms, breaking down barriers between groups, and mediation are critical to the success of professional development programs. Without these basic interaction skills, group project development becomes an uphill effort. For groups with these skills, learning seems to accelerate.

Teachers appreciate the relevance of social skills when connections are made to students in the classroom. For example, a physical educator went through an in-depth professional development program that focused a great deal on social skills. He went back to his school and began to teach many of the same social skills to his students through the use of cooperative games. The rest of the physical education department joined these efforts. The positive impact on students and the school culture was noticed by staff members, administrators, and parents.

Soon, the physical education department was providing social skill development workshops for the entire school staff. In physical education as well as other subject areas, the staff feels that increased social skills have resulted in decreased discipline problems and have helped to create a positive, cooperative learning environment in which all students achieve.

■ Effective staff development is based on knowledge about human learning and development.

In recent years, there has been a great increase in brain research and efforts to connect the results to student learning across all subject areas. Brain research emphasizes the complexities of personal learning processes. For example, new information in physical education is learned best when students have the time to reflect, dialogue, and make meaningful connections between the new information and concepts learned previously. Evidence is mounting that long-range, in-depth professional development approaches for physical educators are far more effective than "one-shot" sessions.

Like classroom instruction, professional development is most effective when it attends to the individual needs of participants through multi-modal (visual, auditory, and kinesthetic) presentations of new information and through strategies that connect to the multiple intelligences: i.e., musical, logical-mathematical, linguistic, spatial, interpersonal, naturalist, intrapersonal, and bodily kinesthetic (Checkley 1997). Although I have seen physical education standards presented in many different ways, the most effective introduction was provided by a physical educator who rotated participants through interactive stations that provided an example of each standard. The participants thoughtfully read each standard, discussed each standard, and physically attempted an activity for each standard.

■ Effective staff development bases priorities on a careful analysis of disaggregated student data regarding goals for student learning.

Student work is a determining factor in selecting focus areas for change in physical education. A wide variety of student data is examined, including achievement scores (in such areas as physical fitness, motor skills, knowledge assessments, and social skill development); attendance and failure rates; portfolios; student surveys; and other norm or criterion-referenced tests. Staff development priorities are made by analyzing these data in relation to desired student outcomes.

The primary purpose of fitness scores may be to help students set and achieve personal goals. However, by reviewing district scores disaggregated by grade, gender, and other factors, one may be able to determine if there is a districtwide need to provide workshops on aerobic activities for all grade levels, upper body strength development programs for particular grade levels, and so on. Sometimes student fitness scores may be high, but student surveys and student failure or dropout rates in phys-

ical education may indicate a dissatisfaction with the manner in which the fitness programs are conducted.

■ Effective staff development uses a variety of staff development approaches to accomplish the goals of improving instruction and student success.

Once the focus strands for professional development have been selected, a wide variety of professional development activities may be utilized to support the achievement of benchmarks and goals for each strand. Sample activities that can be effective are school and classroom visitations, coaching and shadowing, skill development sessions, demonstration lessons, teacher talk and collaboration, networking and teaming, accessing and sharing resources, consultation and reflection, inquiry and collaborative action research (Speck 1996). For example, at one school it was determined that students needed more experience in rhythm and dance. The members of the physical education department, however, had limited experience teaching this area. Therefore, the teachers selected dance as a professional development strand.

Once the professional development strand was determined, the teachers visited schools that had quality dance programs. They networked to locate resources for instructional materials and lessons, audio equipment, and storage facilities. They shadowed effective teachers, tried lessons, debriefed lessons with each other, and tried the lessons again. They shared successes and failures, and worked as a group to solve problems. Within three years, all members of the department were providing a wide variety of rhythm and dance opportunities for students. This department now mentors other schools desiring to improve dance for students.

■ Effective staff development uses content that has proven value in increasing student learning and development.

The content of the professional development activities used to achieve physical education standards and goals should be research-based, and may include physical education specific knowledge and skills. The content also may include cross-disciplinary knowledge and skills such as classroom management, instructional strategies, child development, learning theories, assessment strategies, curriculum development processes, motivation and discipline theories and strategies, group interaction skills and strategies, technology innovation and application, parent and community interaction strategies, interdisciplinary connections, and processes for personal and organizational change. When cross-disciplinary workshops and presentations are provided, examples should always include physical education as well as other subject areas.

The Content of Professional Development

The content of professional development refers to the skills and knowledge educators need in order to be effective. For purposes of discussion, the content standards from the National Staff Development Council can be grouped in four categories: Curriculum, Instruction, Assessment, and Connections.

In the area of curriculum, effective staff development:

■ Enables educators to provide challenging, developmentally appropriate curricula that engage students in integrative ways of thinking and learning

■ Prepares educators to demonstrate high expectations for student learning.

Curriculum is a key area for professional development in physical education because it provides the direction and groundwork on which instruction and assessment are based. Unfortunately, the process of curriculum development is often overlooked in physical education. Preservice programs may focus on class management, instruction, and lesson and unit planning rather than the process for developing articulated standards across grade levels. While most schools and districts focus on articulated curriculum development in areas such as reading and mathematics, physical education is sometimes tragically left out of this loop at regional and school levels.

Physical education teachers in these systems may end up with only a schedule of activities or a series of unit plans. I have seen the frustration of physical educators who attempt to implement authentic assessment or enhance instructional strategies without a standards-based curriculum. The *National Standards for Physical Education* (NASPE 1995) provides an outstanding model on which to base the development of regional or site curricula. (See Chapter 3 for further information about the content of curriculum.)

In the area of instruction, effective professional development:

■ Increases administrators' and teachers' understanding of how to provide school environments and instruction that are responsive to the developmental needs of adolescents

■ Facilitates the development and implementation of school and classroom-based management which maximizes student learning

■ Prepares teachers to use research-based teaching strategies appropriate to their instructional objectives and their students

■ Addresses diversity by providing awareness and training related to the knowledge, skills, and behaviors needed to ensure that an equitable and quality education is provided to all students.

There are so many lenses through which educators can study and evaluate instruction that it is sometimes helpful to select a focus within instructional strategies to narrow the scope of target skills and knowledge. An example of such a focus is examining the extent to which students are encouraged to make decisions about their own learning. This lens is described in Mosston's spectrum of instructional styles, which describes a continuum of teacher control—from command style in which the teacher makes all the decisions about the lesson (for example, in fencing and archery) to the student-designed style in which the student makes all the decisions. For example, a group of students may select a topic in basketball, decide how to study the topic, prepare a project, and present it to the class (Mosston & Ashworth 1994).

Another lens that can be used examines the extent to which we provide equal opportunity within the physical education classroom based on our interaction with individual students. Coding interactions in categories such as wait time, proximity to students, eye contact with students, and quality of feedback provides data to determine the equity of teacher interaction with all students.

■ Effective staff development prepares teachers to use various types of performance assessment in their classrooms.

Professional development helps teachers make the transition from traditional forms of grading in physical education (e.g., focusing on suiting up, tardies, absences, and attitudes) to authentic or standards-based assessment. The lack of standards-based assessment is one of the greatest obstacles to the establishment of physical education as an entrance requirement for higher education. (For further information on student performance assessment, see Chapter 3.)

Effective professional development:

■ Facilitates staff collaboration with and support of families for improving student performance

■ Prepares educators to combine academic student learning goals with service to the community

■ Increases administrators' and teachers' ability to provide guidance and advisement to adolescents.

Connections are a key. The content of physical education professional development is connected to the larger picture of the Coordinated School Health Program (CSHP), with specific connections to health education, health services, nutrition services, psychological services, safe schools, family and community involvement, and employee wellness. For example, professional development on physical fitness may better prepare the physical education staff to provide information and opportunities for employee wellness.

Physical education also is connected to the school mission and goals, and to student standards in other subject areas. For example, members of one physical education department are preparing a workshop session to share the effective interdisciplinary mathematics and fitness assessment module they created in cooperation with the mathematics department.

The Design of Professional Development

As I have mentioned before, the longer I am involved with physical education professional development, the more I note similarities with the physical education class instructional program. Since we tend to teach the way we are taught, the modeling of quality plans in professional development for educators is essential. The steps for creating a professional development plan are similar to the steps used to create an instructional plan for students:

1. Determine the needs of the learners.

2. Establish learning outcomes.

3. Select/design and implement appropriate experiences to achieve the outcomes.

4. Evaluate the extent to which the learners achieve the outcomes.

5. Modify the outcomes and activities as indicated by learner progress.

To determine the needs of the learner, the professional developer needs to gather as much information as possible about the current skills, knowledge, performance, interests, and attitudes of the intended participants in relation to the goals of the district, school, or department. In some cases, the professional developer has the opportunity to assist in establishing the goals. In other cases, the goals for physical education professional development have been established, and the professional developer is responsible for helping physical educators achieve some portion of them. As mentioned previously, it is critical that all professional development programs be part of a comprehensive plan, and not isolated incidents.

Tools I have found helpful to determine learner needs include district and school site plans; program review or accreditation reports as well as staff responses to such reports; observations of random classes; student work; interviews with teachers, administrators, staff, students, and community members; and information about the impact of previous professional development programs for the target group. (If background information is not available, design the professional development as effectively as possible, then begin the session with activities that will allow you to gauge participant needs, and adjust accordingly.)

Once the needs are determined, develop outcomes related to these needs. The outcomes should be stated in participant performance terms. They should be reasonable in relation to limitations of time, facilities, scheduling, funding, and materials. Some professional developers can provide long-range involvement and follow-up. Others may be asked to provide a one-time-only session on a given topic. If I am asked to be involved in the latter situation, I have found it is imperative to connect the session to a larger professional development plan. For example, a school may be emphasizing reading across the curriculum. I then gather the information provided by the reading resource teachers at the school and select physical education resources that connect. If a professional developer needs to make choices among service opportunities to educators, it is helpful to keep in mind that the most effective sessions are usually those that are components of long-range, thoughtful plans.

The next step involves selecting or designing and implementing the activities to achieve the stated outcomes. This step requires artfully combining appropriate content with the appropriate processes. Should, for example, content on instructional styles in physical education be presented in a lecture or an experiential format? To what extent will demonstrations, observations, peer coaching, inquiry, and reflection be used to achieve the performance outcomes for participants?

Research on staff development and personal experience has helped me gain increased respect for the experiential approach as a powerful learning tool. There are many ways to break lectures into bite-sized pieces, to provide time for reflection and interaction, and to present lectures in humorous and multi-modal formats. Yet, I continue to be amazed at the long-range, powerful impact of participant-designed learning experiences. One example that comes to mind is an academy for physical education in which teachers were asked to design a project of their choice that would affect programs and instruction. The projects the teachers designed and shared with others far exceeded the expectations of the professional development program designers! Years later, many of these projects (including curriculum materials, innovative equipment, and public information packets) continue to have a positive impact on teachers and programs.

The next step involves assessment of the extent to which participants achieve the outcomes. This step is relatively easy if the outcomes or objectives are written in performance terms. The evaluation process provides important information needed to appropriately revise participant outcomes and adjust learning activities.

The Evaluation of Professional Development

In many ways, the evaluation of professional development programs is similar to the evaluation of instruction in the classroom. Tests, surveys, and performance rubrics are just a few of the means that can be used to determine the extent to which participants have gained new skills or knowledge.

However, one large difference exists between the evaluation of effective professional development and the evaluation of instruction in the classroom. Funding sources for professional development programs have expectations for accountability. Often these sources expect to see improvement in student achievement as a result of particular professional development efforts. However, there are problems with directly relating professional development efforts to student outcomes. There are simply too many variables within a school community that affect student achievement. To isolate professional development as the key variable for change in student achievement is a foreboding task, since many variables interact to affect student achievement.

Measuring the effectiveness of physical education professional development programs seems to demand a portfolio approach with many types of assessment procedures that add information and data. For example, a portfolio of a teaching strategies professional development program might consist of a self-analysis of a videotaped lesson that displays a teacher's instructional strategies before and after the professional development intervention. The portfolio could include participant reflections and personal perceptions of progress and examples of student work.

Internal evaluation information gathered by workshop providers, and data gathered from external, objective reviewers can contribute to the professional development portfolio. Even when such portfolios cannot be used to "prove" that a particular professional development program is the cause for change in student work, the accumulation of data from a variety of sources can be convincing documentation of positive change.

It is especially difficult to connect professional development to student work when a program is not site-based. Yet, non school-based programs, such as the California Subject Matter Project (CSMP), are particularly effective in the depth of resources they provide for content and process. These projects focus on specific subject areas, connect experienced teachers and researchers in rich dialogue, and recognize time as a valuable resource to promote investigation and innovation.

Firestone and Pennell (1997) recently shared the results of a comparison of two designs for state-sponsored teacher networks—one of which was the California Subject Matter Project. Using interviews and observations, they concluded that state-sponsored networks can improve teachers' knowledge and motivation while at the same time empowering them. The authors offered three recommendations:

1. Networks should use a loosely coupled, capacity-building strategy to promote reform.

2. Extrinsic incentives to help reduce costs to participants should be provided.

3. Networks should offer activities that vary the emphasis on delivering knowledge to teachers and helping teachers to construct knowledge.

Professional development, like teaching, is an art and a science. We continue to base our programs on documented, effective approaches while experimenting with innovations such as the Montana Master Teacher Program for physical educators (see Chapter 12), the Kansas Physical Dimensions Project, the South Carolina High School Physical Education Institute, and the Pennsylvania Physical Education–Learning Is for Everyone (PE–LIFE) Project. We share new experiential data, and we work together to enhance professional development programs and opportunities.

Resources for Professional Development

Every teacher is a potential resource for professional development. There also are associations and groups that provide networks for sharing resources and publications specifically related to professional development. One such association is the National Staff Development Council, which produced *the Standards for Staff Development* that were shared with permission in this chapter. Another valuable network is the Association for Supervision and Curriculum Development.

In terms of specific content and processes for physical education, the National Association for Sport and Physical Education (NASPE) is an outstanding resource, as are the district and state associations connected to this organization.

Many schools, districts, regions, and states employ individuals who specialize in professional development across all subject areas. Most institutions of higher education also have personnel and media resources to support various aspects of professional development.

Technology is an increasingly important resource, one that provides not only access to rich stores of information but also opportunities to network across the miles through teleconferencing, e-mail, and the Internet. Technology for long distance professional development has been effectively implemented at various sites, but is still in the embryonic stages.

Chapter Summary

All educators have roles related to professional development. For some, this may mean taking responsibility to enhance personal effectiveness as a teacher or administrator; for others—whether mentor teachers, department chairpersons, teachers on special assignment, or administrators—it means promoting the professional development of school personnel at site, district, regional, or state levels.

Effective professional development in physical education is thoughtfully designed; it adheres to standards in three critical areas: context, process, and content. Evaluation is important, not only to provide specific program feedback to monitor and adjust programs, but also to add to the growing body of knowledge that supports the education of physical educators— a life long endeavor.

References

Armstrong, T. (1994). *Multiple intelligences in the classroom*. Alexandria, VA: Association for Supervision and Curriculum Development.

Caine, R. N., & Caine, G. (1997). *Education on the edge of possibility*. Alexandra, VA: Association for Supervision and Curriculum Development.

Casey, M. B., & Tucker, E. C. (1994). Problem-centered classrooms: creating lifelong learners. *Phi Delta Kappan, 76* (2), 139-143.

Checkley, K. (1997). The first seven…and the eighth: A conversation with Howard Gardner. *Educational Leadership 55* (1), 8–13.

Clarke, J. H. (1997). Teaching, research, and service in a professional development school. *Phi Delta Kappan, 78* (10), 789-792.

Firestone, W. A., & Pennell, J. R. (1997). Designing state-sponsored teacher networks: a comparison of two cases. *American Educational Research Journal, 34* (2), 237-266.

Fullan, M. G., & Stiegelbauer, S. (1991). *Professional development of educators. The new meaning of educational change*. New York: Teachers College Press.

Hirsh, S. (1997). Breaking ranks recommendations: require standards-based staff development. *The High School Magazine, 4* (4), 4-13.

Killion, J., & Harrison, C. (1997). The multiple roles of staff developers. *Journal of Staff Development 18 (3)*, 33-44.

Kohn, A. (1993). Choices for children: why and how to let students decide. *Phi Delta Kappan, 75* (1), 8-16, 8-21.

Little, J. W. (1993). Teachers' professional development in a climate of educational reform. *Educational Evaluation and Policy Analysis, 15* (2), 129-150.

Mosston, M., & Ashworth, S. (1994). *Teaching physical education*. New York: Macmillan.

National Association for Sport and Physical Education. (1995). *Moving into the future: National standards for physical education*. Reston, VA: Author.

National Staff Development Council. (1995). *Standards for staff development*. Oxford, OH: Author.

Nonaka, I., & Takeuchi, H. (1995). *The knowledge-creating company*. New York: Oxford University Press.

Richardson, J. (1997). Durham's challenge: improve yourself. *Results. 1*, 6.

Schmoker, M. (1996). *Results: The key to continuous school improvement*. Alexandria, VA: Association for Supervision and Curriculum Development.

Sparks, D. (1994). A paradigm shift in staff development. *Journal of Staff Development 15* (4), 26-29.

Speck, M. (1996). Best practice in professional development for sustained educational change. *ERS Spectrum, 14* (2), 33-41.

Shawn, J., & Valle, R. (1997). Lessons about learning. *Thrust for Educational Leadership, 27* (1), 36 - 38.

Westheimer, J., & Kahne, J. (1993). Building school communities: an experience-based model. *Phi Delta Kappan, 75* (4), 324-328.

CHAPTER 5

Decreased governmental spending means increased pressure for programs to be subsidized by private sector support...In order for public education to survive in the 21st century, partnerships among federal agencies and with others in the public and private sector are forthcoming. (DeGraw & McGinnis 1991.)

Creative Funding

Jayne Greenberg

Imagine this: You have just returned from the most innovative physical education conference of your professional career. As you went from session to session, you were inundated with new ideas, new technology, new product lines, and—most importantly—new concepts in curriculum programming.

With catalogs and brochures in hand, you meet with your supervisor expecting to get all—or at least part—of your wish list approved. Unfortunately, within five minutes you are leaving your administrator's office broken hearted. You have learned that there is no money available to fund your programs. If this sounds like a familiar scenario, don't be disillusioned. You're not alone.

Today, when the overall student population is growing and legislative dollars are shrinking, many constraints are placed on all programs, especially when public outcry demands that school resources be spent on increasing student test scores, reducing class size, and instituting tougher academic standards to name just a few.

In these new and difficult financial times, nontraditional funding sources emerge as a key to overall restructuring and modernization of educational programs. Knowing where to find additional sources of revenue can ease your anxieties about additional programmatic needs. Don't despair. Monies are available...if you exert a little time and a lot of effort in finding them.

In this chapter, I will lead you through successful procedures in identifying and securing funds for your programs. These include:

1. How To Secure Existing Dollars, or In-House Funding

2. How To Secure Parent Teacher Association (PTA) Funds

3. How To Secure Outside Funding Through Corporate Donations and Fundraising Strategies

4. How To Secure and Establish Business Partnerships

5. How To Obtain Funding Through Grants

6. How To Write a Simple Grant

7. Some of the Do's and Don'ts of Grant Writing.

Although some monies may be obtained in the traditional manner, it's time to be creative and start looking and thinking "outside the box." The brass ring really is within your reach!

How To Secure Existing Dollars, or In-House Funding

As you probably are aware, individual schools receive money from their respective state Departments of Education in propotionate manner, based upon the number of students enrolled in the school. All of the dollars generated by student full-time equivalent (FTE) are placed in the principal's discretionary account. This is money that the principal can spend any way he or she sees fit, as long as it benefits students.

This account funds all of the educational programs that are considered "basic." All programs not designated as line items—such as vocational education, JROTC, or alternative education—fall into the basic category. How the principal disseminates these dollars is usually based on two simple factors: (1) programs that support the goals and objectives of both the individual school and the school district, and (2) programs that bring recognition to the school. Although physical education programs usually fall into the latter category, they can by no means be eliminated from the former.

So, how do you tap into the discretionary pot of gold? The first way is to show how your program supports the educational goals of the school. To become a part of the solution means becoming a contributing part of the School Improvement Plan (SIP). Although meetings are often held after school, and in many cases interfere in part with your interscholastic practice schedule or intramural after school activity program, it is critical that you initiate creative coverage to ensure your attendance at these meetings.

Utilizing this strategy, you not only maintain high visibility for your program or department, but you get to participate in the inner workings of the decision-making process. For example, at the elementary school level, if you know that one of your school's goals is to improve reading comprehension, then you need to show how your physical education program contributes not only to critical thinking, but to improved standardized test scores as well. At the secondary level, you might add specific reading materials or study guides that would enhance preparation for the PSAT or SAT.

Physical education, by virtue of its strong connection to our cultural heritage, lends itself to interdisciplinary units at all levels of education. Associating what we do in physical education to concepts in science, mathematics, social studies, and language arts is easier than you might imagine. For example, a teacher in Broward County, Florida, recently received funding through an Impact II Grant to develop a program, "Jack Be Nimble," to teach mechanics by integrating math, science, and physical education. Throughout this program, students run obstacle courses to determine distance covered, time, mass moved, work done, speed, and power output.

The key is sharing this concept with other teachers and getting them to buy into it. Once you visibly associate yourself and your program with the school's mission and goals, financial support will come as a necessity rather than as a luxury.

External Recognition

A second strategy is to bring visibility or recognition to your program. This can be accomplished in a variety of ways. For example, at the elementary school level, mall demonstrations, activities during back-to-school night assemblies, or family fitness field days are easy to implement and positively received. At the secondary school level, you might consider putting on health fairs at community gatherings, or conducting an intergenerational golf or dominoes event. Intergenerational events—pairing up a high school student with a senior member of your community—further bring to public attention the impact that your program has in the community as a whole. Community service or volunteerism through physical education is also a good way for your students to meet their community service graduation requirement.

Tagging onto Existing Programs

A third strategy for securing in-house funds is to connect your program with another school-based program whose funding is provided under a different structure. For example, in a traditional school setting, students enrolled in Alternative Education programs usually take physical education with the general population. However, keep in mind that the FTE funding is significantly higher for students enrolled in Alternative Education than for students enrolled in the general educational program. Because every student in Alternative Education has access to all your equipment, you could request that Alternative Education dollars fund a specific piece of equipment.

However, because of auditing issues, be certain that the equipment requested through these funds will be utilized by students enrolled in Alternative Education programs. The same holds true for students enrolled in the Exceptional Student Education (ESE) program. Additional balls, equipment, and supplies can be purchased with ESE dollars as long as that equipment will be utilized by ESE students. Of particular interest would be the purchase of items which could be utilized in the Sports Program for Students with Disabilities, or in Special Olympics competitions. This may not help the overall program significantly, but it will add to the longevity of your consumable items and existing equipment.

With respect to technology, working closely with other faculty members across disciplines is another way to ensure that students enrolled in physical education have access to the latest software and hardware. A common way to accomplish this is by coordinating your assignments with those of other faculty members. Let's say, for example, that the business education teacher is providing lessons in PowerPoint or HyperStudio. By working closely with that teacher you can provide an opportunity for your students to use the software to develop their physical education portfolios. In a win-win situation, the business education teachers would accomplish their instructional objectives by having the students exposed to technology while adding physical education content to their business education applications. Similar lessons could be coordinated in science classes by purchasing heart rate monitors through Urban Systemic Initiatives (USI) dollars when studying cardiac output. (USI is a program that provides money to school systems through the National Science Foundation.) In health classes, nutrition software might be purchased with Drug Free and Safe Schools dollars. In language arts classes, students might conduct physical education research and create reports using the Internet.

How To Secure Parent Teacher Association (PTA) Funds

One of the most highly respected organizations that works closely with the schools is the Parent Teacher Association (PTA). Guided by the mission of supporting and speaking on behalf of children and youth in the schools and community, assisting parents in developing skills they need to protect and raise their children, and encouraging parent and public involvement in the public schools of this nation, members of the PTA play an integral role in the overall development of educational programs.

Because of their high profile and involvement, it is not surprising that we often turn to the PTA to assist in raising funds for individual school projects. After all, isn't it the parents that we see selling paper and pencils before school in the school bookstore, selling physical education uniforms before and after school, selling wrapping paper prior to the holiday season, and selling fresh baked pies and cookies to help fund school specific projects? Although fundraising is not the primary function of the PTA, the National PTA leaflet on "Funding PTA Projects" says, "Funds are raised to carry out PTA work. The real working capital of a PTA lies not in its treasury, but in its members' energy, resourcefulness, and determination to promote the well being of children and youth."

The local PTA usually sponsors one major annual fundraising project for a specific educational purpose. Justifying to the parents your specific need in physical education is one way of getting on their calendar of fundraising activities. Knowing the members of your PTA could also prove to be beneficial in securing funds from the community. Many members of the PTA either work in local businesses or know someone of influence in your community. Networking through the PTA is one of the best vehicles for getting your needs known.

As a case in point, a group of 12 students from South Florida were preparing to go on an Olympic exchange program with students from Canada. The students were from different schools, so a meeting was held with the students and their parents so that they could meet one another. It was made clear that it was up to the group to raise funds for the trip, and it was necessary to raise enough money for everyone to go. The parents went into action. By the time they were through, they not only raised enough money for travel, they raised enough money to purchase souvenirs! This was an example of parents networking with their respective PTAs for the cause of children. Hats off to all those who are involved with their school PTA.

Simply put, money is available, through various sources, to accomplish all your existing instructional objectives and probably even a few new initiatives. You just need to show that what you do contributes to the overall mission of the school. On a final note, don't forget to give public recognition to your school, your supervisor, and your principal in everything you do. That goes a long way.

How To Secure Outside Funding Through Corporate Donations and Fundraising Strategies

Once you have determined that there is absolutely no money in-house to fund your programs or projects, it's time to start looking outward to determine what dollars are available. The two best sources for outside financial assistance are simple fundraising activities and corporate or business donations.

Fundraising

As money becomes more and more scarce in the schools, legitimate fundraising activities become the norm rather than the exception. Once permission is granted from your school or district, a wide range of sales items are available from the several hundred fundraising companies in the country. If you have had a long-standing career in the field of physical education and athletics, chances are you already may have been involved in the sale of items such as ribbons for homecoming, gift wrap for the holiday season, or school spirit T-shirts.

Although there are several strategies you can use to organize a successful fundraiser, the most important thing to remember is to check on the accounting procedures that are required by your school or school district. Depending on the type of product, and length of the campaign, a solid fundraising activity has the potential of bringing in several thousand dollars. And, you will be accountable for those funds at a later date!

Fundraising activities can be conducted by school-recognized groups, such as clubs or athletic teams, as well as by school-related organizations such as PTAs and booster clubs. The major difference between the two groups lies in the accounting procedures they use. For example, the Florida State Board regulations require that all financial transactions related to student activities and conducted by school-recognized groups be recorded in the internal funds of the school. School-related organizations, such as athletic booster clubs, usually handle their finances outside the school and make gifts or donations to the school as they choose.

The second most important factor in the planning stage is selecting a company with which to work. When making your selection, you need to take into account such factors as how long has the company been in business, whether the company guarantees its products, whether the company will give the school credit for—or buy back—unsold items, and whether the company will assist you in your kick-off. It is also a good idea to make sure that the company is not in conflict with the goals of your program. For example, selling candy is probably not the best fundraising activity for a physical education or athletics program.

After your selection is made, the actual planning of the fundraiser begins. According to Zaidel (1996) several strategies exist to make fundraising a manageable activity rather than a burdensome one. These include:

■ Form a committee and divide the workload. Don't feel like you have to conduct the whole campaign yourself. Appointing a co-chair or several committee chairpersons

to assist will ease your tensions. For example, one committee chairperson can assist you in the accounting, another can be in charge of inventory control, and a third can assist in the distribution of the items.

■ Motivate your volunteers. Include students in the decisions made at the early stages of the project. If students are a part of the decision-making team, they will be more apt to have ownership in the project. And, provide incentives, prizes, and a means of tracking sales.

■ Establish a financial goal. Know exactly how much you will need for your project, how large your target sales audience is, and how much time you need to allot for sales. This will assist you in keeping realistic fundraising goals.

■ Choose a quality product to sell. If you are going to put in the time and effort into organizing a fundraiser, be certain that the product you choose to sell is a product that people are willing to buy. People won't pay for inferior or poor quality merchandise. Keeping the customers satisfied will ensure repeat customers if you decide to do a second, or annual, fundraiser.

■ Set specific beginning and ending dates. This will assist you in pacing your activity. Include target timelines so that you can monitor the success of your efforts.

A successful fundraising campaign will undoubtedly provide you with the money you need to implement your program. If additional dollars are required to fully implement your program, then perhaps corporate donations or sponsorships are what you need to explore.

Corporate Donations and Sponsorships

In a manner less formal than a contractual business partnership, many local corporations are willing to assist with school-wide projects through donations or sponsorships. The process begins by developing a comprehensive plan of action before approaching a potential corporate sponsor. Once your plan is conceptualized, the next step involves developing a formal letter. It can be less sophisticated than a comprehensive proposal, yet it should carefully lay out your plan. Before making the initial contact, be certain to acquire the support and approval from your principal, district supervisor, and superintendent.

Having the name of a contact person will greatly enhance the probability of your request being taken seriously. The initial contact is usually made by a one to two-page letter followed up with a phone call shortly thereafter. Once you have an appointment with a member of the staff, you're on your way.

Prior to your meeting, be sure to develop a corporate presentation packet for distribution. Also be sure to have a prepared, established agenda so that you can cover all your points in a controlled manner during the meeting. Continued communication, along with a thank you card, is essential after the initial meeting.

Once your funding request is granted, it's up to you to be the advocate for the company that is supporting you. You must be their best public relations person in the community. This can be accomplished by mentioning the corporation in all of your publications and interviews, as well as using their logo in appropriate places. When corporations donate materials or

GOSHEN COLLEGE LIBRARY
GOSHEN, INDIANA

actual dollars to educational institutions, they usually simply request a letter of receipt on official letterhead for tax purposes. It is up to you to maintain a positive relationship with them throughout the school year. In this type of relationship, the corporation becomes an active part of the school, and the students and faculty become more supportive of the businesses in their community.

How To Secure and Establish Business Partnerships

The local business community—whether large or small, urban or suburban—has a vested interest in the operation of the schools for two primary reasons: the members of the business community are made up predominately of the parents of the children who attend the schools, and the graduates will be the next generation of employees for that business community. As tax paying members of the community, nobody knows better than the business community the financial constraints placed on educational institutions. Knowing the importance of quality education across the board, many businesses in the community have come forward to provide both financial and human resources to public education.

By definition, partnerships achieve mutually agreed upon goals and objectives by matching community resources to identified needs of the school system or individual schools, and by matching school resources to the identified needs of a particular partner, whether it is a business, university, or community group (Dade County Public Schools 1997). The long-term purpose of developing partnerships is to provide greater awareness and understanding of the needs and resources of the schools and the community, to provide ongoing dialogue between schools and the community, and to work together to improve and enhance educational programs responsive to the needs of the students and the community.

Because of the financial responsibilities involved, securing a business partner should be a formal process. Although not as formal as writing a grant, it begins with identifying a need and culminates with an evaluation. (See Figure 5.1.) Of course, the partnership process also should follow the guidelines set by your school system for entering into a contractual agreement.

The first step in developing your potential business partnership is to identify your needs. In essence, you must ask what is lacking in your educational program. Where is the deficiency, and what program can be implemented to correct it? Test your concept by asking yourself some relevant questions. For example: Can you defend the program for which you are seeking funding? How many students will the program impact? What is the importance of implementing this program? And, why should Corporation X fund this program? For example, securing a partnership with a sport beverage company is one way of providing funds for your physical education program while at the same time providing marketing opportunities for the beverage company.

Remember, funding programs through corporate sponsorship is a reciprocal process. While you are seeking funds for your programs, the businesses are asking themselves, "What's in it for us?" Once you have done a complete needs assessment analysis, you're ready to formalize your thoughts. After carefully thinking out your proposal, develop it formally on paper.

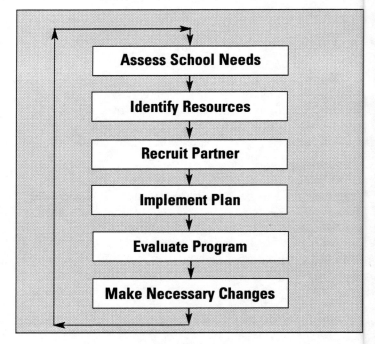

FIGURE 5.1:
The Partnership Process

- Assess School Needs
- Identify Resources
- Recruit Partner
- Implement Plan
- Evaluate Program
- Make Necessary Changes

Ask a colleague who is not familiar with your program to read it over to determine if your request is clear. Now that the proposal is ready for distribution, you're ready to progress to the next stage of the process—identifying resources.

Identifying the business that might be interested in funding your project can take some thought and some time. One good resource is the business listing offered through your local Chamber of Commerce. This directory describes local businesses and the type of service they provide. After identifying several businesses you might approach, do your homework. Learn about the company, the types of community activities with which it already is involved, and the types of services they might be willing to provide for you.

If you are looking for fitness equipment, you might be restricted to an exercise equipment facility that will give you a significant discount or loan you equipment for a year. For example, one local fitness vendor in the Miami area became interested in working with Dade County Public Schools after learning about the "Fit-Tech" Centers that were opening in several of the 51 middle schools. Knowing that the school system was securing funding to place high tech fitness equipment in the schools, they saw a golden opportunity to provide a variety of services to the schools. The most basic service they provided was a significant discount for bulk purchases. In return, they were granted permission for their company's logo to be placed on the base of the equipment. As an extended service, any child or parent who visited that particular vendor and mentioned the equipment at that particular school was given a 25 percent discount on any purchase. This type of agreement not only helps the schools, but helps members of the community as well.

You also might establish a close working relationship with the fitness or health clubs in your community. All commercial fitness clubs must refurbish their equipment every three years,

FIGURE 5.2: Business Partner Introductory Letter

District/School Letterhead
Date

Prospective Business Partner
Address
City, State Zip

Dear _____:

The purpose of this letter is to introduce you to **SCHOOL NAME**, and to invite you to take part in an innovative and exciting new program known as **PROGRAM TITLE**. As a proactive business in the community, I am certain that you will be interested in learning more about this program, as well as how we could work together to improve the educational opportunities of our students.

SCHOOL NAME is comprised of students from **SCHOOL DEMOGRAPHICS**. Our total enrollment is **NUMBER OF STUDENTS.** (In this section you would describe your program as well as the void that it is designed to fill.)

I am enclosing a copy of the formal proposal for your review. I will follow up with a phone call within the week to arrange a meeting with you. If you would like additional information, please contact me at **SCHOOL PHONE NUMBER**. I look forward to meeting with you in the near future.

Sincerely,

YOUR NAME
YOUR TITLE

---

as fitness equipment becomes outdated rapidly—especially with the advent of virtual reality equipment. Many fitness or health clubs would rather donate their old equipment to schools, take the tax write-off, and purchase new equipment for their clubs. This is a win-win situation for all parties involved.

The next step in securing a business partner is the actual recruitment process. There are several ways to contact a potential business partner, depending upon your comfort zone and level of experience. Regardless of how you proceed, be sure to develop a comprehensive plan of action before making a corporate contact. For your own credibility, make sure that all your "t"s are crossed and all your "i"s are dotted. Strategies could include a direct phone call, mailing a proposal on your school's letterhead with a request for a meeting, a cold call visit, leaving the package with a secretary, or asking a friend or neighbor within the company to present the concept to the manager and feel out the response.

It is critical that the proposal be well written and on your district or school letterhead. This will tell the potential partner that your request already has the support of your school system and supervisor. By the way, don't forget to get permission from your administrator to pursue a business partner. It would be embarrassing for yourself and your school or school district if you were to receive support, and then found out for one reason or another there was a conflict with the school system. Once you get the approval, go ahead and draft your introductory letter. (See Figure 5.2.)

Designing and implementing the program are the next steps in the process. This means sitting down with all the players

involved to determine the best strategy. Issues that might arise include how to include members of the business in the program, how to properly publicize the program, and which specific activities will be utilized to fully implement the program. Communicate with your business partners on a regular basis to keep them updated on the status of the program. This gives the business partner a feeling of being a part of the program, rather than strictly a funding source. Having a sense of ownership may help to ensure future funding requests for your ideas. Remember, when a business partnership is formed, the school, business, and community all benefit.

Benefits to the schools include:

■ Additional personnel to enhance educational programs for students

■ Utilization of business perspectives to enhance the present curriculum

■ Increased opportunities to relate academic information to the workplace

■ Assistance in rewarding students for outstanding achievements

■ Reinforcement of good citizenship values by community members.

Benefits to businesses include:

■ Satisfaction in becoming an active participant in the education of our children

FIGURE 5.3: Business Partner Thank You Letter

District/School Letterhead
Date

Business Liaison, Title
Name of Business
Business Address
City, State Zip

Dear **BUSINESS PARTNER**

Thank you for becoming a partner to **SCHOOL NAME**. It is through partnership efforts with distinguished community leaders such as yourself that we can strengthen both our school and our community.

I am especially grateful for your commitment to the students of **SCHOOL NAME**. Your partnership activities, as outlined in the proposal, will contribute greatly to the success of our students, and will make the link between the public and private sector of our community even stronger.

I look forward to a long and positive working relationship with you.
Sincerely,

PRINCIPAL'S NAME
Principal

- Opportunities to motivate students and increase their awareness of career opportunities
- Enhanced corporate image in the community
- Tax benefits from financial and in-kind contributions.

Benefits to the community include:

- Establishment of an ongoing dialogue between the schools and the community
- Increased awareness and understanding of the needs and resources of the schools and community
- Better educated students who become better educated citizens. (Dade County Public Schools 1997.)

After the link is established between the benefits to the schools and the business community and the program is implemented, it is time for evaluation. Knowing that there are several stakeholders in your program should motivate you to continually make changes as they become necessary. Very seldom does the initial plan run as smoothly as envisioned. Most programs undergo change on a regular basis. As your program is ongoing, it makes sense to perform an informal, or process evaluation.

At the conclusion of your initial year, perform a formal evaluation of your program. If an increase in fitness test scores was the culminating factor of your program, did the involvement of the business partner help fulfill that objective? Did your business partner get the recognition that it deserved? Was your partner mentioned in all of your school newsletters? Did you invite a representative of the company to all of your holiday functions? Was your partner recognized at your end of the year awards ceremony?

If all of these criteria were satisfied, then congratulations on your successful implementation of your program. If not, then go back and make the necessary corrections. If, after the first year

of implementation, you honestly feel that the program was successful in making an impact on the lives of your students, then move forward and expand the program.

Expanding a program can include adding more business partners to the same program, but giving the new partners a different responsibility. This will ensure that the first partner is not offended by another company taking part in the project. A second way to expand the program might entail adding more students to the program. This could be accomplished by expanding the criteria for inclusion or asking a colleague to become part of your program. One real test of the measured success of a program is whether the program spreads to other schools in your district, or whether the school district as a whole adopts your program.

After all is said and done, don't forget to formally thank your business partner. This could be accomplished at a PTA/PTSA meeting, end of the year awards ceremony, at a Chamber of Commerce luncheon, in your school newsletter, or simply by a formal thank you letter. (See Figure 5.3 for an example.)

Business partnerships have become a viable way to fund educational programs when state allocations can no longer fully subsidize them. Public involvement in support of primary and secondary education has, through proven programs, yielded many benefits to the educational community and the business community alike. Students benefit from enriched school programs and business partners reap the satisfaction derived from community involvement and helping young children succeed.

How To Obtain Funding Through Grants

Now that you have mastered the less complicated means of securing funding for your programs, you're ready to move on to a more sophisticated means of securing dollars—grant writing. Because grant funding is a competitive process, the important

FIGURE 5.4: Grant Proposal Title Format

Chapter 2 Program Proposal
Title: FIT-TECH: A High Technology Physical Fitness Program for Middle School Education

School/Work Location : _____   Prepared By: _____

Address: _____   Mail Code: _____

---

thing to remember in writing grants is not to take the success or failure of your application personally. In other words, don't be too disappointed if your request is turned down. If you honestly feel that you have a good idea, find out why your application was turned down, revise the application, and either resubmit it to the original funding source or submit it to another funding agency. Writing grants is not an unusually difficult process, but it does require time and perseverance.

Grant writing is similar to developing a business partnership proposal in that there is a set procedure to follow. The initial stage of grant writing requires finding a funding source that is interested in funding your idea. You might contact local or civic organizations, school systems, local or national foundations, and state or governmental agencies to locate potential funding sources. Locally, mini grants for teachers are usually made available through public education funds; Chambers of Commerce; area franchises such as McDonalds, Burger King, Pizza Hut, and Wendy's; and service organizations such as the Rotary, Lions, and Kiwanis Clubs. Foundations such as the Phi Delta Kappa Educational Foundation, also award mini-grants for teachers.

In addition, individual school systems offer several grant opportunities through entitlement programs such as the Safe and Drug Free Schools, Block Grants such as Title 6, as well as through state Department of Education discretionary grants. Federal grants, although extremely competitive, can be located through sources such as The Foundation Center, *The Federal Register, The Catalog of Federal Domestic Assistance, Education Week,* and *Grantsmanship* magazine. Federal grants are disseminated through such agencies as the U.S. Department of Education's National Diffusion Network, the Department of Health and Human Services, the Centers for Disease Control and Prevention, and the National Institutes of Health. Additionally, requests for grant proposals can be located online at various websites.

Before beginning the writing process, be absolutely clear about what you want to achieve through your project and ascertain exactly what the funding agency wants. Reading the grant application carefully will usually tell you exactly what kind of project they are looking to fund and what their priorities are for funding. Educational grants in particular usually target specific types of students such as at-risk, exceptional education students (ESE), Limited English Proficient (LEP), and minority populations; and particular types of programs such as critical thinking, cooperative learning, academic achievement, ecology, and health issues. In many instances, specific geographic locations

also are targeted.

If you feel that your idea falls into a certain area of interest, then begin conceptualizing your proposal. If you feel that your idea is outside of the parameters of the funding interests, then you will need to determine if you could modify your proposal enough to meet the agency's requirements, or if you need to find another funding source. Once you are certain that you have found a match between your idea and a funding source, you're ready to begin writing the proposal.

If you have never written a grant proposal before, relax. Grant writing is basically a systematic process. All grant applications or proposals have basically the same format: title of your project, abstract, proposal narrative, statement of the problem, related research, objectives, procedures or activities, budget, and evaluation. Throughout this section, I will try to ease your anxieties about grant writing by sharing an actual physical fitness grant (FIT-TECH) that was funded for $60,000 through a simple Chapter 2 (federal grant) application.

How To Write a Simple Grant

To begin, the *Title* of your project should be a concise description of the proposed project. The title will usually tell the reviewer whether the proposal falls into the parameters of grants that the agency is seeking to fund. The title should be creative but clearly related to your proposal concept. Figure 5.4 illustrates a basic title format.

A simple yet complete title informs the reviewer of the content of the pages to follow. If the title grabs the attention of the reviewer at the start, you will have his or her undivided attention throughout the rest of the proposal.

Next, you are ready to proceed on to the *Needs Assessment* or statement of the problem. The first statement you make in this section is probably the most important, because this sets the stage for what is to come. Your problem statement should convince the reviewer that what you are proposing is important. It also must show the funding agency that what you are proposing is directly related to the philosophy and goals of that agency's mission.

This section also must establish that the need is great enough for that particular agency to fund the project. The problem needs to be clearly stated with specific data to support it. This section usually includes a short review of literature to lend support for your project's need. In this section, you must convince the reviewer of the need to fund your project. The focus should be on the problem, or the need to be addressed,

FIGURE 5.5: Sample Needs Assessment

NEEDS ASSESSMENT. Briefly explain the problem you are addressing and state why the project is needed. Tell what conditions are believed to have caused the problem and indicate which of these will be addressed by the project.

Recent national and local findings from several fitness and health studies determined that American children in general, and Dade County Public School students in particular, are not developing the exercise and fitness habits that could help maintain their good health as adults; and as many as half are not getting enough exercise to develop healthy cardio-respiratory systems. Studies sponsored by the U.S. Department of Health and Human Services and the President's Council on Physical Fitness and Sports revealed that today's youth have higher absolute and relative weights than their counterparts in the 1960s; 28 percent have higher than normal blood pressure; 41 percent have high cholesterol levels; 98 percent have at least one factor corresponding to heart disease; and many exhibit signs of poor muscular strength, flexibility, and vital capacity.

To a large degree, the conditions believed to cause the problems are exhibited in poor eating habits and exercise patterns, a sedentary lifestyle prevalent among today's youth, an increase in working mothers leading to a curtailment of extracurricular activities, and a reduction in required physical education classes. Through innovative nutrition and fitness education strategies; evaluative feedback to students, parents, and teachers; and enhanced motivational opportunities through the use of the latest technological fitness equipment, it is anticipated that many of the issues confronting enhanced fitness achievement will be addressed.

and how your project will address this problem or need. A sample needs assessment is provided in Figure 5.5.

You are now ready to proceed to that part of your proposal commonly called the *Project Design*. In this section, you have an opportunity to delineate your actual objectives, develop the activities that you will implement to achieve those objectives, and develop a timeline for implementation and evaluation. Keep in mind that as you develop your project design, your objectives should be *clear, specific, measurable*, and written in concise terms. Objectives are usually written in a single sentence, outcome format, and listed in their order of priority. This will tell the reviewer what is to be the expected result of participation in the project.

The methods or activity section of your proposal provides the opportunity for you to describe how you intend to achieve the objectives of your proposal. In this section, you must convince the reviewer that, in essence, you know what you are doing and that your project, or idea, is well thought out. When developing your activities, keep in mind that they must support the intended objectives.

Developing timelines for implementation is a good way to ensure that all of your activities will be completed and the project will progress as planned. When setting timelines for both activities and evaluations, be sure to be realistic. If midway through the development of your proposal you find that you have tried to include more activities than you can realistically accomplish, go back and revise your plan. Professional grant reviewers are usually successful grant writers; they will see through the shortcomings of a proposal with unrealistic expectations. Figure 5.6 provides a sample plan of implementation.

Once your project design is charted, it is often helpful to add a project narrative to assist the grant reader in conceptualizing the project. Figure 5.7 provides a sample project narrative. Remember, follow the directions provided in the grant application packet. If the application packet gives you the opportunity to add a narrative, then do so. If the application packet does not permit any extra sections, do not add anything. This could actually eliminate your grant from funding considerations.

Following the completion of the project design section, the next step is to take a close look at the resources—both human and financial—that you anticipate you will need. Your *Budget* breakdown is critical in showing the reviewer that you have carefully thought out you financial needs and will be spending the money in a cost-effective and efficient manner. Both a budget sheet and budget narrative are required for most grant applications.

When preparing the overall budget, keep in mind that the funded dollars usually are received from six months to one year after acceptance. This in essence translates into developing a budget that is sensitive to inflation. Carefully think out all facets of your project that will need to be funded. These usually include personnel, social security, workman's compensation, insurance, and other fringe benefits (contact your district's personnel office for exact figures); services and materials, including supplies, equipment, professional and technical services, printing and duplicating, and shipping and handling; and transportation costs, whether they involve in-county or out-of-county field trips, your travel expenses, etc. Unless you are writing a continuation grant (grants that are funded for more than one fiscal year, in which re-application is required at the end of the initial funding year), once your funding is received, you cannot go back and ask for additional dollars. You will have to adjust your project accordingly if you under budgeted.

Begin by listing all personnel who have agreed to take part in your project. Do not list people who have not given at least their verbal permission. Once you have secured a list of personnel, develop a short paragraph for each person indicating the title, qualifications, and what part he or she will play in the grant process (i.e. consultant, principal investigator, etc.). As you develop the list of human resources, don't forget to ask if these people need to be included in the budget or if their services will be in-kind. For example, an outside consultant might ask for a flat rate of $5,000 for services throughout the project; a local personal trainer might be so excited about your proposal that he or she will assist you in developing your exercise program as an in-kind service. You might need the services of a full-time

Figure 5.6: Sample Implementation Plan

	Project Design	
	Project To Be Implemented from <u>September 1992</u> to <u>June 1993</u>	
Objective	**Activities**	**Evaluation/Timelines**

1. To increase fitness instruction time to ensure the development of increased levels of physical fitness.	A. Conduct intensive site-based training for teachers focusing on instructional methods and strategies.
	B. Develop curricular activities relevant to the needs of a fitness curriculum. Included will be a scope and sequence of activities as determined by age, grade level, and needs of the students.
	C. Pretest and posttest the student population to obtain a baseline measure of fitness levels and achievement gains.
	D. Utilize state-of-the-art computer technology within the framework of fitness education to expand the program.
		Complete by September 1992
		
		Complete by September 1992
		
		Analyze Data:
		  Pretest - October 1992
		  Posttest - March 1993
		
		Ongoing

2. To increase the amount of instruction for the cognitive development of concepts to enable students to make intelligent decisions about the quality of physical activities that will contribute to life long fitness.	A. Instruct students in the general principles and concepts related to fitness activities. B. Provide students with the opportunity to experience factors associated with assessing, developing, and monitoring adequate levels of fitness.	Ongoing Ongoing
3. To increase participation opportunities to encourage all students to develop positive attitudes toward physical fitness and personal well being.	A. Understand the value of maintaining an adequate level of physical fitness. B. Exhibit positive attitudes that will reflect an acceptance of differences in others. C. Demonstrate the ability to cooperatively work with others through skill development.	Ongoing Ongoing Ongoing
4. To provide increased opportunity for community members to participate in existing and innovative school-based programs and projects.	A. Develop a cadre of additional human resources to enhance educational programs for students. B. Identify volunteers within the community to support new or expanded programs and to work closely with the school population.	Ongoing Ongoing

educational aide, in which case you will have to budget for salary, along with fringe benefits.

Determine where your financial priorities are; keep in mind that the funding agency may fund all or part of your grant request, so be cautious not to over budget in the beginning. It is easier to add services and equipment once you have your actual dollars than it is to eliminate from your master plan if a partial funding request is received. Figure 5.8 is a sample budget work-

FIGURE 5.7: Sample Project Narrative

Problem to be Addressed
The overall purpose of FIT-TECH is to develop a model program of fitness education that will address the urgent need for fitness improvement at the middle school level as evidenced by actual Dade County Public School fitness test results indicating deficient fitness levels among our student population.

Implementation Plan and Strategies To Be Used:
On a rotational basis, all students enrolled in the physical education instructional program will be monitored one day per week with computerized heart rate monitors. As an instrument utilized to measure and monitor cardiac output, the heart rate monitors will assist with the physical education instructional program by providing feedback to the individual students with regard to the amount of time the students exercise in their "target zone." A unique feature of the monitor is the ability to set high and low target zones, which will allow for optimum safe training. When a student exceeds safe limits, based upon his or her individual target zone, the monitor beeps, alerting the student to decrease the exercise intensity until he or she is back in the "safe" training zone.

The students will wear the heart rate monitors for the duration of their physical education instructional period. This will provide evaluative feedback to the physical education instructors as to the amount of quality exercise/activity time the students are exerting during their fitness training time, physical skills activity time, and recovery time. At the completion of the instructional period, the cardiovascular data will be downloaded to a personal computer by means of a special interface module and software. Data can then be analyzed for the purpose of making individual fitness prescriptions for the students, and reports can be prepared and sent home to parents.

In addition to the heart rate monitors, computerized exercise equipment will be utilized to enhance cardiorespiratory training. Students will not only be given the opportunity to develop cardiovascular fitness through jogging, walking, and other selected aerobic activities, but they also will be provided the opportunity to utilize electronic treadmills, climbers, steppers, cycles, and ergometers. Cardiovascular activity also will be monitored while on the fitness equipment. By focusing on the "process" of fitness education through motivational high-tech experiences it is expected that the "product"—enhanced fitness levels—will be a natural consequence.

This approach was selected because of its utilization of the latest technological fitness equipment; enhanced motivational and educational instructional methodologies; and ability to provide evaluative feedback to teachers, parents, and students.

The approach selected is further expected to change the problem situation by providing students with the educational means of taking responsibility for their own fitness gains. The focus shifts from a teacher-centered orientation to a student-centered educational process.

---

sheet that was developed by the Dade County Public Schools Grant Administration Office.

Make sure you familiarize yourself with the format that the funding agency requires. For example, if the funding agency will only fund projects that provide for equipment and supplies for students, don't write yourself in as the project manager for a salary. This will not be within their parameters, and your grant application will be denied.

The next to last step of the application process is writing a formal *Evaluation* for your project. An evaluation is important to both the school system and funding agency, as it serves to determine if you were able to do what you proposed to do, and how you can do it better next time. An evaluation also will help the funding agency decide whether to extend funding for your project. When planning your evaluation, be specific as to what evaluative instruments will be utilized and who will conduct the evaluation. In the end, the evaluation should determine the degree to which you have met your intended objectives and whether your project design was fully implemented.

Evaluations can be either process or product in nature. A process evaluation, or formative evaluation, looks at the procedures carried out throughout the length of the grant contract. This is a way to determine if the process of the project was beneficial in achieving the objectives or whether changes need to be made. A product evaluation, or summative evaluation is used to determine whether or not your project achieved its objectives. Figure 5.9 provides an example of both.

The final phase of your proposal writing is the development of the abstract. Although first in order of appearance, the abstract is usually written last. The abstract is used to give the reviewer an overview of your proposal. Written clearly and concisely, it should explain the need for your project and the major objectives and procedures of your proposal. It should be limited to one page, or approximately 250 words. After the first phase of reading all grant applications, it is usually the abstract that the reviewers look at when making their final decision. Therefore, key facts, activities, and outcomes are critical to this section of the proposal.

Some of the Do's and Don'ts of Grant Writing
As noted earlier, grant writing is not a difficult task, but it does take time. And, there are several rules that you should adhere to ensure that your grant has a fair chance of being funded. First, follow the guidelines on the grant application precisely. Second, write in language that is understood by all; avoid using educational jargon or slang. Third, show how your

FIGURE 5.8: Budget Worksheet

Project Title: FIT-TECH: A High Technology Physical Fitness Program for Middle School Education

Project No:_____1234_____   Date:___2/28/93_____

Project Manager:___<Name of designated manager>____   Telephone No:___<Where manager can be reached>___

Location :_____<Name of school>_____   Mail Code _____<In house mail>_____

Function of Focus of Proposal

Instruction to Students:_____X_____   Student Services:_____

Curriculum Services :_____X_____   Instructional Staff Training:_____X_____

PERSONNEL

Object	Number	Description	Cost
5149	<5 days @ $75 per day>	<Substitute Teacher (Training)>	
5144	<1>	<Full Time Teacher - $38,500>	

FRINGE BENEFITS

5210		Retirement <16.45%>	
5220		FICA (Social Security) <7.65%>	
5230		Workman's Comp. <2.24%>	
5240		Insurance <$3,342>	

SERVICES AND MATERIALS

5510		Supplies	6,000.00
5640		Equipment	45,000.00
5310		Professional and Technical	7,000.00
5399		Printing and Duplicating	2,000.00

TRANSPORTATION

5330		In-County Field Trips	
5332		Field Trips	

OTHER

Total: 60,000

< > = Provided as sample data only; not part of actual FIT-TECH grant proposal.

proposal can be replicated in other states, regions, communities, and school systems.

Conversely, when writing your proposal, don't promise more than you can deliver, don't think that a longer application will increase the probability of getting funded (the reverse is actually true), and don't over extend your budget.

When seeking corporate funding, be assertive in stating what benefit your project will have to the corporation. Make reference to key documents from the corporation, including the mission statement, strategic plan, etc. In other words, do your homework thoroughly.

Obtain advice and assistance from colleagues or other professionals in the field who have experience in working with corporations or foundations. Not only can they lend assistance in the preparation of your proposal, but they could serve as an external support network. And finally, give a draft copy of your completed proposal to a colleague or friend to proofread. By this time, you have probably spent so much time on your application that you may not see your own grammatical errors.

Grant writing is a fun, yet challenging experience. Following the steps listed above should assist in guiding you through the application process. As you achieve success, you'll begin to feel more comfortable writing subsequent grants. If you are not successful in winning a grant award and are still convinced that you have a unique project, then re-evaluate your proposal, make revisions, and seek funding from other sources.

Chapter Summary

At this point, you should feel a little more comfortable in seeking funding through alternative strategies. From the simplest form of fundraising to the more complex form of proposal writing, money is available to fund your programs and projects if you approach the task in a systematic and controlled manner.

As legislative dollars for education continue to shrink, the challenge to seek funding sources for new and innovative projects and programs will increase. As you venture out into the corporate world, accept the challenge by knowing that the business community is behind you. Don't hesitate to make securing funds a group or team project; it becomes less burdensome when you have a support group to assist you in developing proposals. Additional assistance can always be secured from the community relations or grants administration office in your school system or university.

There is a pot of gold out there just waiting to be tapped. Go ahead and go after your share!

FIGURE 5.9: Evaluation

The evaluation of the FIT-TECH project will contain both process and product elements; that is, it will document both the activities that will take place under the grant as well as the impact.

The process aspect of the study will document such information as the demographics of the student population, the nature of staff development activities, and the nature of the "fitness" and "cognitive" activities. The grant proposal call for extensive computer stored information descriptive of the students who will participate as well as the nature and duration of participants. These computer files will serve as an important source of input for both process and product aspects of the evaluation.

Process data will be gathered from available student records and from specially developed evaluation forms. As part of the product evaluation, the impact of different durations of exposure to this project, including pre- and posttest measures will be assessed. A final evaluation report will be prepared to document both project activities and project impact.

References

Brewer, E. W., Achilles, C. M., & Fuheiman, J. R. (1995). *Finding funding: Grantwriting and project management from start to finish* (2nd ed.). Newbury Park, CA: Corwin Press.

Dade County Public Schools. (1997). *Dade partners: Schools and community working hand in hand. Guidebook for schools.* Miami, FL: Author.

DeGraw, C., & McGinnis, J. M. (1991). Healthy schools 2000: Creating partnerships for the decade. *Journal of School Health, 61* (7), 294–296.

Hunter, B. M. (1995). *From here to technology, how to fund hardware, software, and more.* Arlington, VA: American Association of School Administrators.

Moursand, D. (1996). Grantwriting for technology in education: Part 2—The dollars and cents of grant writing. *Learning and Leading with Technology, 23* (5), 34-37.

Ruskin, K. B., & Achilles, C. M. (1995). *Grantwriting, fundraising, and partnerships: Strategies that work.* Newbury Park, CA: Corwin Press.

Smith, S. H., & McLean, D. D. (1988). *ABCs of grantsmanship.* Reston, VA: American Alliance for Health, Physical Education, Recreation and Dance.

Worth, M. J. (1993). *Educational fundraising: Principals and practices.* Washington, DC: American Council on Education.

Zaidel, L. B. (1996). Raise funds, not hackles. *Learning, 25* (1), 47-49.

CHAPTER 6

Utilizing Technology

Bonnie Mohnsen

Technology can be defined as anything that facilitates the accomplishment of a task. A separate chapter on the topic may seem redundant in this book, since technology can be infused into every other chapter. However, because many professionals are having a difficult time adjusting to the rapid changes in technology, we choose to devote one chapter to the use of technology and how it applies to the various aspects of leadership.

Ten to 20 years from now this chapter will likely be analogous to a chapter on the overhead projector in a book on teaching today. The focus in the future won't be on the technology itself, but rather on the purpose or process of the task.

The seven major points for this chapter include:

1. Model the Use of Technology

2. Organize Time and Connections

3. Establish Telecommunications

4. Use Technology To Stay Accountable

5. Assess Instruction Using Technology

6. Encourage Staff Use of Instructional Technology

7. Provide Professional Development Related To Using Technology.

Model the Use of Technology

In 1949, Henri Fayol listed the five basic elements of administration as planning, organization, command, coordination, and control. During the past 50 years, the basic elements of administration have changed only slightly. However, the efficiency with which they are performed has greatly improved. The emergence of new technologies has reduced the amount of time necessary to perform the five basic elements of administration. This has provided the educational leader with more time to concentrate on improving the instructional program.

Our ultimate goal as leaders is to facilitate the use of the most efficient and effective tools. Modeling the use of current tools is the first step in facilitating their use by others. This includes selecting computer hardware and software, and using word processing, data base, and spreadsheet applications.

Selecting a Computer

The first decision when selecting a computer is whether to use the Macintosh Operating System or the Windows Operating System. When making this decision, consider the following:

▪ Which type of computer is more predominant at your site?

▪ Are the software programs you want to use available for Macintosh, Windows, or DOS?

▪ Do you or your staff have personal preferences?

▪ Is there technical assistance for only one type of computer at your site?

Remember, Macintosh computers with a DOS card (piece of hardware that is placed inside the computer) or SoftWindows (a piece of software) can run both Windows and DOS programs.

The second thing you must determine is what size computer will best meet your needs. There are basically four sizes of computers: desktop, notebook (5 to 10 pounds), sub-notebook (less than 5 pounds), and handheld. Ideally, we would have one of each and use each one for different jobs. However, most of us will need to select the one that best fits most of the tasks we perform. When making this decision, consider the following:

▪ Where do you normally work (in a chair, at a desk, or on the run)?

▪ What kind of tasks will you be performing with the computer?

▪ Do you have a personal preference?

My personal preference is the notebook computer. It provides me with mobility; I can continue to work whether I am on a plane, at my desk, or in my rocking chair. I find that it is not too heavy to carry, and it allows me to accomplish most of the same tasks as a desktop computer and more tasks than a handheld computer. However, I no longer work in the field, so my preference might be the handheld if I were still teaching.

Most handheld computers can interface with either a Macintosh or Windows-based computer. Popular models include the Apple MessagePad (Newton Operating System), Windows-CE based devices, Psion Series 3, and 3Com Pilot. Basic word processing, data base, spreadsheet, calendar, address book, to-do lists, time accounting, and telecommunication features discussed in the following sections are available for handheld computers. However, for teachers, the Newton Operating System (no longer produced, but still in use) currently offers the greatest number of titles in the area of grading. These include Sunburst's Grade Point and Sunburst's Learner Profile.

Now we get down to the specifics of speed: how much RAM (active memory), how big a hard drive (storage memory), and which computer. The answers are as fast as you can afford, as much as you can afford, as big as you can afford, and—finally—it depends. Any recommendation on a specific computer is outdated as soon as it appears in print. So, I suggest that when you are ready to buy, purchase a few magazines that contain reviews on computers and compare the top three or four recommendations.

Then, consider your finances and computer needs, and select one. For example, if you don't plan to take advantage of the audio features on the computer, then you may select a less expensive computer with inferior audio quality.

Software

The three most common uses of a computer include the inputting and printing of data (word processing), the organization of data (data base), and the manipulation of data (spreadsheets). When it comes to the use of technology, it can be helpful to use non-technical analogies. Thus, think of word processing as type-writing. Anything that once was created on a typewriter now can be created using word processing software. The non-technical analogy for a data base is a Rolodex, and the non-technical analogy for a spreadsheet is a ledger. These three tools are so commonly used that software publishers sell them as an integrated package along with art software, draw software, and communication software. Examples are Microsoft Works, Claris Works, and Microsoft Office.

Word Processing. Word processing is one of the most frequent uses of the computer in leadership. Supervisors used to sit at their desks and write memos using a pen and paper. Their secretaries were left to decipher the handwriting and produce the final docu-ment. Today, supervisors type rough drafts directly into a computer using word processing software. The draft is then sent through a local area network (LAN) to the secretary, who uses a computer to format the memo, select a font and style, correct for spelling and grammar, and print the final document.

Curriculum guides, agendas, evaluations, minutes, and policy statements are typical word processing files. The ability to save on a disk allows for quick updating when it is time to revise any of these items. No longer do we need to retype an entire document; changes are literally made in a matter of minutes.

In the past, if you wanted to create a more sophisticated layout for a document, you had to use special desktop publishing soft-ware, such as PageMaker. However, today many word processing programs provide the necessary tools for developing newsletters, flyers, task cards, and anything else that requires the manipulation of text and graphics. Most word processing programs also come with templates (predesigned forms ready for the user's data) for flyers, certificates, brochures, and newsletters.

The mail merge option adds a new dimension to letter writing. A form letter can be personalized for each recipient by placing a list of names, addresses, and any special information in one file, placing the letter in a second file, and using the mail merge feature available with most word processing or integrated software pack-ages to merge the two files. The final product is a series of person-

FIGURE 6.1: A file of physical educators sorted by expiration dates for cardiopulmonary resuscitation certification.

	A	B	C	D	E
1	**First**	**Last**	**School**	**CPR**	**First Aid**
2	Juan	Garcia	Roosevelt	Nov-98	Nov-98
3	Brenda	Adams	Roosevelt	Nov-98	Nov-98
4	Jenny	Smith	Santa Ana	Nov-98	Nov-98
5	John	Chan	Bell Gardens	Nov-98	Nov-98
6	Steve	Samuels	Roosevelt	Nov-98	Nov-98
7	Jesse	Gomez	Franklin	Feb-99	Nov-99
8	Kelley	Thompson	Santa Ana	Feb-99	Nov-99
9	Jason	Washington	Bell Gardens	Feb-99	Nov-99
10	Alicia	Gonzales	Roosevelt	Feb-99	Nov-99
11	Jane	Kennedy	Bell Gardens	Feb-99	Nov-99
12	Valerie	Johnson	Bell Gardens	May-99	Nov-00
13	Steve	Brown	Franklin	May-99	Nov-00
14	Jeramie	Bradley	Roosevelt	May-99	Nov-00
15	Joshua	Jones	Franklin	May-99	Nov-00
16	Mariz	Gonzalez	Franklin	May-99	Nov-00
17	Amy	Woo	Santa Ana	May-99	Nov-00
18	Hvong	Chung	Franklin	May-99	Nov-00
19					

FIGURE 6.2: A curriculum file sorted by grade level to produce the scope for each grade level.

StandardNumber	Grade	Standard
1	7	Student sets goals and monitors change in movement skill development.
2	7	Student applies locomotor, nonlocomotor, and manipulative skills to a variety of activiti
3	7	Student creates an individual/dual game with scoring options and a penalty system.
4	7	Student analyzes movement performance using spin and rebound principles in order to im
5	7	Student designs a one week personal fitness plan.
6	7	Student assesses personal fitness, compares scores to a health-related standard, and se
7	7	Student explains the growth rates of her body segments and the relationship to movemer
8	7	Student demonstrates risk-taking through participation in individual or dual movement ac
9	7	Student values personal identify and the development of aesthetic features of her perfor
10	7	Student displays collaborative problem solving techniques during risk-based initiatives.

alized letters, each addressed to an individual, and containing information specific to that individual. And the initiator need only type one letter!

Data Base. Data base software organizes data into records and fields. A record is equivalent to a card in a Rolodex file: It contains a variety of related information. A field represents one piece of information, such as a name or address. Information can be sorted (alphabetized or placed numerically) based on one or more fields

Scheduling facilities, updating eligibility lists, organizing locker assignments, scheduling teachers, and monitoring information is done more efficiently using data base software. Once a data base file is created, the user can sort the information within a matter of seconds using one or more of the fields. For example, a file that contains teacher's names, schools, expiration dates for first aid certification, and expiration dates for cardiopulmonary resuscitation certification can be sorted on the expiration date for first aid certification in order to determine which teachers have the same renewal dates (see Figure 6.1).

Another feature of data base software is its unique ability to filter information. In the previous example, the file can be put through a filter or selection process so that only the names of those teachers who need to renew their cardiopulmonary resuscitation certification during the coming month are displayed. A more complicated filter can display the names of those teachers who need to renew both their first aid certification and their cardiorespiratory certification. The same file can be sorted, filtered, and printed in many different combinations.

A data base program also can be used to facilitate the curriculum development process. Each record contains the grade level, standard number, and standard. The file can be sorted by grade level to produce the scope for each grade (see Figure 6.2) or sorted by standard number to produce the sequence for each standard (see Figure 6.3).

*Spreadsheets:*Spreadsheets facilitate the manipulation of numbers. They are made up of rows and columns. Each row (see Figure 6.4) is designated by a number, and each column is designated by a letter. The intersection of each row and column is called a cell and is referenced by the column letter and row number (e.g., A1, C3, E7). Data in the spreadsheets can be manipulated using operators (+, -, *, /) and special functions. Even though spreadsheets may appear complicated, they are in fact one of the easiest programs to use, once you learn a few basics.

Spreadsheet programs are typically used to create files for inventories, purchases, and budgets. Income, expense, and payroll files can all be maintained with current information. The grant development and implementation process is greatly simplified by using a spreadsheet file to create the original proposal budget and to maintain the budget once the grant is received. Spreadsheets also can be used for grading and fitness testing, although specific programs do exist for these tasks.

Organize Time and Connections

As leaders, we often find that we have more to accomplish than time permits. We can make better use of our time while simultaneously modeling the use of technology in our everyday work. Electronic address books, electronic calendars, time accounting programs, and "to do" lists are four specialty programs available to assist us in this area.

All of these programs are available for desktop, notebook, sub-notebook, and handheld computers. The handheld computer or "personal assistant" is ideal for these applications, since it can be easily used away from the office. Once back in the office, the handheld computer can be connected to a desktop computer via either a cable or infrared connection and the new data transferred to the desktop within a few minutes.

Electronic address books provide easy access to addresses, phone numbers, fax numbers, and e-mail addresses without the need to fumble with loose business cards. Associates can be sorted by first name or last name, or any other field. Specific individuals can be quickly located using the "find" command. Many of these software programs also provide automatic dial service; simply click on the person's name you wish to call, and your computer (connected to your phone) automatically dials the number for you.

Calendar programs produce daily, weekly, and yearly displays of appointments. Audible signals from the software alert you to meetings or special appointments. Calendar programs on a networked system even allow users to schedule meetings by

FIGURE 6.3: A curriculum file sorted by standard number to produce the sequence for each standard.

StandardNumber	Grade	Standard
1	1	Student explains that the desire to learn increases learning.
1	2	Student explains that mental practice assists with improving or learning movement ski
1	3	Student uses cue discrimination when involved in movement activities.
1	4	Student develops a practice plan using the variables of whole and part practice.
1	5	Student constructs practice programs for increasing speed and accuracy in movement-
1	6	Student applies appropriate feedback to a partner while developing or improving moven
1	7	Student sets goals and monitors change in movement skill development.
1	8	Student applies the principle of transfer of learning in order to learn a new skill.
1	9	Student develops a practice program for an open skill and for a closed skill.
1	10	Student develops a practice plan for himself taking into consideration his stage of learn

viewing the calendars of colleagues.

Time accounting programs track time spent on specific tasks. Type in the name of the activity, the starting date and time, and the ending date and time, and the computer calculates the total time and stores the information. This can be a helpful feature if you are working on a number of different grants and each requires a precise accounting of time. These programs also can be used to help you determine whether time is being used effectively.

Electronic "to do" lists can serve as a management tool for a multi-manager project. The computer allows for sorting and viewing of the list by deadline date, task priority, project name, or person responsible. Multi-manager project software often provides a number of organizational charts, including Gantt charts designed to monitor the development and implementation of a project that involves a number of people.

Establish Telecommunications

The ability to communicate is a leader's most important asset. Too often, we don't have time to pick up the phone and contact one another. This is where telecommunications can come in handy. During the last several years, use of the Internet has literally exploded. The Internet provides users with the opportunity to send messages to and receive them from one or many colleagues simultaneously. In addition, the Internet provides each user access to vast amounts of information.

The Internet is, simply, a connection between computers located around the world. The World Wide Web (WWW) provides users with a graphical user interface for finding and using Internet resources. In addition to a computer, Internet users need a modem (converts the computer's digital code into the telephone's analog code and vice versa); a direct connection to the Internet or an Internet Service Provider (e.g., America Online, Earthlink, local school district); and Internet connection software, software for electronic mail, and software for browsing the WWW. Such software is generally provided by the Internet Service Provider.

E-Mail

Using a real life analogy, e-mail is like having your own post office box. Your friends and colleagues send mail to your post office box and, when you have time, you go to the post office, open your box, and retrieve your mail. With electronic mail, your mail box is located on the server (computer) of your Internet Service Provider.

All electronic mail software programs provide you with a template for sending mail. Eudora is a popular e-mail program, and Netscape Navigator and Internet Explorer are popular web browsers that also have e-mail features. The process for preparing an e-mail message is very similar to preparing a regular (snail) mail message. You type in the address of the individual to whom you are sending mail, type your message, and send the message (by clicking on the "send" button).

Electronic mail can facilitate communication between a leader and other educators in a school district, a region, or a state. It also can bring leaders together for articulation and problem solving, regardless of where they are located geographically. Finally, electronic mail seems to eliminate the artificial boundaries of title and position. It allows for communication between first-year teachers and senior university professors. Asking a question of an expert is as simple as clicking on a button—as long as you know the expert's e-mail address.

Listserv

Listservs provide an opportunity to communicate with tens, hundreds, and even thousands of individuals simultaneously. In order to send a message to a listserv, you must first be a member of that listserv. There are many listservs available for physical educators. A roster is available at http://www.stan-co.k12.ca.us/calpe/.

Typically, listservs have two electronic addresses—one for administrative purposes (i.e., joining the list), and the other for communication purposes (i.e., sending a message). When using the administrative address, you are communicating with a software program, so you need to use special commands. Common commands include:

FIGURE 6.4: A sample spreadsheet.

	A	B	C	D	E
1	**Inventory**	Bats	Softballs	Footballs	Volleyballs
2					
3	Room 1				
4	Room 2				
5	Room 3				
6					
7					
8	**Totals**	=Sum(B2:B5)	=Sum(C2:C5)	=Sum(D2:D5)	=
9					
10					
11					
12					

SUB or SUBSCRIBE	To join a list
UNSUB or UNSUBSCRIBE	To leave a list
DIGEST	To have messages accumulated and sent to you once a day
HELP	To get a list of all commands

The Council of School Leadership for Physical Education (CSLPE),which exists under the National Association for Sport and Physical Education (NASPE) umbrella, provides a listserv service for its members. If you are a CSLPE member, you can join by sending the following in the body of the message and leaving the subject line blank:

To: listserv@host.fsd.k12.ca.us
From: (Your e-mail address)
Re:
SUB CSLPE YourFirstName YourLastName

Then, you may send messages to everyone on the list by addressing the e-mail to:

cslpe@host.fsd.k12.ca.us

Listservs are especially effective when you need a quick answer or input from several persons regarding the same topic, or when you need to communicate/disseminate something to a large audience. Perhaps you are on a curriculum writing team and you want sample curricula from several other districts or regions. You can simply send a request to the CSLPE listserv and it will go out to hundreds of physical education leaders across the country, many of whom have already developed and implemented new curricula. What a listserv does not provide, however, is a live interaction. You must wait for the receivers to check their e-mail before you will get a response.

Chatting and Conferencing

Live, interactive sessions are available via the Internet through chat sessions (written communication) and audio/video conferencing. Unlike listservs or e-mail, all users are on-line simultaneously so a constant dialog can occur. As long as you have an Internet connection and the appropriate software you may use any of these services without incurring an additional time charge. Unlike a telephone system, you don't have to pay for the length of the conversation.

There are several sites on the World Wide Web where chat sessions occur. Some of these sites do not require special software. You simply go to the web page, type in the message you wish to share, and click on "send" to send it, and "listen" when you want to view what others are inputting. At other sites, special "chat" software is required. The software allows you to immediately see the messages written by other users.

Video conferencing provides audio and video communication; the users hear one another and see one another. They can pick up the subtle forms of communication that come with body language and facial expressions. The bandwidth (data transmission speed) requirements for video conferencing are great; they require at least an ISDN (Integrated Services Digital Network) line. Video conferencing software such as CU-See-Me is freely distributed over the Internet.

Each form of communication (e-mail, listserv, chat, video conferencing) can put you in contact with new resources for information and the sharing of ideas. These resources can be from the other side of the country or the globe. In addition, these new forms of communication are much more efficient when compared to traditional meetings, which often require more time for transportation than for the meeting!

Searching the Web

Sometimes acquisition of knowledge or information, not communication, is the primary purpose of going online. Since the Internet is a connection of computers around the world, a wealth of information is available. In order to maneuver through the World Wide Web, you will need a browser like Internet Explorer or Netscape Navigator.

There are two major strategies for searching the World Wide Web. The first is used if you already have an address for the site that has the information you need or for a general site (i.e. physical education) that contains links to the information needed. In this first example, you simply type in the address and the browser brings the information to you (see Figure 6.5).

The second strategy involves conducting a search using one of

FIGURE 6.5: Locating a specific Internet address using a World Wide Web browser

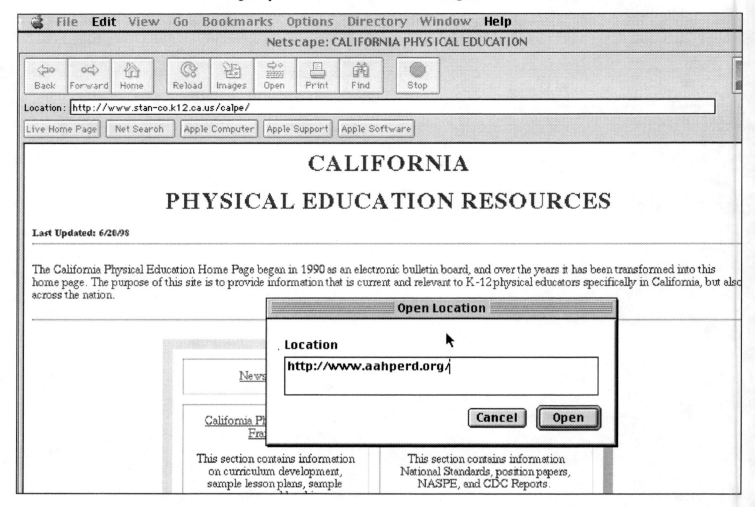

the search tools available on the web. The choice of search tools depends on the information you are seeking, but popular tools include Excite, Yahoo, and AltaVista. Each of these tools has its own home page which has space for you to type in your topic (i.e., social skill development).

The difficulty lies not in finding information, but in limiting the parameters of your search. A search for physical education leadership may result in several thousands entries (see Figure 6.6). Thus, it is helpful to apply a filter (selection process) so that fewer "hits" (number of times a search word is found) occur during a search. Using the previous topic, you may wish to put quotes around physical education leadership so that you only get references to information where these three words appear together. You may want to further reduce the number by adding AND "middle school." Using this search string, you will only get physical education leadership references that also relate to middle school.

Using the world wide web as a personal library is a very effective tool for the busy leader, since access to current events, research, literature, grants, laws, sample curricula, and assessment data is immediate. Sites visited often (e.g., Centers for Disease Control, AAHPERD) can be bookmarked (the name of the site and its address are added to a list), so that you can return to the site quickly.

Designing Web Pages

Once you have had an opportunity to search the World Wide Web, it will only be a matter of time until you will want to contribute to this international library. A few years ago designing a web page required the skills of a computer programmer. Today, anyone with word processing skills, an idea, and time can design a web page.

You can learn the basics of web creation tools such as Microsoft Front Page, Adobe PageMill, and Claris HomePage. With a few hours of personal study or class time, you can have your web page up and running in an afternoon. So, the question is not, "Can I learn how to create a web page?" Rather, the question is, "Do I have something significant to contribute?"

Many leaders create web pages to share their physical education programs; others create web pages to educate parents on quality physical education and the importance of physical activity; and still others create web pages that include or link to curriculum samples, lesson plan samples, and assessment ideas.

Once you have designed your web page, the next step is to post it on a server so that everyone can see your work. Many school districts have their own servers and encourage contributions from teacher/leaders and students. If your school district doesn't currently have its own server, you can secure an Internet account through an Internet Service Provider such as America Online or EarthLink.

FIGURE 6.6: Locating information on the Internet using a search tool.

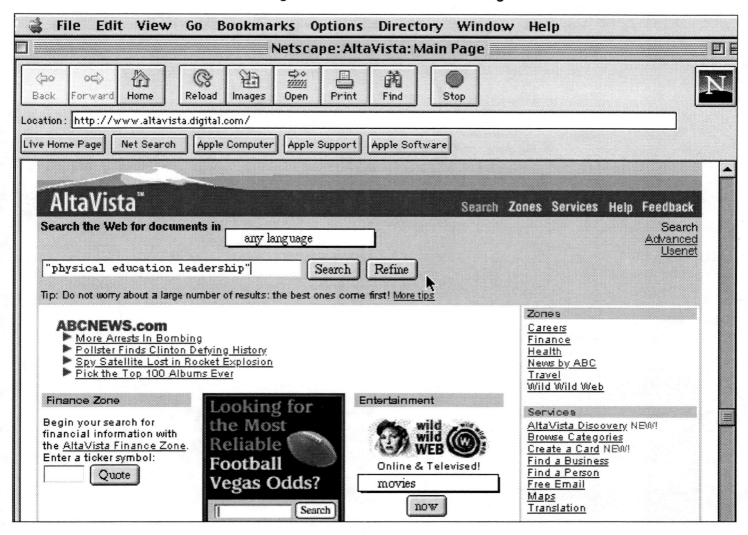

Use Technology To Stay Accountable

Manipulating numbers and information is what computers do best. Therefore, an obvious use for technology is the management of assessment data. By keeping track of core objectives/standards and assessment results, teachers are better able to evaluate the current performance level of their students and determine future learning experiences. By aggregating student achievement, leaders can demonstrate the importance of physical education in the total school curriculum.

Management Software

Management software facilitates the input, organization, and storage of standards and individual/group achievement data. Basically a management program is a data base that is predesigned to monitor data for an entire school or school system. Popular management programs include Abacus and Instructional Management.

Electronic Portfolios

Electronic portfolios are similar to management software, except that each student is responsible for maintaining his or her own individual portfolio. A number of generic portfolio software pieces are available on the market, including Grady Profile

(Grady) and Scholastic's Electronic Portfolio. These programs are templated to assist both students and teachers with the formatting.

Teachers and students also can create their own portfolios using authoring programs such as HyperStudio, SuperLink, HyperCard, and NewtCard. A number of preformatted HyperCard Stacks (Macintosh Operating System), NewtCard Stacks (Newton Operating System), and SuperLink Folders (Windows Operating System) also have been created to serve as templates for electronic portfolios in physical education. These programs, available from Bonnie's Fitware, include: Health-Related Fitness Tutorial/Portfolio, Portfolio, and Volleyball Complete Tutorial/Portfolio.

The electronic portfolio picks up where the paper portfolio leaves off. It allows the collection of written information, audio records, pictures, drawings, handwriting samples, and even video clips to document student learning. Using a video card, users can connect either a video cassette player/recorder or camcorder to their computers (similar to the process of connecting a VCR to a television set) and convert analog video into digitized video that is ready for computer use. Video clips are ideal for showing student performance on a motor skill prior to practice and after several weeks of practice.

Fitness Reporting

Fitness reporting was one of the first uses of the computer in physical education. Fitness reporting programs analyze raw fitness scores, print summaries (tables, charts, graphs) that can be sent home to parents, and store data for pre/post-test comparisons and statistics. From a leadership perspective, fitness reporting is an ideal use of technology. Fitness scores are maintained in a master file, so that charting a student from kindergarten through twelfth grade becomes possible regardless of which schools the student attends. In addition, the summary sent home to parents is an outstanding public relations tool and encourages parental involvement in the child's fitness development.

Assess Instruction Using Technology

Many leaders are asked to do some teacher observation and assessment. The ability of the leader to document what is actually occurring in the class or gymnasium increases the credibility of the assessment. The type of data collected should reflect the experience and abilities of the teacher being observed. Time on task, number of specific feedbacks, and ratio of boys and girls asked to demonstrate a new skill are all good starting places when the leader doesn't know the background of the teacher being observed. When visiting classes, the quantitative data can be collected on either a notebook computer or a handheld device like the Sharp Wizard or the Apple MessagePad (Newton).

Popular software programs include ALT-PE (Microcomputer Data) and OARS (Maze Products). Most of these programs prompt the user for the type of activity occurring. The computer then notes the time when the activity (roll call, exercise, transition) was selected and continues to monitor the time until a second activity is selected. At the end of the lesson, the computer calculates the amount of time spent in each activity. (It should be noted that although these software programs have been used for some time by faculty at many colleges and universities, they are fairly new to most leaders, teachers, and master teachers.)

Encourage Staff Use of Instructional Technology

Being a leader in the area of technology means more than using technology for management purposes. It also means seeing to it that the teachers in the field have access to and use technology to prepare and deliver instruction to students. Every physical education teacher should be equipped with at least one teaching/presentation computer workstation. (Grants and other avenues of financial assistance are available where funding is an issue.) The workstation should ideally consist of a notebook computer with a modem and CD-ROM drive. The portability of the notebook computer provides teachers with the opportunity to work on the computer regardless of location—both on and off the field and at home.

The workstation also can be used with students to learn physical education concepts during the instructional period. Presentations are easily developed using software programs such as Microsoft PowerPoint. The teacher simply develops an outline of his or her presentation and the software program converts the outline to slides. The teacher then connects the computer directly to a projection system or through a television encoder to a large monitor, so that the entire class can see the slides as the information is discussed.

Teachers also can use this arrangement with instructional soft-ware programs. These programs run the gamut from drill/practice (ask a question and the user provides an answer), tutorial (provide the user with some information and then ask a question), and resource information such as encyclopedias, to simulation programs that require users to solve a problem in order to demonstrate their understanding of the concept.

It is our responsibility as leaders to encourage teachers to select high-quality simulations and resource software. For information on the software available for physical education, consult *Physical Education Sourcebook* (Hennessy 1996), and *Using Technology in Physical Education,* Edition 2 (Mohnsen 1998).

The selection of instructional materials is an important leadership responsibility. It is not unusual for school systems to put committees together to review textbooks and make recommendations for school board adoption. However, when it comes to instructional software, it is not uncommon for teachers to be left on their own in the selection process. Some states, including California, have created state software clearinghouses where teacher/reviewers try out software, use it with students, and make recommendations on its appropriateness. The reviews from California can be found at http://clearinghouse.k12.ca.us. In addition, the International Society for Technology in Education publishes an annual review of recommended software that includes programs for physical education.

It is not enough to simply put hardware and software into the hands of physical educators, however. They need to observe other physical educators using technology effectively. It takes time to learn to use a computer well enough to begin saving time. So, it is crucial that physical educators can see the long-term benefits of the time they must invest. They also must observe the increase in motivation and learning of students who are engaged with technology. A visit to a nearby school where physical educators are using technology will provide such a view.

Provide Professional Development
Related To Using Technology

Teachers will need sufficient inservice time in order to become comfortable with the computer. According to Boudrot et al. (1988), while teachers need 20 to 100 hours of inservice training to adequately learn to use the computer, most teachers get between 5 and 15 hours of training. Training should be specific to how the physical educator will use the technology, and ability grouping is a must. In my region, we have developed a three-level approach (beginning, intermediate, and advanced) to professional development in the area of technology.

Our Level One courses focus on teacher utility. The teachers learn how to work the operating system and to open, close, copy, move, and save files. In addition, they create word processing, data base, and spreadsheet programs. They receive their e-mail addresses and learn how to use their electronic mail accounts. Depending on the needs of the group, special grading software or fitness reporting software also is introduced. The instructor for the Level One courses uses a command style of teaching initially with the participants, then as the course progresses the participants are given task cards to follow in order to progress at their own rates.

At Level Two, it is assumed that the teachers have had an opportunity to work with the programs taught during Level One and have begun to feel comfortable using the computer for their own teaching duties. Level Two focuses on the use of instructional software with students. We have found that teachers are unlikely to use the software with their students until they feel some comfort with computers in general, as well as with the specific software they will be asking their students to use. During this time, teachers have the opportunity to experiment with the instructional software, follow task cards, and participate in online tutorials. Then, they work in groups and create lesson plans that take advantage of the instructional software programs.

Finally, at Level Three, it is assumed that the teachers have interacted with their students using instructional software. And, like most physical educators, they have found that there are only a limited number of software programs available. This inservice, then, provides them with an opportunity to learn an authoring language such as HyperCard, HyperStudio, or SuperLink so that they can create their own instructional programs or electronic portfolios. Learning to use an authoring program also provides the participants with the necessary skills to teach their students how to create their own multimedia projects to demonstrate what they have learned. It is at this level that interested participants are taught how to create web pages.

My region also uses technology as the process for delivering professional development. By offering professional development via the Internet (see Chapter 11), we provide simultaneous learning opportunities for physical educators. They not only learn the content of the professional development, but also the necessary skills for navigating the WWW and using other Internet tools. Many colleges and universities now offer degree programs through the Internet. As leaders, we can use this vehicle for professional development as well.

Chapter Summary

Whether it be as a user or an advocate, physical education leaders have a role to play in advancing the new technologies of our day. Those who are novices must update their skills, and those who already are familiar with the technology must stay abreast of the latest advances. As leaders in the field of physical education, we must show the way for the teachers in our district and enable them to become more efficient in the instructional tasks they perform each day.

References

Boudrot, T., Hertzberg, L., Leonard, J., McKinnon, G., Newmark, A., Pankin, J., Pogue, L., Solomon, G., Stanton, D., & Vernont, D. (1988). One hundred and one things you want to know about educational technology. *Electronic Learning, 7*(8), 32-48.

Hennessy, B. H. (Ed.). (1996). *Physical education sourcebook.* Champaign, IL: Human Kinetics.

Mohnsen, B. S. (1991). Using computers—helping physical education administrators. *Journal of Physical Education, Recreation & Dance, 62*(1), 40–44, 48.

Mohnsen, B. S. (1998). *Using technology in physical education, edition 2.* Cerritos, CA: Bonnie's Fitware.

Mohnsen, B. S. (1997). *Teaching middle school physical education.* Champaign, IL: Human Kinetics.

Mohnsen, B. S. (1997). What's the ideal system. *Teaching Elementary Physical Education 8* (4), 14-15.

Mohnsen, B.S. (1997). Technology and special events. *Teaching Elementary Physical Education 9* (1), 27-29.

Software Resources

Adobe PageMaker, Adobe PageMill: 800-833-6687
Apple HyperCard: 800-776-2333
Bonnie's Fitware Health Related Fitness Tutorial/Portfolio, Bonnie's Fitware Portfolio, Bonnie's Fitware Volleyball Complete T/P: 562-924-0835
Claris HomePage, Claris Works: 408-727-8227
Eudora: 800-338-3672
Maze Products OARS: 2610 Commonwealth Dr., Charlottesville, VA 22901
Micro Computer Data ALT-PE: Virginia Tech, Department of Physical Education, Blacksburg, VA 24061, c/o Michael Metzler
Microsoft (Front Page, Internet Explorer, Office, Works): 800-426-9400
Netscape Navigator: 650-937-2722
NSBasic NewtCard: 416-264-5888
NCS Abacus Instructional Management System: 503-224-2152
Roger Wagner HyperStudio: 1050 Pioneer Way, Suite P, El Cajon, CA 92020
Scholastic Electronic Portfolio: 800-SCHOLAS
Software for Teachers Grady Profile: 800-77-GRADY
Sunburst Grade Point, Sunburst Learner Profile: 800-321-7511
Washington Computer Services SuperLink: 360-734-8248
White Pine CU-See Me: 603-886-9050

Hardware Resources

Apple Newton: 800-776-2333
Sharp Zaurus: 714-903-4600
Psion Series 3: 800-997-7466
US Robotics Palm Pilot: 800-881-7256

Internet Service Providers

America Online: 800-827-6364
Earthlink: 800-395-8425

Internet Search Tools

Excite: http://www.excite.com
Yahoo: http://www.yahoo.com
AltaVista: http://altavista.digital.com

Part 3. Assuming the Role

"The original Greek idea of pedagogy had associated with it the meaning of leading in the sense of accompanying the child and living with the child in such a way as to provide direction and care for his or her life. Teachers practice a form of pedagogical leadership directly, because in schools they stand first and closest in a caring relationship to children. They have the major responsibility for guiding children academically, socially, and spiritually through the world of childhood to adulthood. Indeed, the process of education in itself implies leadership."

–Thomas Sergiovanni

CHAPTER 7

Elementary Teacher Leadership

Dorri Hawkes

They call me a leader at my site, in my district, and even throughout the state. But I have always believed myself to be unremarkable. I care about kids, have a passion for teaching and learning, and love to share and grow professionally.

I am a steward of information, a troubleshooter, a listener, an advocate, a model for life long learning, a willing hand when something needs to be done, and an active participant in the decision making process. I am a catalyst for interdisciplinary connections, critical thinking/problem solving activities, student social development, positive discipline, instructional strategies, brain compatible learning, organizational strategies, and ordering equipment and instructional materials. My role evolves from doing research, consulting, listening to a multitude of teachers and innovative thinkers, borrowing ideas, applying what I learn with my students, and securing the trust of positional leaders.

My primary goal has always been to be a good teacher. Teachers who take pride in their performance and profession and gain personal satisfaction from their work are the ones who leave lasting impressions on their students. It is not just through the knowledge they impart, but by the example they set.

It may be difficult to perceive of yourself as a leader until you understand that leadership is not limited to one type of behavior. Nor must leadership be delegated to be realized. Leadership occurs in many ways and on many levels: You can lead by example, by being a facilitator, by directing a change effort, by inspiring others, or by a combination of these. Schools that demonstrate positive performance and attitudes among their students and teachers usually have strong leaders.

This chapter will address teacher leadership in terms of:

1. Identifying Effective Teacher Behaviors
2. Building Relationships
3. Improving the School Physical Education Program
4. School-Site Leadership
5. School-to-School Leadership
6. District Level Leadership
7. Leadership in Professional Organizations.

Although these topics are similar to those listed for middle and high school teacher/leaders, I will address each through the lens of an elementary physical education leader.

Identifying Effective Teacher Behaviors

There are official leaders such as mentor teachers or project coordinators, but there are far more unofficial leaders in successful elementary schools. These leaders may include talented teachers who rarely supervise or train other teachers but whose professionalism is demonstrated continuously by their knowledge, skill, and enthusiasm. Leadership begins with effective teaching. Effective teaching can be divided into three segments: (1) instruction, (2) curriculum and assessment, and (3) professional behavior and life long learning.

Instruction

Instruction encompasses the range of methods that can be applied in working with students in physical education. Generally, the more teachers know and practice a variety of instructional strategies the more likely they are to meet the diverse needs of students. Instructional strategies appropriate for elementary physical education include cooperative learning, reciprocal teaching, guided discovery, movement exploration, and direct instruction. While balancing strategies takes skill and experience, choosing the most appropriate strategies for meeting specific curricular objectives requires continuous thoughtful consideration. For example, cooperative learning is a great strategy to use to teach social interaction skills, while direct instruction is useful for introducing a specific motor skill.

Perhaps one of the most significant challenges to physical educators is that of creating an environment where all students—regardless of gender, size, skill, ability, or cultural background—can flourish and feel confident in their performance, knowledge, and skills. It is not an accident that three of the seven National Standards for Physical Education focus on student self-image, personal development, and social development:

■ Standard 5. Demonstrates responsible personal and social behavior in physical activity settings.

■ Standard 6. Demonstrates understanding and respect for differences among people in physical activity settings.

■ Standard 7. Understands that physical activity provides opportunities for enjoyment, challenge, self-expression, and social interaction. (NASPE 1995.)

These standards focus on the way students feel about themselves and each other, and their valuing of physical activity. To teach to these standards requires much more knowledge and understanding of the multitude of instructional strategies than is typically available to physical educators. These strategies are most often taught within the context of other content areas such as language arts, social science, and math. Physical education teacher/leaders would benefit from attending workshops, inservices, and trainings in these content areas and adapting the strategies learned to physical education content.

Constructing a thinking/meaning centered curriculum, using multiple intelligences and authentic assessment can provide students with great motivation for self-expression, enjoyment, and challenge. Some models of cooperative learning, such as David and Roger Johnson's, offer more of an emphasis on social skills instruction than others. Social skills instruction can be applied to reciprocal teaching, conflict resolution, and any partner or small group strategies. Individualized instruction, guided discovery, and critical thinking/problem solving can help develop student self-awareness.

Physical educators know that if elementary students are to develop a desire for being physically active for life they must acquire skills and abilities beyond fitness knowledge and motor skills. Students need to feel connected to their learning and to each other while developing a realistic and positive sense of self. These are the motivators that drive the desire for life long health and wellness, which includes physical fitness and motor skill acquisition.

How can we make physical education a positive experience for every student? We can do it by ensuring physical and emotional success for all students.

Emotional success for all students will be determined in large part by the elementary physical education teacher's willingness and ability to teach and model appropriate social skills. Physical education is one of the most natural places to teach students how to interact successfully, because it is highly interactive in nature. One way to create a positive learning experience for students is through the use of cooperate teams or groups where two or more students work together in a structured process to accomplish a common task or goal.

Cooperative learning strategies focus on the skills necessary for students to be successful, contributing members of a group. These skills include facilitating, recording, time keeping, equipment/materials monitoring, reporting, and social skills monitoring. An abundance of interaction occurs in the performance of movement activities, and we can ensure a physically and emotionally safe environment by teaching students to be encouraging and caring, to disagree in a positive manner, and to show respect for diversity.

Teachers can be role models by using positive versus punitive discipline; holding class meetings; using techniques such as journaling, peer feedback, peer discussions, and small-group processing; modeling critical thinking skills; and encouraging students to problem solve and share problem-solving processes. For a physically and emotionally safe environment to exist and endure, not only in physical education but in all classrooms and throughout the campus, staff and students must demonstrate respect for each other, while supporting the development of the appropriate skills in every individual and every aspect of schooling.

Physical success in elementary physical education encompasses both movement performance and cognitive understanding of movement related concepts. It is important to use a variety of instructional strategies because it is impossible to meet all student's needs with direct instruction alone. Some students learn best alone while others learn better in groups; some learn sequentially (one thing at a time) while others are more global learners. Students can be more visual, auditory, or kinesthetic. They can come from diverse cultural backgrounds and speak any number of languages. And, they can vary widely in ability level. There are instructional strategies to meet the needs of all students, and these strategies can be used together with ease once the teacher becomes familiar with them.

The importance of effective instruction cannot be overstated. Effective instruction is a fundamental building block for leadership. Although teachers can become leaders in varying arenas without these skills, authentic leadership necessitates a solid foundation of professional instructional expertise. Without it, credibility cannot be established.

Curriculum and Assessment

Curriculum, instruction, and assessment are inseparable. A strong instructional knowledge base prepares teachers for teaching critical knowledge and skills identified in the curriculum. Authentic assessment is embedded in instruction: It should not look very different from instruction, it should be performance and product-based, it should be ongoing, and it should provide meaningful information to students to help improve their skills.

Effective teacher/leaders research current information and resources, and they examine their own site/district goals and student outcomes to determine the content of the physical education curriculum. *Moving into the Future: National Standards for Physical Education* (NASPE 1995) and *Concepts of Physical Education, What Every Student Needs To Know* (Mohnsen 1998) are excellent resources to begin to explore curriculum standards.

The primary question that needs to be answered before developing curriculum is, "What do students need to know and be able to do to be physically educated for the twenty-first century?" Teachers may have a curriculum in place that is mandated by the school district or school site, and some of these may not meet the needs of twenty-first century students. Aligning outdated curricula with National Standards and state standards and guidelines is a worthwhile leadership project.

A powerful curriculum includes attention to higher level thinking skills and meaningful interdisciplinary connections. When I arrived at my first teaching assignment as the sole physical education teacher for 800 elementary students, I began by visiting other teacher's classrooms and asking questions about the most important aspects of their curriculum. I watched them teach and invited them to watch their students in physical education class. This process created a natural medium for shared curricular outcomes and mutually supportive approaches to achieving those outcomes. Curriculum development can provide teacher/leaders with an invaluable opportunity to nurture strong and enduring advocates for quality physical education.

Assessment in physical education is as valuable to learning as are curriculum and instruction. After elementary physical education teacher/leaders have determined what students need to know and be able to do (curriculum), assessment tools should be developed that enable teachers and students to know whether they have achieved the curricular goals. If multiple instructional strategies are used effectively, assessment can occur both formatively (ongoing) and summatively (at the end). Formative assessment can include student self-checklists for designated motor, social, and personal skills; teacher observations and checklists; skills and knowledge tests; journals; etc. Summative assessment may include skills and knowledge tests, portfolios, pre and post-fitness assessments, student projects, and exhibits.

Assessment should include self-evaluation, student-to-student, teacher, and group evaluation strategies. The goals of assessment should be to provide students with useful feedback for monitoring progress, making adjustments in their performance, and achieving their goals. It should provide teachers with information regarding curriculum and instruction, program effectiveness, and student enjoyment.

One example of student self-assessment is a three-point rubric that students use at the end of physical education class to assess their social performance.

---

3 I was successful at completing the tasks. I cooperated with others and encouraged others.

2 I completed most tasks successfully. I cooperated and encouraged others most of the time.

1 I was unable to complete the tasks successfully and work cooperatively with others.

Students can explain to one another how they assessed themselves. They can discuss why they were or were not successful, what they said or did to encourage others, and what they will do differently next time. They also can use the rubric for self-reflection when they return to class by writing about it in their journals. A prompt might be: Write about a way that you encouraged others in your group to accomplish the task.

Professional Behavior and Life Long Learning

Starting in my first year teaching, I began to recognize the importance of learning about other content area goals and how they relate to physical education. I noticed that classroom teachers had a common language that did not include me, as a physical educator. It was not intentional, but I knew that physical education would never be integral to the school unless I had access to the knowledge, language, and skills that the majority of teachers shared. So, I began attending every professional development inservice required of classroom teachers as well as other content inservices provided by the district. I observed in classrooms, participated on school-site leadership committees, and asked a lot of questions.

When committed teachers lack the content or process knowledge necessary to meet the needs of their students, they do whatever is necessary to learn. They attend workshops and professional development programs. Physical educators who do not have access to the range of necessary instructional strategies in their own content area seek out the strategies in other content areas.

I have always been interested in teaching as a process, and in the many ways teachers can reach children and facilitate learning. I have learned about cooperative learning models, multiple intelligence strategies, learning styles instruction, meaning centered activities, metacognition, authentic assessment, technology applications, English language learning techniques, diversity sensitivity (cultural, gender, ability), and more. A majority of the training sessions I have attended have been in content areas other than physical education—most often language arts and math. These are the disciplines where cutting edge research on teaching and learning seems to be focused first. At the same time, I continue to attend workshops to expand my physical education content knowledge and skills.

In my pursuit of continuous improvement, I have noted a number of behaviors that have transformed me over time. These behaviors have become the foundation for my professionalism. I have learned to:

- Ask questions for clarity and understanding
- Model every skill and behavior I ask of my students
- Be courteous and considerate of all students, staff, and community members
- Enthusiastically research knowledge and information to improve learning
- Actively listen and participate in meetings
- Participate on committees and in professional groups
- Take an active role in both site and district-level decision making
- Be a life long learner.

Teachers are not assembly line workers, manufacturing "educated" children. We are facilitators of learning, innovators for using technology to enhance living and learning, and guides for positive interaction. When we work to consciously meet the needs of all students we realize the need to take responsibility for developing our own skills. Teachers are always at the helm; therefore, we must advocate for the necessary time and resources to cultivate knowledge in our discipline, knowledge across the disciplines, teaching and learning techniques, and continuous sharing and interaction among educators. These processes provide the source of professionalism that can breed pride, integrity, personal accountability, efficacy, and desire for excellence in all caring teachers.

Teachers are expected to adapt and change. Societal needs change over time, as does the knowledge and information in our profession. Teachers who do not attend to societal needs and the changing knowledge base may be providing information that is neither needed nor wanted. With the acceptance of change as a reality comes the necessity and willingness to prepare for it. Teachers must recognize their need for continuing education and acquire it through research, ongoing staff development, seminars and courses, site visits, etc.

I realized early in my career that if I was to foster student growth I must nurture and develop my personal and professional knowledge and skills. If I continually ask, "What is it my students should know and be able to do?" it leads me to ask myself, "What should I know and be able to do?"

The sense of wonder and awe I feel when immersed in the process of teaching and learning compels me to seek more: "Why did Marie develop the ability to demonstrate opposition while Jorge is struggling with extension errors?" "Can I affect the social interaction skills of individuals who are from vastly disparate backgrounds and who have vastly different temperaments?" "What skills and abilities will my students need to be successful in movement activities and life in the 21st century?" These questions, and thousands more, drive my thirst for continuous life long learning.

Building Relationships

Building relationships with and among staff members, administrators, parents, students, and community members has enormous implications for successful program implementation and leadership endeavors. The nature of the relationships that the elementary physical education teacher leader develops can be readily correlated to the success that teacher has in implementing program outcomes. Although there are numerous ways to approach successful interactions with others and to advocate for quality physical education, I have found some tenets to be particularly helpful:

- Always be forthright and sincere in professional relationships.

- Be knowledgeable about and interested in the goals, wants, and needs of other persons and assist them to the best of your ability.

- Know the language ("educational lingo") of those in your school-site/district, and be part of the discussions. Shared knowledge is shared power. Teachers own responsibility for acquiring knowledge. Leaders do not wait for someone else to determine what knowledge and skills they need to possess; they learn as much as they can about every aspect of teaching and learning.

- Turn negative comments about physical education into "teachable moments" instead of defensive posturing. People base their opinions on their own experiences. Tell them about the concepts that students learn in motor learning, exercise, physiology, biomechanics, social skills, etc. Offer opportunities that will provide them with new, more positive experiences; invite them to observe your program.

I have noticed a lack of awareness among many elementary school staff members regarding the knowledge, skills, and behaviors that quality elementary physical education programs can produce. To some, physical education is games and sport. To others, it is fitness or exercise. One aspect of leadership that I fervently pursue is urging all educators on staff to view physical education in the same light as all other content areas. This begins with conveying to the entire staff the effects that a quality school wide physical education program has on the school learning environment.

I must be certain that the physical education program is delivering on the claims I make and then ensure that those claims are attributable to the physical education program. When students demonstrate improved concentration, higher test scores and academic performance, reduced disruptive behaviors,

reduced susceptibility to stress, and positive social skills as a result of cooperative learning in physical education, the program value is enhanced.

Forging positive relationships also contributes to allocation of necessary funding and resources. We need facilities, equipment, and materials. By networking with other teachers, parents, and community members, I discovered a variety of strategies for obtaining sufficient equipment and materials. We found ways to make our own equipment. We had parent volunteers supply the PVC pipes, paint, and other materials, but they also constructed the equipment. On family fun nights, these parents received rave recognition. Parents saw the equipment being used and enjoyed, which encouraged more parents to donate or build equipment. Building relationships with businesses also can result in an increase in resources. Consider, for example, carpet stores (for carpet squares), hardware stores (PVC pipe, rope, wood, boxes, crates, etc.), sporting goods stores, businesses specializing in technology, etc.

There are several additional ways to nurture professional respect. I met with the staff development coordinator for our site and offered suggestions for training related to the school's improvement plans in addition to physical education topics. I consulted respected experts in the field who provided both wisdom and encouragement. I researched materials written by reputable physical educators and other content specialists. I prepared myself for those "teachable moments."

Jesse Jackson once said, "Excellence is the best deterrent to racism." I believe the same is true of misperceptions of physical education. Excellence in teaching, learning, professionalism, and leadership are the best possible forms of physical education advocacy. Excellence always speaks for itself.

I believe that one of the most critical aspects contributing to my effectiveness as a teacher is my desire to establish a learning environment that reinforces the value of relationships. Rather than isolating ourselves from one another and from the community outside the school, we can benefit by cultivating relationships with colleagues on and off site, students, volunteers, parents, members of community and professional organizations, and administrators.

For elementary physical educators, this can be done by working with the school nurse for height/weight/body composition testing, volunteering for school/community collboratives, co-sponsoring events with local recreational organizations, inviting your school community to participate in a local 5K walk/run, or organizing an after-school or evening bicycle, skateboard, skating, jump rope, bowling, or movement rally for students, staff, and families.

Finding enough time to network with colleagues is a constant challenge. When appropriate, engage in professional talk during lunch or recess, before and after school, during staff meetings, and during school social events. Since opportunities for meaningful dialogue with colleagues are rare, we can't afford to miss them.

Quality instruction is expected of all teachers. An equally significant characteristic of elementary physical education teacher leadership is the ability to nurture positive, productive interactions among teachers, students, administrators, and community members.

Improving the Elementary School Physical Education Program

An effective physical education program balances and contributes to children's academic learning. It is not separate from the core curriculum (California Department of Education 1994).

Marc, a second grade student, says, "Physical education is something we do in the morning. I exercise and run, learn how to play new games with other kids, and I learn why I run and jump and play games and make my body fit and healthy from my mind to my feet."

This second grader's concept of physical education isn't very different from what educators recognize to be components of quality physical education. He's learning how to move, developing social behaviors by working with others, and gaining an understanding of the importance of developing and maintaining fitness. Marc, although he didn't use these terms, probably is developing locomotor and non locomotor skills, learning biomechanical principles, studying the human body, appreciating and analyzing movement, and strengthening his self-image.

My goal as an elementary physical education teacher is to provide a quality, comprehensive physical education program. This includes facilitating student learning, which can lead students to pursue healthier lifestyles as well as to meet other challenges that are inherent in our changing world.

If it is true that effective teachers consistently address the question, "What is it that students should know and be able to do?" then it follows that the next question would be, "What is it we must do to make it happen?" Since we are evaluated based on the performance, behavior, and products of our students, it is prudent to implement programs that enhance our desired outcomes.

Physical education state frameworks/curriculum guides/content standards provide philosophical insight and well-researched perspectives on curriculum and instruction. These types of guidelines serve as a primary resource for developing the district and school-site curriculum. However, the guidelines alone are not sufficient. Philosophical tenets, core values, and beliefs about teaching and learning need to be explored with everyone who will be responsible for implementing the curriculum.

Before implementing new curriculum or other innovations, teachers should consider specifications for texts/instructional materials; requirements of what, when, and how much to teach; and district/school policies. They also should consider the professional development that will be needed to implement necessary instructional strategies, student wants and needs, and availability of equipment, facilities, and staff to optimize skills and expertise.

Political decisions regarding testing, standards, and curricular priorities can have a profound effect on the teacher's decisions. A practice such as using fitness scores to determine adequacy of the physical education program provides an opportunity for the elementary physical education leader to demonstrate the fallacy of this conclusion. Another example of the way in which political decisions affect instruction involves the distribution of program funding based on a curricular priority, such as reading. The curricular priority is seldom physical education. However, it is prudent for the elementary physical education leader to find a way to access "priority" funding for elementary physical education program improvement. This is most likely to occur if the physical education program is making meaningful interdisciplinary connections to the subject area being prioritized for funding.

Elementary physical education teachers can receive professional development, equipment, planning time, new technology, etc. to accomplish the interdisciplinary objectives funded through the related content priority. Thus, elementary physical education teacher leaders need to think globally to access additional funding. Don't be afraid to offer creative ideas for funding program improvement. The networking alone that the resourceful elementary physical educator cultivates will produce new ideas and opportunities.

It is difficult to discuss funding sources without thinking of the huge disparity in the times per week students receive physical education, the qualifications of the elementary physical education teachers, the length of periods, and student/teacher ratios. In my experience, I have found two tenets to be true:

- Improving the quality of instruction, curriculum, and interdisciplinary connections of the existing physical education program—even if it is once a week with 60 students at a time—is more likely to produce additional resources than waiting for the resources to improve the program.

- In negotiations for funding to improve the physical education program, describe what your program can do to contribute to the broader educational goals and priorities of the school/district.

Improving the school's physical education program includes a combination of advocacy, networking, assessment, content knowledge, and professional development—all of the recommendations discussed in this chapter. With teacher/leaders who can organize and motivate others to use new strategies and ideas, the elementary physical education program can flourish.

School-Site Leadership

A teacher/leader's role can range from moderate, reliable involvement in critical school issues to being a catalyst for whole school transformation. The choices a potential teacher/leader makes in initiating leadership actions depends largely on self-reflection as to skills and abilities, as described earlier in this chapter, and the circumstances in which the teacher finds him or herself. What level of involvement and actions are actually necessary? Although the possibilities are virtually unlimited, I have found some general precepts to be helpful.

Capable school-site leaders have an intimate understanding of the school's vision, and they cultivate this vision in others. They use both people (the ability to get along well with others), and process (the knowledge and understanding of how the system works) skills. They are energetic, enthusiastic, and insightful role models. Their spirit and enthusiasm influences others. They gain the respect of others through their contributions to the success of the school.

Our staff decided on a goal to create a positive schoolwide learning environment by consistently reinforcing social skills. Students learned social skills in physical education and practiced them throughout the day in cooperative activities. Together with a classroom teacher, we trained the entire school staff (including classified personnel, supervisors, and instructional aides) to teach, practice, and reinforce student social interaction skills.

The physical education program led positive schoolwide change for students. There was improved achievement, acceptance, and support among peers; increased self-esteem; and dramatic improvement in classroom behavior. While modeling the skills in staff interactions contributed to the success of the program, it also improved the morale of the staff. It created an avenue for approaching another critical component of educational leadership—interdisciplinary connections.

As noted earlier in this chapter, the physical education curriculum must be an integral part of the school curriculum; it must be integrated with other subject areas. This requires physical education teacher/leaders to pursue content knowledge in other areas. It also means talking to other teachers, deciding on concepts that can be taught and reinforced across the disciplines, developing a schedule for instruction, and identifying key assessment strategies and shared projects and activities. Some examples include vocabulary reinforcement, math/science/language and health concepts, cross-cultural games and activities from social studies, and social, personal, critical thinking, and problem-solving skills.

Change can be generated both by inspiring others and sharing in the ideas of others. Enthusiasm is infectious and will certainly spread. To become an integral part of the school, participate in projects like science fairs, history days, read-a-thons, and literacy fairs at your site. Initiate projects such as jump rope for heart, jog-a-thons, dance-a-thons, and school wellness or family fitness nights. Create student/staff running or aerobics clubs. Invite input from other teachers, parents, and students. Of course, all of this requires doing more listening than talking. And when you are introducing an idea, proposing an activity, or describing an event, invite the others involved to share in the presentation.

Learn as much as you can about the goals, programs, and operations at your site. Listen to the administration to find out about the school's goals and significant activities. Then, share your thoughts in terms of relevance to the school. Because the principal or leadership team determines how change is implemented and sustained at your site, it is important to nurture this relationship continuously.

Leadership roles can involve researching special projects and writing or participating in the writing of grants. Volunteer for (and chair, when appropriate) committees to give input about schoolwide policies, and align your program with them. For example, fundraisers that include selling candy may not reinforce nutrition education goals. If you like a challenge, and you have a strong contingency of teachers supporting you, perhaps you can affect policies regarding candy sales and other school practices that do not align with physical education and health curriculum goals.

More elaborate leadership pursuits can include changing the structure of the school day to accommodate longer periods, reducing class size to maximize positive outcomes of your program, reorganizing lunch/recess schedules and activities to increase student learning opportunities, developing cross-age playground leadership programs, organizing peer conflict reso-

lution managers, and supervising daily multi-class physical fitness stations and student aerobics programs.

The number and kinds of activities that can be pursued is limited only by your imagination and capacity to follow through. Keep in mind that over-extending yourself can lead to ineffectiveness and burn-out. It is extremely important (and for some most difficult) to know your own limitations in terms of time, energy, and level of commitment.

School-to-School Leadership

School-to-school leadership can be the precursor to district level leadership. Teachers with expertise in a certain area can begin by sharing this information at local and state AAHPERD meetings. Enterprising teachers also can invite other physical educators, teachers, and administrators to observe their programs. They can invite local media to cover programs and events, and write articles or proposals for local conferences (both general and physical education related), and network with involved, action-oriented teachers in other schools.

As individuals began to learn about my expertise, I received more and more requests to share what I knew with other teachers in other schools—both physical educators and classroom teachers. I did not initially seek out these experiences, but as I began to see the value of raising a regard for physical education in other schools, I realized that I needed to do more of it. I became a resource for training in any area related to physical education—from curriculum writing and planning, to content area instruction, program development, and playground organization. As I continued to develop my interdisciplinary skills and teaching/learning strategies, I was able to provide inservices to classroom teachers on more general educational areas such as cooperative learning, conflict resolution, positive discipline, interdisciplinary/thematic teaching, also including examples of how I use these strategies in teaching physical education.

I believe that these kinds of inter-school workshops and consulting services provided the opportunity for general educators to value physical education in a way that they may never have, had I not reached out to them. It also became another step in my journey toward personal and professional growth that would include districtwide leadership.

District Level Leadership

District level leadership can mean many things in relation to elementary physical education program development. It may mean effecting change by developing professional relationships with influential district personnel, such as board members, curriculum directors, project specialists, assistant superintendents, superintendents, etc. Some districts appoint teacher leaders as resource specialists, content area specialists, or project leaders for a period of time to write curriculum, lead major reform efforts, and implement new instructional strategies. Whether it is a formal assignment, such as a resource specialist, or an informal, self-directed leadership effort such as offering to provide workshops in elementary physical education for classroom teachers, staying in the hearts and minds of the people who are most influential in the system creates great leveraging power for improving the quality of elementary physical education programs.

One good way to access the expertise of outstanding teachers in a district is through mentoring or merit pay programs. In mentor teacher programs, teachers usually apply for predetermined positions. Some districts require mentor projects, others select teachers based on certain criteria, some are selected exclusively to "buddy with" new teachers. There is great potential for physical educators in a mentor program to influence change in perception and valuing of physical education. Interested physical educators should check with their district offices to request information on the criteria for selection into a mentor or merit pay position in their district.

My pursuit of quality physical education lead me to assume responsibility as lead writer of our district curriculum, a considerable undertaking. I was given the task of organizing a team of writers who were experienced in interdisciplinary teaching, had extensive knowledge of the state framework and National Standards, and who were eager to transform the district physical education program. It was a two-year process that involved frequent meetings during and after school and on many weekends. It was extremely time intensive but also profoundly rewarding. It offered a real sense of ownership to all involved.

Teacher/leaders who have developed a relationship with district level leaders can use this relationship to advocate for improved professional development opportunities for elementary physical educators. As stated earlier in this chapter, elementary physical educators usually have to attend inservices in other content areas to receive information on the latest research-based instructional and assessment strategies. Although there is great value in the interdisciplinary aspect of attending these workshops, they should not be the only way that elementary physical educators can access this information.

Because I have knowledge and expertise in both elementary physical education content and current research on instruction and assessment from attending hundreds of hours of cross-discipline training, I am able to provide elementary physical educators the information within their content. Elementary physical education teacher leaders who are prepared to take on this role will be a tremendous asset to their peers as well as to classroom teachers, administrators, and staff developers/curriculum coordinators.

General education instructional leaders are not intentionally avoiding including the content of elementary physical education in their offerings. They may simply not have the necessary content knowledge to make the connection for physical educators. Sometimes we must do it ourselves.

District level leadership is best characterized by a level of involvement that includes but also transcends site and program distinction. Most district level work will require a teacher to have a solid reputation for site level program excellence. The district's purpose is to build districtwide capacity by allowing experienced teachers to share their expertise.

Leadership in Professional Organizations

Professional organizations offer extensive access to other professionals, the latest research and methodology in the field, vast support and encouragement networks, legislative services, conferences and workshops, information dissemination avenues, resource materials, and experts in many areas. The national professional organization for physical educators is the American Alliance for Health, Physical Education, Recreation and Dance (AAHPERD). There are affiliate associations in each state. They are separate memberships with separate fees for each association. Membership in one is not a prerequisite for the other.

Professional involvement can occur by being a member in the national and local professional AAHPERD unit, or helping to start a local organization if one doesn't exist. A full range of roles within the organization are possible. These include participating in meetings, volunteering to help with activities, and holding office.

Typically, professional organizations initiate advocacy campaigns, support legislative issues, raise money for special projects, provide grants or scholarships, offer workshops and conferences, provide networking opportunities during monthly/bimonthly meetings, and keep members appraised of all of the latest innovations/changes in the field. Professional organizations provide a way for educational leaders to access information and resources that will allow them to enhance their leadership knowledge and skills. Vital, active professional organizations benefit the individuals in the field and strengthen the discipline.

Chapter Summary

Elementary physical education teacher leaders are knowledgeable about current research and practice in elementary physical education curricula and have interdisciplinary knowledge and skills. They know and apply a variety of instructional strategies to meet the diverse learning needs of all students. They use authentic, meaningful assessment strategies that help students improve their performance and give feedback on program effectiveness to teachers.

Building positive relationships among staff members, administrators, parents, students, and community members is critical to creating and sustaining successful elementary physical education programs. Improving the school's physical education program requires a combination of advocacy, networking, ongoing assessment, content and general education knowledge, and professional development. The teacher/leader's role may include, but is not limited to: modeling excellence in teaching, participating in school site decision making, networking with teachers at other schools, becoming a resource at the district/county/state level, and contributing to professional organizations.

Leadership in elementary physical education is exhilarating for the infinite possibilities and challenging for the dilemmas it presents. As a teacher who was drawn to a leadership role, one thing is very clear to me. I have always believed that students deserve the best education that we as a society can offer. I read the professional literature, networked with committed individuals in the field, and decided that daily, quality elementary physical education was not a luxury for students; it was a necessity. I have wished many times that I had a manual on leadership for elementary physical educators along the way. I struggled through many mistakes but learned from them as well. This chapter is a testament to the fact that acting on one's beliefs and passion for excellence does make a difference.

References

Joyce, B., Weil, B., & Showers, B. (1992). *Models of teaching.* Needham Heights, MA: Allyn and Bacon.

Mercier, R. (May-June 1993). Student-centered physical education strategies for teaching social skills. *Journal of Physical Education, Recreation & Dance.*

Mohnsen, B. (Ed.). (1998). *Concepts of Physical Education, What Every Student Needs to Know.* Reston, VA: NASPE.

National Association for Sport & Physical Education. (1995). Moving into the future. *National standards for physical education: A guide to content and assessment.* St. Louis, MO: Mosby.

California Department of Education. (1994). *Physical education framework for California public schools, kindergarten through grade twelve.* Sacramento, CA: Author.

CHAPTER 8

Middle School Teacher Leadership

Karen Mendon

Sometimes we don't even realize we've become teacher/leaders until someone points it out. That's what happened to me! I had standards for my students in terms of their learning, and I had standards for myself in terms of my teaching. Each year, I made improvements to what I had done the previous year and tried new things to enhance student learning.

I constantly asked myself, "Am I doing what's best for kids?" And, as time went on, I found myself sharing ideas with other teachers in my department. I also found myself completing departmental tasks and taking on leadership responsibilities both for the department and the school.

Fifteen years into my career, I became the team leader as we began to restructure our physical education program. During this restructuring period, I became more involved with districtwide projects and activities related to physical education. I also took on some leadership responsibilities. As I reflect on my career, perhaps the reason that I didn't realize that I had become a teacher/leader was because the process was so gradual.

In order to gain the respect of administrators and other staff members, a teacher/leader must first set high standards for him or herself, model effective teaching, and share the significance of physical education with everyone in the school environment. With that in mind, here are the seven major points for this chapter:

1. Be an Effective Teacher

2. Develop Relationships

3. Provide Department/Team Leadership

4. Participate in School Site Leadership

5. Initiate School-to-School Leadership

6. Broaden Your Impact: District Level Leadership

7. Assume a Leadership Role in Your Professional Organization.

Although these topics are similar to elementary and high school, I will address each topic through the lens of a middle school teacher.

Be an Effective Teacher

In order to write this chapter, I had to reflect on my growth as a leader and the many leadership roles that I have assumed throughout the years. This led me to believe that an effective leader must first and foremost be an effective teacher—one with a vision of quality physical education, who is capable of demonstrating effective teaching strategies, and who is willing to be a life long learner.

Vision

My vision of a quality middle level physical education program is one where all students understand the need to involve their young and growing bodies in vigorous activities. Students seek a variety of physical activity experiences, are challenged to meet their full potential, develop the necessary skills to be competent in the lifetime activities of their choice, and experience success that is so important to the middle school student at a time when self-esteem is developing. As a teacher/leader, I hope that all middle school teachers feel the same way, and that their programs provide students with optimal learning opportunities.

Regardless of the circumstances, you must maintain your vision of what a quality physical education program should be in middle school. Stay positive and don't let others pull you down. If you are respected because of your teaching skills and expertise, collaboration and change will be easier. Your colleagues will have a tendency to trust and accept your suggestions when collaboration is needed. Lead by example.

Teaching Strategies

It is of vital importance that you understand how your state physical education framework or district curriculum aligns with the National Standards for Physical Education. This document contains standards, benchmarks, and assessment strategies that address what a physically educated person should know and be able to do. The National Standards are a guide to assist local districts in developing curricula that meet the needs of their students. (See Chapter 3 for a list of the standards.) Curriculum provides direction for instruction.

Middle school students are like fingerprints; they're all different - They come in all sizes, shapes, and levels of maturity. Their levels of intellectual, physical, psychological, and social development are extreme. In order for students to learn, an effective teacher must use a variety of teaching strategies. Being able to match teaching strategies with student learning styles and standards promotes student learning. While it is beyond the scope of this chapter to go into detail about a variety of teaching strategies and styles, there are many good books on the market.

Some of these include: *Teaching Physical Education* (Mosston & Ashworth 1994), *Teaching Middle School Physical Education* (Mohnsen 1997), *Teaching Physical Education for Learning* (Rink 1993), and *Developing Teaching Skills in Physical Education* (Siedentop 1991).

I have found that teaching stations and cooperative learning are very effective with middle school students. Middle school students' attention spans are short, and the variety of activities and the freedom to move around give them a feeling of independence. Fortunately, both strategies also work well with my limited-English-proficient students. The more hands-on and student-centered the instruction, the more learning can occur. If each student has a piece of equipment or task to complete, and the activities (i.e., high risk) are relevant to middle school student's interests, student behavior is more on task. Be creative and adjust teaching strategies so all students have a chance to enjoy learning.

Teaching stations allow small groups of students to rotate from one learning area to another. They allow students to peer coach, practice on their own, and monitor their own progress through check sheets. This leaves me time to give individual feedback to students as well as to monitor group work. We need to provide activities that are active, not passive, real-life scenarios, and use a variety of activities and instructional strategies to promote success. A variety of situations can be used at the different stations to practice a particular skill or concept, and more learning occurs than when I am working with the class as a whole.

I use teaching stations in gymnastics, for example. Students rotate from station to station in groups of four or five. Each station has a task card, so students know what they are expected to accomplish or practice at that particular station. Each student also has an individual check sheet in order to monitor his or her progress over time. Other group members act as spotters and give corrective feedback. Every student has a responsibility; this keeps active middle school students on task.

The same benefits occur in cooperative groups. Such groups also foster a sense of belonging. Cooperative learning promotes the development of social skills through team building activities. Social skills are important to middle school students because their behavior is erratic and inconsistent, and personal-social concerns dominate their thoughts and actions. They are loving, caring, and willing to please, but they also will test the limits of acceptable behavior. Middle school students have all the capabilities to succeed but they expend a great deal of time and energy on trying to beat the system. However, students must be instructed in how cooperative learning groups work. Each member of the group shares a responsibility for the successful completion of the assigned task. Students learn to work together by helping one another, listening to all ideas, and then coming to consensus to solve the problem or complete the task. Through cooperative learning, students learn to trust each other and value others' opinions. And, their self-esteem is enhanced.

An example of cooperative learning is when students are to learn the five concepts of health related fitness. Students use the jigsaw strategy, where each student becomes the expert on one fitness concept and then teaches that concept to the other members of their group.

I am constantly trying new ideas and teaching strategies. Some are more successful than others. And, when I find something that works for me and can demonstrate its effectiveness, others around me are more willing to try it. Teacher/leaders share their ideas with others and are willing to experiment with new ideas.

Life Long Learners

Ideas and concepts are constantly changing. Therefore, everyone needs to be a life long learner. A major change for me was going from the junior high school model to a middle school model. Teachers in particular need to be life long learners as models for the students in their classes. I have found the best way to stay abreast of what is happening in the field is to join professional organizations, attend conferences and workshops, network with others in the field of physical education, take college courses, and read books and journals.

Professional organizations will keep you updated on current events in physical education through conferences and publications. They also support legislative issues concerning physical education. I belong to the American Alliance for Health, Physical Education, Recreation, and Dance (AAHPERD), the National Association for Sport and Physical Education (NASPE), and the California Association for Health, Physical Education, Recreation and Dance (CAHPERD).

I also belong to other educational organizations outside the field of physical education, such as the National Education Association (NEA), California Teachers Association (CTA), California League of Middle Schools (CLMS), Computer Using Educators (CUE), and Association for Supervision and Curriculum Development (ASCD). Their conferences and journals also are beneficial. You will find ideas and strategies that can be applied in physical education such as portfolios, authentic assessment, cooperative learning, gender equity, block scheduling, technology, and meeting the needs of middle school youngsters. Much of the information also can be used to integrate physical education with other curriculum areas.

There are many types of conferences and workshops available—AAHPERD, NASPE, and state and local conventions are examples. Sessions focus on teaching strategies, curriculum, assessment, research, specific activities (i.e., golf, tennis, dance), and standards. Other conferences and workshops are built around specialized areas such as assessment, cooperative games, effective teaching, technology, coaching, integrating curriculum, Project Adventure, and specific activity workshops.

One extremely effective professional development workshop I attended was Teacher Expectations and Student Achievement (TESA). TESA was developed by the Los Angeles County Office of Education for teachers throughout the curriculum; however, it can be applied specifically to the physical education setting.

TESA is based on expectation theory. Teachers form expectations for individual students' learning based on their own perceptions (i.e., race, class, physical appearance, gender, and physical and emotional challenges). Teachers also base expectations on other information, such as past achievement, labeling, test scores, and placement. In this workshop, teacher awareness is heightened concerning perceptions and how those perceptions affect expectations for all students. Teachers are encouraged to give low achievers more opportunities to perform in the classroom, to receive feedback, and to establish personal relationships with the teacher. TESA is not only concerned with the quantity of interactions but also with the quality.

The networking that goes on at conferences is invaluable. By networking at conferences, one can gain new ideas and strategies for use in the classroom. I share ideas with colleagues whom I have met at conferences or workshops in other parts of the state or nation. One idea I learned from a colleague is using stations in square dance and having students work in their squares to learn the basic moves.

Another benefit of networking results in making lifetime friends. Attending conferences and networking also provides many new contacts for supplies and equipment. Colleagues have asked about my sources for fitness equipment, golf clubs, best buys on jump ropes and physical education uniforms, etc. I have conferred with colleagues about resources on Olympic material and about making my own equipment. Why should each of us spend our precious time developing materials and finding resources when we can share what is tried and true?

In addition to conferences and workshops, college courses are a great way to gain new information. Several years ago, I took a college class—"Advanced Teaching: Analysis of Teaching Physical Education"—that had a significant impact on my teaching. In this course I was able to review research on teaching effectiveness, identify my own weaknesses, work on classroom management techniques, and increase my effective teaching behaviors. I was videotaped by my peers, and we did some peer coaching. When you peer coach (charting specific behaviors and videotaping), you are able to work on specifics and monitor your progress. I learned effective teaching doesn't just happen; it takes a lot of work.

Reading is an important avenue to being a life long learner. I subscribe to *NEA Today, California Educator* (CTA), *Physical Education Digest, Teaching Elementary Physical Education* (which addresses K-8), *JOPERD, California League of Middle Schools Journal*, and other sports and health publications. A few include: *Shape, Healthline, Conde' Nast Sports for Women, Living Fit, Golf, Kids Discover*, and *Sports Illustrated for Kids*.

Books I have read that include good sources of information are: *School Leadership and Administration* (Gorton 1987), *Using Technology in Physical Education, 2nd edition* (Mohnsen 1998), *Physical Education Sourcebook* (Hennessy 1996), *Teaching Middle School Physical Education* (Mohnsen 1997), *Adventure in the Classroom* (Henton 1996), *The Middle School–And Beyond* (George 1992), and *Turning Points* (Carnegie Foundation 1989).

You are probably asking yourself, "When does she do all this reading?" Often I do get behind; however, I catch up during holidays and vacations. Airports and plane rides are another good time for reading. And, I recently found the perfect time: When I do my hourly cardiovascular workout (stationary bike or stepper), I can get through a publication or make great headway through a book.

We must keep pace with the ever changing world around us. This means we need to be life long learners. Sometimes the challenge can be overwhelming. Just about the time I have

mastered the latest in technology, I find I am two years behind what is current. So, I must push myself to keep learning that which society expects me to be teaching my students, so that they can be productive members of society in the twenty-first century.

Develop Relationships

Effective middle school teachers and teacher/leaders develop a variety of significant relationships: with your students, with a mentor, and with fellow teachers both inside and outside your content area. Relationships with administrators, principals, parents, board members, community members, business people, university people and members of professional organizations also are valuable and should be pursued.

Middle school students need to know that they can have a relationship with you; that you trust them, you are fair, and you care about their well being. For example, I recall one student who was having great difficulty with her lock. I sat down with her during lunch and helped her learn to open it. Later in the day, she came by and thanked me for taking the extra time to help her. Even though this student was not in my class, every time I saw her, she smiled and said hello. Even small actions like this can help to build relationships and help students develop a positive attitude toward physical education.

One of the most significant relationships for a teacher or teacher/leader is the one he or she establishes with a mentor. The mentor should be someone who is not only an effective teacher but also someone whom you respect because of his or her knowledge, expertise, and ability to guide or assist. It is important that this person also be someone whom other people respect, who works within the system, and who helps you get established.

A mentor is someone with whom you can work closely and share ideas. Many times you will find more than one person to serve as a mentor due to the many areas of expertise needed in teaching. I have two mentors. The first was my master teacher. She has so much common sense and a feel for how middle school students learn. The most important attributes I learned from her were class management and class control. This mentor had the first-hand experience and wisdom in dealing with individuals and everyday situations that I needed early in my career. And, I still talk with her and seek her advice.

My second mentor came along later in my career. She came to the district as a coordinator for health and physical education. Here again, there are many things that I have learned from her. The two areas that I feel are most significant are leading me into leadership and advocacy roles and expanding my knowledge of using technology in physical education. By sharing with these mentors, I now have more ideas to try—whether it is with classroom management or creative teaching strategies.

The next relationship to develop is with fellow teachers. Physical education teachers are typically an isolated group due to their location on campus. You may end up spending more time with these individuals than with your own family. And just like families, these relationships will have their ups and downs. Teacher/leaders handle these ups and downs with patience. They are good listeners, flexible with other's ideas, and nonjudgmental. A teacher/leader can minimize the "down times" by valuing the efforts, ideas, and accomplishments of others and encouraging them to be the best they can be.

It is also important to develop relationships with teachers outside the physical education department. Other teachers need to understand what we do and how we can collaborate to enhance student learning. To that end, our physical education staff put on a full day staff inservice on cooperative activities, developing trust, and teamwork. (These three are so important to middle school students in all areas.) Along with four district counselors who also had been trained in this area, we took the entire staff through a series of cooperative activities that culminated with problem solving activities on a low ropes course. Each activity was debriefed, and participants were allowed to participate in their own comfort level. The day was very successful. It brought the staff closer together, and many positive relationships were developed between the physical education teachers and the rest of the staff.

It is important to gain the respect of administrators, especially your principal. Respect is earned by demonstrating your effectiveness as a teacher and your willingness to help with activities on campus, and by the input you give to improve the school environment. If you are respected, you can better educate administrators about the important role physical education plays in the total middle school educational program.

Site administrators will support you and your program by providing additional supplies and equipment, time in the curriculum (minutes), and by making it possible for you to attend conferences. And, they will use you and your program in public relations efforts.

Because of the respect we have developed at my school, our department yearly receives equipment that we would not ordinarily receive due to cost. During the past several years, we have received four tumbling crash mats, apparatus to increase upper arm strength, and six computers. The administration sees the value of what we are doing, and they consider our requests on an equal level with those of other staff members.

A positive relationship with the board of education is very important. If board members know you and understand and respect what you are doing for the students, physical education will be considered when important decisions are being made. Relationships can be developed with board members in a variety of ways. You might have board members' children as students. Through parent conferences and school events they can see the effort you are making to prepare their children and the other students for a lifetime of fitness and wellness.

Working on a campaign for a board member's election can help that board member get to know you outside of the classroom on a more personal level. Making a presentation to the board on quality middle school physical education and what's happening in your classroom is another effective technique. What is happening in your classroom today very likely is considerably different than when the board members were in junior high school physical education classes!

Partnerships with community members can be very beneficial to your physical education program. The best way to establish such relationships is to make direct contact by going out into the community. Community clubs and service organizations—such as Rotary, Kiwanis, Lions, and Optimist—usually invite school administrators to their monthly meetings. Many administrators belong to such organizations and if they don't, encourage yours to join one. They usually have a guest speaker or entertainment section on their agenda. Ask to be a guest speaker or to bring a group of students to explain your program and how they might be able to help you. Or, write a letter, on school letterhead, explaining your middle school physical education program and how you can use their assistance. Most of these kinds of organizations have money set aside in their budgets for donations or special projects.

You also could invite members of the community to your school to see what you are doing and how they might help. I have worked with community members by providing advertisement in exchange for donations. Community members have participated in school career days and fundraisers. The principal has taken me to a Rotary meeting to receive an award. Because members of these groups know what I am doing in physical education and support it, I have received donations.

Relationships with parents are vital. Teachers need to take the initiative and invite parents to the school. Parents need to feel welcome and convinced that you value their input. Middle school parents tend to be overprotective and concerned about the welfare, progress, and behavior of their youngsters, so keep parents informed and encourage two-way communication by phone contacts, special progress reports, and monthly newsletters.

In order to build effective relationships with our parents, we make sure they understand our program and what we are doing for their children. During open house, conferences, and back-to-school nights, our physical education staff presents our program to the parents. And, we welcome parents to visit our classes anytime. We send home flyers asking for volunteers or equipment we might need when special events are scheduled. In the past, we have held student-parent nights where students and parents can engage in physical activities and then have refreshments.

Because we have built effective relationships, we have parents volunteer to assist with our program. They work as coaches in the intramural and extracurricular sports programs, as cooks and servers at sports banquets, and as chaperons for extracurricular sport trips. They also readily donate sports equipment, such as stationary bikes, for our fitness lab. The PTA is another organization that is willing to help when you take the time to attend their meetings and explain what you are doing for their kids.

Business relationships are not only beneficial for the school, but also for the businesses. The business usually profits through increased sales or advertising. One example of working with a local business involves our local bowling center. We take our classes on field trips to the bowling center, where the employees provide a tour and a bowling lesson. Each student is then allowed one free game of bowling. Students are given discount cards to use for leisure bowling, and a percentage of each game is refunded to the school.

A second example of working with a local business involves the local golf course. Free lessons are offered to students during the summer. And, a local recreation department brought in area golf pros and gave a workshop for interested students.

As you can see, relationships are important to a quality physical education program. Time and money are limited, and any assistance received is a great benefit. But, it does take time and effort to establish these relationships. Having established a collaborative working relationship with my fellow physical educators, I earned their respect to work with them as a team leader.

Provide Department/Team Leadership

Teacher/leaders volunteer to take on leadership assignments instead of waiting to be assigned a job. Your first leadership role will probably be within the physical education department or team, where there are many opportunities to assume leadership roles—leading up to and including the role of department chairperson.

In this section, I will be using two terms that can be synonyms but also can take on different characteristics depending on how your site is organized. The term "department chair" refers to an individual who is appointed by an administrator (sometimes with additional pay) to oversee a particular department (curricular area). The physical education department chair meets periodically with other department chairs and the administration to discuss what is happening in the department, and to receive information and assignments for the department. The other term is "team leader." Some middle schools are not set up by departments, so a team may be an integrated curricular group (social studies, language arts, math, science, and physical education), or a curricular area that self-appoints an informal leader. In a curricular area that self-appoints an informal leader, a large number of the responsibilities are shared. Personally, I use these terms interchangeably.

Department chairs are ultimately responsible for departmental tasks. These include:

- Ensuring that the middle school physical education curriculum and instructional schedule is being followed. This can be a grueling experience or a collaborative effort. My department meets to collaboratively develop the yearly plan. All members give input into the scheduling of activities. As team leader, I make sure the curriculum is being followed by monitoring grade level activities. I also make sure there is no overlap of facilities, type up the schedule, and distribute copies to all members of the department. (See Figure 8.1.)

- Scheduling staff supervision. In my department this also is a collaborative effort. In many departments, however, individuals rely on the department head or team leader to do the scheduling. If teachers are asked which areas (locker room, outside areas) they would like to supervise, or a rotating system is used so supervision is seen as fair, then teachers will be more likely to carry out their responsibilities. Middle school students can be aggressive, daring, and impulsive. They look to peers as sources for standards and models of behavior. If left unsupervised, peer pressure can result in unusual behavior leading to risk of accident or injury. It is extremely important to provide adequate supervision for the safety of middle school students and to avoid negligence lawsuits.

- Budgeting and ordering of supplies and equipment. School budgets are set up differently. In some departments there is a set budget for ordering supplies and equipment for the year; in others, staff members simply request what they need. We have no set budget and request what we need. After getting input from my department, I take our prioritized list, make a budget, and submit our equipment and supplies order to the administration. Another responsibility along these same lines would be to submit work orders for repairs.

- Chairing department or team meetings. Effectively chairing a meeting means allowing others to feel they have a say by getting their input and providing discussion time. We have weekly meetings in my school. The topics vary from week to week, but we always start with general housekeeping items such as adjustments in the school calendar or general routine, due dates, problems that have come up during the week, rainy day plans, and announcements. Additional topics might include a report on a conference attended, curriculum, specific activities, upcoming inservices, assessment, and how literacy can be include in physical education.

- Serving on the schoolwide professional staff development committee. Many times, staff development is not seen as relevant to physical educators. If the team leader is on the committee, however, he or she can suggest ways to make a topic relevant to physical education, or volunteer to lead a session that would be relevant to physical education teachers.

- Keeping the department members abreast of current trends and professional development opportunities. One way to do this is to share relevant articles with others. After conferences or workshops, we meet as a department to share information we learned.

- Writing letters of recommendation for colleagues. I recently wrote several letters of recommendation for student teachers who were applying for jobs. I have also written letters of recommendation for colleagues who were applying for recognition awards.

Our physical education program has received a professional development grant for the past seven years. The goal of the grant is for middle schools to develop ways to deliver programs rich in problem solving activities to all students, but especially to disadvantaged students, to English language learners, and other student populations that have traditionally been denied such access. The funds are used mostly for staff development, so teachers can deliver curriculum richer in content and tailored to the unique learning styles of these students.

Because of our involvement in this grant, our program and instructors are respected by the other staff members for our accomplishments. As the team leader, I also have served as the grant coordinator. After our department meets and plans for the coming year, I write up the proposals, objectives, accomplishments, and budgets. I oversee the implementation of the grant, and keep department members informed about the correspondence between our school and other interested schools as well as with the funding agency.

A team leader learns to delegate tasks to other department members. By knowing their strengths and weaknesses, tasks can be assigned that are suitable to each department member. I have

FIGURE 8.1: Physical Education Instructional Schedule

Date	APE	5th	6th	7th Teacher 1	7th Teacher2	8th Teacher 1	8th Teacher 2
9-2 1	Opening						
9-8 2	Cooperative Games and Activities						
9-15 3							
9-22 4				Fitness Testing			
9-29 5	Maple cts.	Rhythms Tininking Jump Rope	Jump Rope	Fitness LAB	Tennis	Football (field)	Gynastics
10-6 6		(sm. gym)	(Vail cts.)	Track & Field	(tennis cts.)		(gym)
10-13 7						Fitness LAB	
10-20 8		Fitness Testing	Fitness Testing				
10-27 9					Fitness Testing		Fitness LAB
11-3 10	Sm. field	Stunts & Tumbling	Basketball Skills	Fitness Testing	Fitness LAB	Fitness Testing	
11-10 11		(lg. gym)	(Vail cts.)	Fitness LAB	Combatives (sm. gym)	Volleyball (Maple cts.)	Golf (whole field)
11-17 12				Tennis (tennis cts.)		Fitness LAB	
11-24 13						VB	
12-1 14	gym	Throw & Catch	Softball Skills				Fitness LAB
12-8 15	sm. field	(1/2 field - west end)	(1/2 field - east end)		Fitness LAB		Basketball (gym)
12-15 16	tennis courts			Fitness LAB			(Vail cts.)
12-22 17 / 18	WINTER RECESS						
1-12 19	East end field	Foot Skills (1/2 field)	Paddle Tennis	Combatives (Sm. Gym)	Tumbling (gym)	Fitness LAB	(Maple cts.)
1-19 20	Vail cts.	(west end)	(tennis cts.)			Volleyball (Maple cts.)	Fitness LAB
1-26 21				Fitness LAB	Fitness LAB	Fitness Testing	

FIGURE 8.1: Physical Education Instructional Schedule (continued)

Date	APE	5th	6th	7th Teacher 1	7th Teacher2	8th Teacher 1	8th Teacher 2
2-2 1	Vail cts. tennis cts.	Striking Skills	Dance (sm. gym)	Fitness LAB	Tumbling (gym)	Basketball	Project Adventure
2-9 2	↓	(1/2 field) west end	↓	Soccer (1/2 field) (east end)	↓	Fitness LAB	↓
2-16 3	↓	↓	↓		Line Dance	Basketball	Fitness LAB
2-23 4	Vail/Maple cts. tennis cts.	Project Adventure	Stunts & Tumbling		Fitness LAB	Softball	FieldSports
3-2 5	↓	(sm. field) courts	(sm. gym)	Fitness LAB	Line Dance (gym)	(1/2 field) (west end)	(1/2 field) (east end)
3-9 6	↓	↓	Fitness Testing	Tumbling (sm. gym)	↓	Fitness Testing	
3-16 7	Vail cts.	Bowling	↓	↓	↓	LAB	Volleyball (Maple cts.)
3-23 8	↓	(tennis cts.)	Circus Skills	(big gym)	Fitness LAB	Softball	Field Sports
3-30 9	1/2 field Maple cts.	↓	(sm. gym)	Testing	Project Adventure	(1/2 field) (east end)	Fitness LAB
4-6 10	SPRING VACATION						
4-13 11	Vail cts.	Fitness Testing	Street Hockey	Fitness LAB	Track & Field	Fitness Testing	
4-20 12	↓	↓	(tennis cts.)	Dance gym	↓	Fitness LAB	Volleyball (Maple cts.)
4-27 13	Field	Aerobics Parachutes	↓	sm. gym	↓	Gymnastics (gym)	Fitness LAB
5/4 14	↓	Jump Rope (Vail cts.)	Project Adventure	sm. gym	Fitness LAB	↓	Volleyball
5-11 15	Maple cts.			Fitness LAB	Soccer	↓	
5-18 16	↓			Project Adventure	(1/2 field) (east end)	Th/F LAB	T/W ↓
5-25 17		Folk Dance (sm. gym)	Soccer (1/2 field) (west end)			Square Dance	
6-1 18				↓	↓		
6-8 19	↓	↓	↓		Fitness LAB	↓ Locks	↓
6-15 20	CLOSURE					Portfolio Assessment	

found that when department members share the responsibilities, they have a tendency to buy into department policies and feel valued. This creates a department that works more like a team. However, someone needs to be the leader to make sure everyone does his or her part, and to assist those members who are having difficulty carrying out specific assignments.

A team leader needs to demonstrate leadership skills to make things run smoothly. The team leader needs to listen to others. Get input from all members, be nonjudgmental, and don't dictate. A team leader also needs to be a good negotiator and possess consensus-building skills to resolve conflicts. If conflicts continue, it is important for the team leader to seek outside assistance from a neutral person who is knowledgeable in conflict management and who is respected by all team members.

Being a good department chair means representing your department and getting involved with other school leadership activities. A team leader needs to have good organizational skills to get things done in a timely manner and be able to communicate thoughts and ideas to team, staff, administrators, parents, and students.

Participate in School Site Leadership

There are many types of leadership opportunities one can pursue at the middle school site level. It is important to get involved in leadership positions to ensure that the views of physical educators are represented. Remember that administrators, teachers, and support staff look to members of committees as school leaders.

Some examples of school site leadership opportunities include decision making committees (i.e., school site council), Parent Teacher Organization, school improvement committee, safety committee, and school-site grant committees. Several years ago, I was on the earthquake committee for my school. Not only did I give input, but I ended up getting equipment for the physical education program.

In discussing how to evacuate the second story of our main building if all stairwells were blocked, I suggested cargo nets. I also reminded them that students should know how to climb them. One is now hung from the ceiling of our gymnasium, so students in physical education can practice and learn safety procedures for using the net.

I am currently on the technology committee. I represent physical education and educate others as to how technology is being used as an important part of the physical education curriculum. As a result, we have received more than our fair share of computers. We also have been trained to use the school computer lab, and I have explained to the committee that our physical education fitness lab needs to be wired to the Internet.

Physical educators can provide inservice instruction to other teachers on various aspects of the physical education curriculum. Teachers are respected for their expertise and willingness to share that expertise with other teachers. In our school, the fifth and sixth grade teachers are self-contained and teach physical education to their own classes. We have provided instruction to them in teaching the physical education curriculum, and we also provide peer tutors to assist them occasionally.

When physical educators make the effort to contact teachers in other subjects areas and express an interest in promoting interdisciplinary instruction, physical education begins to be seen as a "subject area" with academic meaning. Physical education teachers are then held in higher esteem by the rest of the staff. In addition, they will have classes that are equal in size to those in other subject areas. And, when students can make connections through interdisciplinary instruction, learning is enhanced.

An example in my school is when our seventh grade students study the medieval era in their history/social studies class. The seventh grade physical education teachers teach a combatives unit. The culmination is an afternoon activity for all seventh grade students. A local theater-restaurant (Medieval Times) brings horses and riders outfitted in medieval attire, and they put on a demonstration using combative techniques. Seventh grade students also study Africa. Physical education can use the orienteering unit and survival skills to relate to the topography of that continent. When sixth graders study Greece, we offer a unit on the Ancient Olympics.

In eighth grade, students study U.S. history. In eighth grade physical education, during our basketball unit, we have students relate the history of basketball and why it was invented to what was going on in that era. We also offer square dance to further emphasize the type of physical activities that people were involved in during that time.

Physical education teacher leaders also can assume leadership roles by coordinating schoolwide events. For example, I have organized student/teacher basketball, softball, and volleyball games; coached after-school sports teams; and organized schoolwide field trips (roller skating, trips to theaters and amusement parks).

Initiate School-to-School Leadership

Once a physical educator has had department and school-site leadership experiences, he or she may want to branch out and work with other schools. Expertise needs to be shared between schools within the same district and beyond. This can take the form of shared inservice days and articulation days.

Teacher/leaders can assume the responsibility to organize, plan, and present sessions at district-sponsored inservice days. Our school has cluster meetings (staff and teachers from the high school and the feeder middle schools) on school inservice days.

Last year, I took the responsibility to organize two inservice day activities for the cluster physical educators. The first day, we shared curricula, assessment, teaching strategies, and innovative ideas. The second day was spent on reviewing and participating in Project Adventure activities. Teachers from the other sites appreciated the opportunity to work with cooperative initiatives and set up the low ropes course, and to practice management techniques for using the low ropes course within a classroom setting. Teachers commented that these were the two best inservice days they have ever experienced because they were relevant and meaningful to them.

Articulation between elementary schools and the middle school is important. Instead of blaming the elementary teachers for not teaching the students anything, set up a meeting with feeder schools and find out what they are doing and why. In the discussion, suggestions can be made to enhance their programs.

Because elementary teachers in my district are not physical education specialists, they are thrilled with new ideas and suggestions. Recently, we also began articulating with our local high school. Both feeder middle schools and the high school shared their programs. Each school felt it had problems that were affecting student learning. These were discussed by all, and possible solutions were suggested.

This was the first articulation that has occurred between the middle schools and the high school in the 25 years I have taught in the district. Everyone was pleased about how the day went, and we decided we needed more time together to make physical education a continuum of learning experiences for our students. Having a district curriculum with standards and outcomes makes this easier, because it sets expectations for each grade level.

Experience in school-to-school leadership prepares the physical educator to assume even more responsibility and affect more schools through a district level leadership role.

Broaden Your Impact: District Level Leadership

The step up to a district level leadership role is a big one. Some of the district leadership tasks include mentor projects, inservices, committee work, and special projects. Mentor projects allow an exemplary teacher to share his or her expertise with colleagues by developing education-oriented materials (task cards, sample lessons), activities, teaching/learning strategies and programs, or by providing staff development. Teacher/leaders can affect many individuals and students by volunteering or applying for these types of leadership opportunities.

I have served at the district level as a mentor teacher for physical education. In that role I instructed and provided inservice to elementary teachers on our district's physical education curriculum, since we have no physical education specialist at the elementary level. I also provided demonstration lessons so that elementary teachers could observe a physical education lesson.

As a mentor, I also have co-chaired the physical education curriculum ad hoc committee as the middle school facilitator. The purpose of the committee was to bring our district's curriculum in alignment with the state framework. Each middle school and high school selected one teacher to be a representative on the committee.

We started by asking the committee what they thought the characteristics of a physically educated person should be. Having agreed upon our definition of a physically educated person, we then asked each member to identify what he or she wanted twelfth graders to know and be able to do when they left our school system. From there we worked through each grade level. We looked at other curricula and designed ours to best fit the needs of the students in our district.

Throughout the process, committee members took information back to their school sites for additional input. Using this process, everyone has a buy in, so implementation goes smoothly. Other possible mentor projects might include developing instructional units, developing assessment materials, or working with other physical educators to implement a new curriculum.

Teacher/leaders can provide a variety of inservices or workshops for other physical educators. And, these do not need to stop at your district level, but also can be provided for neighboring districts. Inservices and workshops should be planned based on areas of need. Examples include middle school assessment, curricula, specific units of instruction (i.e., juggling, a variety of lead-up games, jump rope, and medieval times activities), fitness testing, dance, technology, cooperative activities, team and trust building activities, and idea swap shops.

For example, I presented a session of golf at a district workshop. Information was provided on where to obtain equipment at a reasonable cost, available resources, and teaching ideas and strategies. I also provided practice opportunities for the teachers to improve their skill levels. The teachers were very appreciative, because for many this was an activity outside their comfort zone. They felt able to return to their school sites and teach a beginning golf unit.

Teacher/leaders play an important role by participating on or chairing districtwide committees. These committees can include recreation advisory, comprehensive school health, curriculum, textbook adoption, site-based decision making, professional development, and the teacher contract negotiating team.

The recreation advisory committee develops guidelines for the district's after-school sports program. At least one teacher or coach from each middle school makes up the committee, which meets quarterly. Our district's comprehensive school health committee is made up of representatives from health services, counseling service, nutritional services, health education, physical education, special services such as our pregnant minors program, the police department, and the American Heart Association, as well as other interested or invited community members.

Teacher/leaders become committee members in a variety of ways. My experience has been that the teacher/leader is asked by the chairperson of the committee to be a member. Other times the district sends a letter to the schools and asks for teacher representatives. In these cases, the teacher/leader may volunteer to be a member.

Personally, I enjoy knowing what is happening at the grass roots level and being part of the decision-making process. Professionally, I want the district to know what is happening in middle school physical education and its benefits for our students, so that physical education is considered when decisions are made.

Teacher/leaders take on special projects, generally in areas that are of interest to them. Some examples include making board presentations, developing a middle school web page, printing a district newsletter, developing and distributing informational packets (i.e., middle school assessment samples and middle school interdisciplinary ideas), and overseeing your district's state-mandated testing program.

As a teacher/leader at the district level, you can influence a great many people, which will in turn affect many students. To broaden your influence, you need to move outside your geographic area and increase the number of people you can affect. Assuming a leadership role in your professional organization is the next step.

Assume a Leadership Role in Your Professional Organization

Professional organizations always need new leaders and new ideas. Without new ideas, conferences become repetitive, attendance drops, and the organization becomes stagnant. Teacher/leaders can assume leadership roles in their professional organizations by volunteering for committee work, assisting at conferences, presenting at conferences, and writing articles for the organization's journal.

Volunteering for committee work is an important step for the emerging teacher/leader. You can initially get involved by talking with a conference manager or one of the officers and letting them know you are interested. You will learn how the organization works, and you can provide the necessary "personpower" to make the committee successful. You also can organize and oversee the creation of a middle school workshop or conference.

Committee work is time consuming, but when the final product is completed it provides a sense of satisfaction and the joy of knowing that you did the best job possible. I have worked on several committees, and the type of work I like best is planning and organizing. I have helped organize workshops and mini-conferences, and it makes me feel good to see each event become a success. Most important, however, I enjoy seeing the participants learning and gathering valuable information and ideas.

Assisting at conferences starts with the role of introducing a speaker. It also can include committee work such as helping with registration or hospitality, setting up equipment, and decorating for luncheons or special events. These roles are learned by watching others and "pitching in" to help. Volunteering at conferences is a great way to get involved in a organization and learn first-hand how conferences are run. Whenever there is an opportunity to volunteer, approach an officer or the conference manager!

Teacher/leaders share ideas with others in the field through their involvement in professional organizations. One way I have done this was by opening up our middle school for visitations during our state conference. Middle school teachers were invited to come for a full day to see our program in action, and to talk with the students and staff.

Another way to share is by being a conference presenter. Not only do you share your ideas and teaching strategies but you gain new ideas from those in your sessions. The more presenting you do, the more proficient you become. Presentation skills are fine tuned and you become more comfortable speaking in front of a group.

I enjoy providing information to others, knowing that teachers will use the information to make learning more meaningful to their students. Time is a commodity that is in short supply for most of us. Why should each person reinvent the wheel? I highly recommend presenting as a learning and growing experience.

Finally, you can share information by writing articles for professional journals. The way to begin would be to submit articles to your state association journals. As you become more proficient, submit articles to the national journals, such as *Teaching Elementary Physical Education (K-8)*, and *Strategies*.

Chapter Summary

Becoming a leader is like training for a marathon. Your sphere of influence starts small, but you continue to add to it because of the satisfaction and enjoyment that comes from sharing. You start with yourself and your classes by being an effective teacher. As you establish relationships with those around you and you grow in confidence and expertise, your sphere of influence grows from your department to your site, to the district and the professional community.

As a teacher/leader, your sphere of influence continues to grow as you begin to touch lives at the professional level. Being a marathon runner, you will cross the finish line, but you will continue to train. Middle schools are unique settings and you will hit the wall many times. But just as a life long learner continues to learn, a teacher/leader continues the journey to lead.

References

Carnegie Council on Adolescent Development. (1989). *Turning points: Preparing American youth for the 21st century.* Washington, DC: Author.

George, P. S., Stevenson, C., Thomason, J., & Beane, J. (1992). *The middle school–and beyond.* Alexandria, VA: Association for Supervision and Curriculum Development.

Gorton, R. (1987). *School leadership and administration* (3rd ed.). Dubuque, IA: William. C. Brown.

Hennessy, B. (1996). *Physical education sourcebook.* Champaign, IL: Human Kinetics.

Henton, M. (1996). *Adventure in the classroom.* Dubuque, IA: Kendall/Hunt.

Mohnsen, B. S. (1998). *Using technology in physical education.* (2nd ed.). Cerritos, CA: Bonnie's Fitware.

Mohnsen, B. S. (1997). *Teaching middle school physical education.* Champaign, IL: Human Kinetics.

Mosston, M., & Ashworth, S. (1994). *Teaching physical education.* New York: MacMillan College.

Rink, J. E. (1993). *Teaching physical education for learning.* St. Louis, MO: Mosby.

Siedentop, D. (1991). *Developing teaching skills in physical education* (2nd ed.). Mountain View, CA: Mayfield.

CHAPTER 9

High School Teacher Leadership

Carolyn Thompson

As a child, the act of playing allowed you to lead, follow, or get out of the way. Leadership opportunities may have occurred for you as a youth in the scouts, or later, during the teenage years, when you joined athletic groups, clubs, or organizations. Responsibilities were given to those who demonstrated initiative, direction, respect, and accountability. These beginning steps toward leadership taught you communication skills and assertiveness. You probably even discovered that great feeling of pride and accomplishment when a task was completed or someone noted that it was well done.

I personally began to demonstrate leadership characteristics as a student body officer and a club president in high school. My leadership skills were honed as a playground leader for the parks and recreation department during the summer while still in high school. Each Monday morning, the recreation supervisor met with the playground leaders to plan the schedule for the following week. This is where I learned to create a matrix. It showed the time of day, activities, crafts, and special events. The job was wonderful and it taught me to be creative, to have fun, and to guide the heads and hearts of youngsters.

As a college student majoring in physical education, I continued my quest for playing, learning, and leading with youngsters in the summer as a program coordinator at a private camp. My organizational skills continued to flourish as I became proficient at creating a variety of activity schedules, delegating responsibility, and influencing program change. By the time I completed my student teaching experience, my self-confidence had escalated and I was ready to become a professional educator.

Leadership roles can vary according to the professional situation. In this chapter, I will share the journey I took, along with the lessons I learned through study and experience. This chapter centers around seven steps to becoming a teacher/leader. You will notice that the steps are similar to the steps in the elementary and middle school chapters; however, the implementation in this chapter is specific to high school physical education.

The high school structure and how that structure functions is unique. There are teacher/leaders who are department chairpersons, and there are curricula that focus on career paths for students. High school issues tend to be more severe, and they often take longer to change. Consider, for example, educational reform. Many secondary teachers are entrenched and resist such changes as block scheduling, integration of curriculum, and career paths.

I hope these steps will provide you with guidance and ideas for becoming an effective high school teacher/leader.

1. Be an Effective Teacher
2. Develop Relationships
3. Provide Department Leadership
4. Participate in School-Site Leadership
5. Initiate School-to-School Leadership
6. Broaden Your Impact: District Level Leadership
7. Assume a Leadership Role in Your Professional Organization.

Be an Effective Teacher

Why did you go into teaching? I chose the teaching profession because I wanted to make a difference in the lives of young people. I wanted to affect the future and encourage youngsters to become life long learners. Physical education is the vehicle that I use to challenge my students' minds, bodies, and creativity. The first step in becoming an effective leader is to be an effective teacher. In fact, research has shown that the most effective teachers possess effective leadership traits (Mohnsen 1984).

As educators, we all know that the real challenge in teaching lies in designing motivational and inclusive lessons which allow "all" students to succeed and to discover the power of knowledge. Let's examine how this occurs in one high school physical education class.

In groups of four, the students execute a warm-up run by holding onto a jump rope and jogging as a team. They are laughing and encouraging one another as they finish the warm-up laps around the gymnasium. The teacher greets the students returning from their fun run with a smile and directions to read the white board resting against the equipment cart for further instructions. The members of each group form a circle and immediately begin chatting and discussing how they contributed to the group fun run.

"I would like each group to share one example of how their group worked together during the fun run," says the teacher. "Jose, please share your group's discussion."

"Our group used encouragement by saying one another's names."

"Thank you, Jose. Carmen, what did your group discover?"

"We decided to use the pace of the below average person so the fastest person had to slow down and encourage the slowest person

FIGURE 9.1: Learning Stations: Newton's First Law of Motion

Station 1.	IBM Personal Computer System 2 with M-motion and audio playback cards for presenting video motion on the screen and producing sound. The concept is presented followed by several examples including live action "clips" from a laser disc entitled "Physics of Sport."
Station 2.	Read page 65 and answer question 14 in the textbook. (*Moving for Life*. Dubuque, IA: Kendall Hunt.)
Station 3.	Toss a tennis ball in the air but do not catch it. What eventually happens to the ball? Why?
Station 4.	Drop a basketball. What eventually happens to the ball? Why?
Station 5.	Place a volleyball and ping pong ball on the floor side by side. Blow on each. What happens and why?
Station 6.	Kick a ball into a net or wall. What happens? Why?
Station 7.	Roll a ball on different surfaces. What do you notice? What type of external forces do different surfaces represent?
Station 8.	Using three of each (marbles, ping pong balls, and tennis balls), play a game of marbles. Place half of the objects in a rope circle while using the other objects as your shooters. Play until you have observed each ball hit and moved. What did you notice?
Station 9.	Run as fast as you can, then stop as quickly as possible. What caused you to start, and what caused you to stop?
Station 10.	Place a whiffle ball on a tee. Hit the ball off the batting tee and let it come to rest on its own. What caused the ball to move?
Station 11.	Using a golf putter and golf ball, putt the ball on different surfaces. What do you notice? What effect do different surfaces have on the ball?
Station 12.	Put a tennis ball in your left hand and a basketball in your right hand. Roll both balls at the same time, using the same force. Which ball travels farther?
— Analysis of Movement Unit Plans, Bonnie's Fitware	

to speed up a little. The groups' intensity level continued to be safe for everyone. We communicated by tugging on the rope."

"Thank you, Carmen," responds the teacher as she continues to direct the attention of the class to each of the group's responses.

"The purpose of this activity is to demonstrate that communication is important when working together. Today, you will work as a group to learn about Newton's first law of motion. The concept being learned today is: An object that is at rest will remain at rest, and an object in motion will remain in motion unless acted upon by an outside force. Your groups will need to be able to explain how Newton's first law of motion affects human movement. The groups will perform and discuss the tasks at each station. The group members must agree on their conclusion and record it on the team task sheet. Encourage one another to problem solve the task and listen to all team members ideas at each station." The stations around the gym have been set up prior to the class. A task card and equipment are placed at each cone marking one learning station.

"I would like one person from each group to come get one pencil and a team task sheet for your group. Record your answer next to the number that corresponds with the task card. Each station is numbered. You will rotate on my whistle command," directs the teacher.

The groups scatter to the stations. Each group reads the task card (see Figure 9.1), discusses the assignment, performs the task, and records its response. The teacher moves from group to group

giving feedback, checking on task responsibility, and asking probing questions like, "What did you observe and how does Newton's first law affect the ball?" Laughter, encouragement, cooperation, and feedback is observed throughout the lesson.

The teacher signals the students to bring in the equipment from their stations and place it in the equipment cart. Two students collect the pencils and the worksheets. The class sits in their groups, facing the white board. The board displays the concept being addressed. The students discuss the various stations and how they relate to Newton's first law.

If an answer is incorrect, the teacher asks probing questions like, "What caused the ball to stop bouncing?" "What are the outside forces that are affecting the object?" "How does the mass of the object come into play with the principle of motion?" "What causes the ball to move?"

In the closure, the teacher summarizes Newton's first law of motion, explaining that "objects only move when acted upon by an outside force and once in motion remain in motion until acted upon by another force (such as gravity)." This prepares the students for the homework assignment. The students are asked to identify another example of Newton's first law that applies to their daily lives. The teacher thanks the students for their help and a job well done. The class is excused as squad four returns the equipment cart to the locker room.

Good teaching results in a behavioral change in student performance. As a result of this lesson, students can apply Newton's first law of motion to correct poor technique.

This lesson is a model of effective teaching. The content is appropriate for high school. The teacher was organized, as demonstrated by equipment and learning stations being set up prior to the beginning of class. The learning environment was warm, friendly, and safe. Students are still developing their self-confidence in high school. Inclusion and positive reinforcement are essential when teenagers are required to take risks in learning new content.

The lesson addressed Standards 3 and 5 during warm-ups, and focused on Standard 2 during the lesson. The instruction was student-centered and utilized a variety of teaching strategies, including practice style and cooperative learning strategy, that are especially effective for high school students. The same lesson can be taught using other teaching styles, such as reciprocal, guided discovery, divergent, and congruent. These styles are effective as well, because they require students to use problem-solving skills. (Mosston & Ashworth 1994). The students were kept on task and accountable for learning through the use of a worksheet. The worksheet also served as one form of assessment for the lesson. It provided feedback for the teacher, with information as to who was still not clear about the concepts. During the closure of the lesson, the teacher summarized the key points. Homework was assigned to further the students' understanding of biomechanics and the role it plays in all movement forms.

This is good teaching for high school because the teacher understands how to teach to standards, and how to engage students in learning through performance exploration and movement analysis. The use of a worksheet for student responses and a homework assignment in physical education provide strong evidence of what students know and are able to do. Each student's grade is clearly based on meeting the standards and not on attendance and uniform. New teachers can get to this level of teaching by attending workshops, taking additional classes, reading professional journals and books, and observing good teachers.

Develop Relationships

Research has shown that teachers progress through several steps during the first few years of their teaching. Initially, new teachers are concerned only with their classes; they gradually become concerned with the physical education program at their school. Then, they become concerned with the entire school system. The relationships teachers form during their first several years of teaching seem to match their areas of concern. Initially, teachers develop relationships only with "their" students, then with "their" students' parents, then with other department members, and finally with other members of the school environment.

As soon as you become a teacher, you become a leader; if only in your classes. For an effective teacher to become an effective leader, relationships must progress through the leadership continuum (teacher, teacher/leader, administrator). Your first relationship as a teacher/leader will be with your students. It is important for teachers to meet the needs of their students so they will stay in school. Providing motivational lessons and understanding student learning styles will help to build a level of trust between the teacher and the students. The effective

teacher/leader must show that he or she cares equally about each and every student. The first step in establishing rapport with students is to learn their names.

I use social initiatives in my warm-ups to help students bond and to establish a safe and friendly environment. During the first week of school, the students learn one another's names through fun, safe, and challenging activities. One example is "Name Game." Students form groups of six to eight people. One object (ball, beanbag) is given to each group. People in the group introduce themselves as they toss the object from person to person. Once everyone has been introduced, the ball is tossed randomly as the person throwing calls out the name of the intended receiver. As the teacher and students begin to learn one another's names, students are rotated to different groups to meet new classmates.

High school students complain at first, but join in the challenging activities as they witness the laughter and fun of their peers.

There are many social initiative books available to assist you in building camaraderie in your classes. I recommend *Curriculum and Instruction, The Secondary School Physical Education Experience, Silver Bullets, Cowstails and Cobras II*, and *Team Building Through Physical Challenges for High School Teachers*.

The relationship between a teacher and a student is strengthened when the teacher/leader is just and impartial. It is important to be firm but not harsh. You want to reward with kindness when the student has done what is asked, and admonish only when the behavior interrupts the teacher from teaching and the other students from learning. Clearly explain why the conduct was wrong and how the student can prevent it from happening again. Discuss the matter in an appropriate and reassuring way. It is vital that the student believes in you. Convince the student that you will not allow him or her to fail this class. Explain that you will continue the pressure until he or she takes personal responsibility for his or her education.

The teacher/leader needs to foster a relaxed, yet respectful, learning environment. Be aware of body language: Keep the corners up on your smile and let your eyes sparkle with an invitation to learn. The teacher/leader must be able to "hear" what is being communicated by the student. Is there a plea for challenge, guidance, friendship, or fairness? The teen years are a confusing time for kids, so there are likely to be many emotional ups and downs along the way. Fairness and reassurance affects the heart of a straying student, so inclusion is the key here. Be sure to reinforce each students' sense of worth and celebrate his or her successes. Teenagers appreciate it when they receive the trust that they have earned by being responsible, dependable, and accountable. Both trust and respect are the outgrowth of a good relationship between a student and the teacher/leader.

Parents continue to play an important role in their children's education, even at the high school level. However, it is a constant challenge to get parents of high school students involved in school activities. High school teacher/leaders need to develop specific strategies to get parents involved with the school and the physical education program. A parent newsletter, mailed twice a year, describing the calendar of events and

FIGURE 9.2: Stations for Parent Fitness Assessment

1.	Blood pressure
2.	Calculate target heart rate zone (computer program by Bonnie's Fitware Health Related Fitness)
3.	Lower back flexibility
4.	Vital lung capacity
5.	Height
6.	Weight
7.	Amount of activity and intensity (computer program—"Dine Healthy," by Dine Systems, Inc.)
8.	Body composition using Futrex or Tanita
9.	Calculate metabolic rate (computer program by Dine Systems, Inc.)
10.	Recommended caloric intake based on this data (computer program by Dine Systems, Inc.)

special activities, along with the date and time for the next Parent Teacher Student Association meeting, provides parents with information. A personal letter describing your physical education program and asking for parental support will keep you in touch with the parents.

Back-to-school night and open house provide parents with an opportunity to visit their teenager's classes and listen to teachers describe course expectations and content. The physical education department can distribute a pamphlet at this time describing the curriculum and student expectations. NASPE's pamphlet, "The Physically Educated Person" is a wonderful handout for parents. The NASPE public service announcement video can be shown, followed by sample lessons. Use the open house to model what students know and are able to do. Let the students help monitor the parents through a variety of self-assessment stations (see Figure 9.2) to learn about their personal wellness.

Invite the parents to plan physical activities involving the entire family, and encourage them to help their teenager practice skills and share information learned in class. Extend an invitation for parents to come and visit the physical education class or to work out in the fitness center after school.

A parent volunteer program at the high school will allow parents to assist in the classroom, library, attendance office, and gymnasium. Parents also can serve on the School Site Council, which makes financial decisions on federal and state funds. Parents can be required to visit the school at the end of each semester in order to pick up their teenager's report card, and the parent and teacher can discuss the student's performance in relation to content standards. It is important that parents are kept informed about their youngster's growth and development throughout the year—both when the progress is positive and when it is negative. A short note or a quick phone call can go a long way to establishing a personal relationship with the parents of your students. Remember, parental support is crucial to keeping teenagers in school.

Once your relationships with students and parents are in place, you will want to expand your circle. This is an opportune time to select a mentor. Pick someone whom you really admire. This person should be someone who gets things done in a timely manner. The individual does not necessarily have to be a physical educator, since leadership is found throughout the disciplines. It is wise, however, to select a mentor who is on campus. This allows you the opportunity to talk on a daily basis. You also can observe one another's lessons and discuss teaching strategies, senior projects, community service, curriculum paths, educational reform, and other high school issues.

It certainly is possible to have more than one mentor. Our professional organizations provide us with networks of leaders at the local, state, district, and national levels who can help answer questions regarding leadership, curriculum development using National Standards, powerful teaching methods, authentic assessment ideas, cutting edge grant writing, implementing current research into the daily lesson, using technology in physical education, etc.

I find that a knowledgeable role model brings out the best in me and strengthens my self-confidence. Teacher/leaders need reinforcement, too. Be sure to seize opportunities to work with your mentor or with other professionals in order to learn and grow together. Working collaboratively on projects often fosters creativity, inspiration, enthusiasm, and mutual respect.

Relationships within your department are significant, and we will explore these in the next section. However, we often overlook relationships with faculty members in other subject areas. As a physical education teacher in the Health Careers Pathway (school within a school), I work closely with five other teachers. Using our common preparation period, we collaborated and designed four thematic instructional units (see the example in Figure 9.3) for the year involving math, science, physical education, history/social science, language arts, and health occupation. We spent many hours over the course of the year communicating content with one another. We learned to integrate content from one another's disciplines into our daily lessons. As a result students experience the continuation of thematic instruction being delivered from one class to another.

The Health Careers Pathway also helped me to develop important relationships with other groups through participation on an advisory board that consisted of health professionals, community members, administrators, Pathway teachers, parents, students, and district personnel. The purpose of the board was to assist in the design of curricula and partnerships for the Health Careers Pathway. We met once a month for a year to discuss Pathway needs, resources, partnerships, academic curricula, and the personal job skills needed to enter the work force. Partnerships were developed and put into place with a nearby rest home, two clinics, and one hospital.

It also is important to foster a relationship with members of the school site council. This can be achieved by attending the monthly meetings, taking an interest in the school-wide plan, or becoming a committee member. This committee monitors state and federal funds at the site level. Its job is to make decisions regarding submitted proposals for additional funding.

FIGURE 9.3 : Thematic Instruction for First Nine Weeks

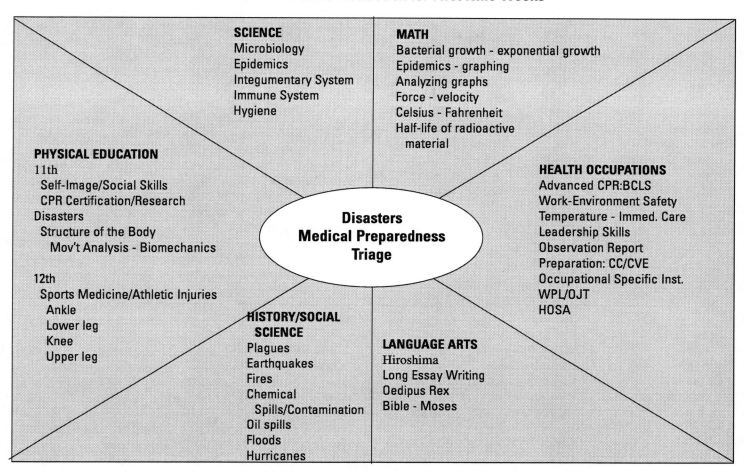

SCIENCE
Microbiology
Epidemics
Integumentary System
Immune System
Hygiene

MATH
Bacterial growth - exponential growth
Epidemics - graphing
Analyzing graphs
Force - velocity
Celsius - Fahrenheit
Half-life of radioactive
   material

PHYSICAL EDUCATION
11th
 Self-Image/Social Skills
 CPR Certification/Research
Disasters
 Structure of the Body
  Mov't Analysis - Biomechanics

12th
 Sports Medicine/Athletic Injuries
  Ankle
  Lower leg
  Knee
  Upper leg

**Disasters
Medical Preparedness
Triage**

HEALTH OCCUPATIONS
Advanced CPR:BCLS
Work-Environment Safety
Temperature - Immed. Care
Leadership Skills
Observation Report
Preparation: CC/CVE
Occupational Specific Inst.
WPL/OJT
HOSA

**HISTORY/SOCIAL
SCIENCE**
Plagues
Earthquakes
Fires
Chemical
   Spills/Contamination
Oil spills
Floods
Hurricanes

LANGUAGE ARTS
Hiroshima
Long Essay Writing
Oedipus Rex
Bible - Moses

Recently, our physical education department received $24,000 (the largest amount given for one proposal) to develop a wellness center in a vacant industrial art shop. The entire school community is benefiting from the allotment. The wellness center is open before, during, and after school. This is an opportune time for parents and community members to visit the school grounds and enjoy working out in the center. Physical education is now viewed in a new light by many members of the local community!

Teacher/leaders need to foster a relationship with administrators. These individuals can strengthen your physical education program. The rapport you establish with the administration needs to embrace trust, honesty, loyalty, and commitment. Communication also is important. Invite them to visit the physical education classes. Let them see your program in action. Ask them what they want to see in your program. Talk about ways you can work together to improve the program. A teacher/leader needs to be willing to take on additional responsibilities to show support for the principal's ideas. This support is often returned through permission to attend professional development seminars, conferences, and conventions to stay abreast of events in the profession.

How do you communicate with an administrator who chooses never to leave his or her office? Possible strategies include flyers, copies of pertinent information, e-mail, or verbal communication. Even a personal note is effective. Identify the things you think are important enough for administrative

update. These might include articles about physical education legislation; research that promotes your program requests; a definition of physical education in high school and how it differs from athletics, pep squad, band, and other non-equivalent activities; supportive documents that guide quality physical education; information about the National Standards; a curriculum model that you support; examples of instructional strategies; or even a brief note that updates the progress of the physical education department toward school site goals.

But wait a minute! What about resolving the current issues in physical education? How do you approach your administrator for support? How do you propose ideas, strategies, or solutions to your administrator and not have to wait forever to get results? These are viable questions that the teacher/leader must be able to address.

The first step is to identify the current issues within the department. Your list of concerns might include: facility upkeep, lack of equipment, acquiring instructional technology, having a classroom, getting textbooks, getting materials for student projects, equitable class size, and sufficient class time. The second step is to prioritize the list according to cost. For each item listed, the department can then brainstorm solutions. The teacher/leader can now take the third step: Make an appointment to talk with the principal and share the list of concerns and solutions.

The discussions with the principal should lead to action. Action will occur when task responsibilities are assigned and a timeline is established. Schedule a follow-up meeting to report

FIGURE 9.4 : High School Committees

1.	School Inservice Committee (organizes school inservice days)
2.	Technology Committee (writes the vision and designs the technology plan for the school)
3.	School Site Safety Council (makes policy with the school district regarding personal items, school site, facilities, security system, and equipment safety)
4.	Curriculum Development Committee (designs and integrate curriculum)
5.	Restructuring Committee (alternative bell schedule, career pathways, and pathway courses)
6.	Focus on Learning Committee (accreditation process)

on the progress being made. If the principal is unable to follow through on the identified task, ask who you can work with to complete the task with administrative support. The teacher/leader needs to keep the principal informed on the progress and outcomes achieved. Be assertive, persuasive, and persistent in your mission. Show the administrator that you are willing to do what it takes to solve department issues.

As a teacher/leader, you should volunteer for committees on campus to ensure that physical education has a voice in the school (see Figure 9.4). Some high schools have a leadership council. This council is made up of department chairpersons and the principal, and meets monthly to discuss school issues, inservice days, and school reform. The principal uses this forum to give and to receive feedback from the departments. However, all school committees can benefitfrom physical education.

For example, the teacher/leader can use committees to educate other staff members and to share the status of physical education as a component of education. You can describe what a comprehensive physical education program looks like and share what research says about the value of physical activity. You can explain today's trends for curriculum and instruction in high school physical education. School committees are helping to create the school of the future, and physical education needs to be active in this planning process.

Once the teacher/leader is comfortable with these relationships, the next level of leadership is to make a connection with the media—newspapers, magazines, radio, and television. The local media may already by aware of the *Physical Activity and Health, A Report of the Surgeon General Executive Summary* published in August 1996. Use it to promote the Centers for Disease Control recommendations and reports in the *Guidelines for Schools and Community Programs to Promote Lifelong Physical Activity Among Young People.*

Pose questions to the media about what the community is doing to increase physical activity for its youngsters. What are parents doing to increase physical activity within the family structure? Then, communicate what physical education

programs are doing in schools.

How do you make this all happen? Who should you contact first, and how do you promote media relationships? The best way to prepare for this new challenge is to learn how to develop a relationship with the media. I highly recommend the National Association for *Sport & Physical Education's Sport & Physical Education Advocacy (SPEAK) Kit.* This is an excellent resource for training yourself on how to take the first steps in building relationships with a variety of audiences. It contains sample letters, suggestions, and ways to make contacts, presentation skills, and resources for supporting quality physical education.

My first media experience was an interview for *Shape* magazine (Weider & Weider 1994) where, along with other teachers, I responded to questions regarding student-centered learning in physical education. Another event with the media occurred a year later, when a reporter from the *Los Angeles Times* visited our campus. The article conveyed the message that an educated and fit youngster is likely to be a healthy active adult. This kind of media visibility, with a positive view on physical activity, will bring pride and recognition to your physical education program, the school, the district, and the community. As your program becomes more progressive and moves into the future, contact the media and inform them of the new age of physical education.

Another important relationship that many physical educators shy away from is with the district's board of education members. These generally are informal as well as formal opportunities to meet with board members. Attend receptions and other events at which board members will be present. Be visible, and advocate quality high school physical education. Extend an open invitation to visit your program.

Making a presentation to the board on behalf of high school physical education is a worthy and educational endeavor, and it provides a forum for changing "old attitudes" about physical education. You can focus on quality physical education, ranging from curriculum development, to restructuring, to powerful teaching and learning, to a word of gratitude for the board members' support of quality physical education. Don't hesitate to seek board member support.

Another vital relationship that will help the program flourish is the relationship with your fellow department members. These are the individuals that lift you up or load you up on a daily basis. As an evolving leader, you must be able to listen, support, promote, collaborate, encourage, and commend your colleagues.

All of the relationships discussed here are essential to a successful teacher/leader. Each is able to give you a different perspective, which in turn gives you the larger picture. The total program will prosper with such a broad perspective.

Provide Department Leadership

Where does one begin to establish relationships with other department members, and how does one grow through this process to become a change agent, and eventually the department chair? In this section, we will look at sharing instructional materials and ideas with colleagues, volunteering for additional department responsibilities, and becoming an effective department chairperson.

As a young professional in an experienced department, you will be seen as a breath of fresh air. You bring with you a level of enthusiasm and zest that has possibly faded through the

FIGURE 9.5: Physical Education Exit Standards Aligned with California Physical Education Framework

Region 9 Sample Physical Education Curriculum

Motor Learning
1. Determine a movement-related goal and develop a practice plan to meet that goal.
2. Apply the correct technique for fundamental movement patterns in activities of choice.
3. Create a new movement-related game.

Biomechanics
4. Analyze movement performance using scientific principles of movement to learn or improve movement skills.

Exercise Physiology
5. Create an individualized wellness program for various stages of life.
6. Meet standards on health-related fitness test.

Growth and Development
7. Plan appropriate movement-related activities according to developmental levels.

Psychology
8. Participate regularly in movement-related physical activities.

Aesthetics
9. Appreciate and value the aesthetic features of movement and appreciate how these features contribute to movement activities.

Sociology
10. Demonstrate appropriate interpersonal skills in a movement-related experience.

Historical Perspectives
11. Analyze the relationship between a movement activity, its culture of origin, and how it has evolved.
12. Describe the historical and current interrelationship between physical education and issues in a global society.

years. You also bring with you the concepts of the new physical education. This alone may be threatening to the experienced teacher who is not professionally involved or is not knowledgeable of the direction that physical education has taken.

This is when you need to exert your charm and begin working to influence opinions. You need to infuse your expertise gradually. Take the inquisitive position as the new kid on the block. Ask each colleague, in an appropriate one-on-one situation, what the department policies and procedures are; how the department issues are addressed; what curriculum is taught at each grade level; what content is covered in the units; who gives instructional assistance with unfamiliar curriculum content; and how discipline problems are handled. Each of these questions demonstrates that you have a vested interest in the department and in teaching physical education. But they also will provide you with a very clear picture of how your colleagues view one another and the curriculum, and their philosophy of physical education.

With your colleagues' opinions tucked away in the back of your mind, the next step is to identify a variety of strategies that will move the department forward at a pace that will keep them at ease. The best strategy is to share lessons, teaching styles, task cards, worksheets, tests, and assessment strategies. Invite your colleagues to share their expertise in an inservice environment. Inclusion is the key here, so that everyone shares his or her area of expertise.

Does your administration provide inservice days, or a block of time within the day to share new knowledge and skills with department members? My high school has a modified schedule on the first Wednesday of each month, when the students arrive one hour later than usual. The early morning meetings are most beneficial to the physical education department, since most of the teachers have coaching responsibilities after school. The agenda for these morning meetings relates to the schoolwide

plan. For example, my school is focusing on how to write and teach to standards. The staff addressed the following questions: What is a standard? How do you teach to a standard? What does the lesson look like when teaching to standards? How do you assess a standard?

Using the National Standards document, *Moving into the Future*, our physical education staff learned that content standards describe "what students should know and be able to do." The staff recognized this definition because it is something we are implementing with our district physical education curriculum (see Figure 9.5). We decided to focus on one grade level a year to establish familiarity and better usage of the standards. For example, the ninth grade units are fitness, team sports, aquatics, and gymnastics (see Figure 9.6). The number next to each unit standard addresses the exit standard.

The department decided to model a lesson by teaching to the standards. The staff members selected partners and instructional units. Dates were selected for each group to present. The task consisted of the following steps:

1. Review the exit standards in the physical education curriculum guide.

2. Review the grade level standards and content.

3. Study the grade level standards addressed in the unit of choice.

4. Prepare worksheets, rubrics, and practice tasks for each of the standards.

The process is going well. Packets are prepared by the presenters for the teachers to use with their students. The worksheets are products of student learning; they are placed in the students' portfolios. Each worksheet states the standard that is being addressed in the lesson. The task is described, and a

FIGURE 9.6: Ninth Grade Units and Standards

I. Introduction (2 weeks)
6– prepare for fitness pretest
10– become acquainted with team members and review class rules

II. Fitness Unit (8 weeks)
4– analyze movement using principles of resistance
5– create and implement individualized fitness plan
6– assess personal fitness, compare data to health standards, and set goals for maintenance and improvement
7– analyze body types within and between age, gender groups, and fitness levels
8– set goal for out-of-school fitness participation/activities
9– use aesthetic features of movement qualities to create an aerobic routine
11– describe historical trends in fitness participation/activities
12– describe events in fitness history that have had an impact on current physical education and sports.

III. Team Sports (8 weeks)
1– compare practice variables for open and closed skills
2– apply fundamental movement skills to a team sport of choice
3– create a variety of offense/defense strategies for a new team sport
4– analyze movement using principles of resistance
5– monitor implementations of fitness plan
6– perform exercises
7– analyze body types and efficiency at playing different positions in a team sport
8– participate in out-of-school activities
10– demonstrate conflict resolution skills

IV. Gymnastics: tumbling, rhythmic gymnastics (8 weeks)
1– develop practice plan for a closed skill
2– apply fundamental movement skills to tumbling/gymnastics
4– analyze movement using principles of resistance
5– monitor implementation of fitness plan

6– perform exercises
7– analyze body types in relation to different gymnastics activities
8– participate in out-of-school activities
9– use aesthetic features of movement qualities to create a tumbling routine

V. Aquatics Unit (8 weeks)
1– develop a practice plan for a closed skill
2– apply fundamental movement skills in aquatics
4– analyze movement using principles of resistance
5– monitor implementation of fitness plan
6– perform exercises
7– analyze body types in relation to floating techniques
8– participate in out-of-school activities

Aquatics Unit (dry land incorporated one day a week within an additional team sport unit)
1– develop a practice plan for a closed skill
2– illustrate the use of fundamental movement skills in aquatics
4– analyze movement using principles of resistance
5– monitor implementation of fitness plan
6– perform exercises
7– analyze body types in relation to floating techniques
8– participate in out-of-school activities

VI. Closure Unit (2 weeks)
1– analyze the difference between the practice plan for a closed skill and an open skill
5– assess ability to implement fitness plan and modify plan as needed
6– assess personal fitness and compare to personal goals and to a health-related standard
7– analyze the variety of body types within and between age and gender groups and their efficiency at different skills
8– assess out-of-school participation for the year

6 –*Region IX Physical Education Curriculum, Region IX.*

rubric is placed at the bottom of the task sheet so the student is able to measure his or her performance. Needless to say, the model lessons have been a fun departmental activity, and they are a very valuable part of our training to become more effective teachers.

Another technique is to volunteer to assist with additional responsibilities. Actually, this is the first step in developing your department leadership skills. Typical duties within a physical education department include monitoring the budget, scheduling facilities, maintaining the locker system on the computer, preparing work orders for equipment and facilities, inventorying equipment, ordering uniforms, and representing the department on various committees (professional development, leadership, restructuring, technology, etc.). Often, the department chairperson will request that each staff member select one of the duties to perform each year. If this is the case, be sure to volunteer for your fair share, if not more, and select different tasks

each year in order to expand your knowledge and skills at leading a physical education department.

Lead sessions on school improvement days for your department. If you are working on curriculum reform, your colleagues need to see that you have areas of expertise (i.e., self defense, dance, authentic assessment, writing standards, etc.). This is a safe and nonthreatening environment in which to "shine" by sharing your knowledge as a young professional, and you will have the opportunity to work collaboratively with other department members. It will also afford you the opportunity to implement your strategies to deal with difficult personalities while working toward a common goal a "quality physical education program."

Teacher/leaders are busy people, so learn to manage your time. Use a daily organizer and a monthly calendar. All events are recorded on the due dates. Outline the tasks that need to be accomplished by working backward from the due date. Items are checked off as they are accomplished. Others are included as you move toward the completion day. Once you learn to manage your time, you will reach expectations above and beyond anything you thought possible, and you will lead with confidence.

Through various leadership responsibilities, both in and out of the physical education department, you have learned to plan and organize, conduct meetings, accomplish assigned tasks, ask questions, listen to others, lead discussions, follow through on tasks, and still remain prepared to teach. You are now ready to become a department chairperson. A good first step as a new department chairperson is to revisit what your department does well and where the weaknesses lie.

I recommend that you look at these eight program areas:

- Department philosophy of physical education
- Content standards
- Learning environment
- Instructional units
- Instructional strategies
- Assessment and grading procedures
- Facilities, instructional materials, and safety practices
- Professional development.

An assessment survey is a good way to accomplish this. A sample survey can be found in *Handbook for Physical Education, Framework for Developing a Curriculum for California Public Schools, Kindergarten Through Grade Twelve* (California Department of Education 1986). Once the assessment survey is completed, the department needs to interpret the results and create a strategy to improve areas of weakness. The department chairperson (you) leads the discussions on how to prioritize the areas of weakness and ways to put them into motion.

There are numerous responsibilities that come with the role of being a department chairperson. They include:

- Facility assignments
- Facility maintenance
- Supervision assignments
- Inventory
- Monitoring the budget
- Locker system
- Uniform orders and sales
- Professional development.

At least four of these tasks—facility assignments, supervision assignments, professional development, and budget—should be handled by the department chairperson. The other tasks can be delegated or selected by other department members. Delegating responsibility will help ensure that the department is run efficiently. However, it is the department chair's responsibility to follow up and to make sure deadlines are met.

A matrix is very helpful for viewing the entire year's curriculum when making facility assignments (see Figure 9.7). The grid shows all of the units and facilities for each grade level

FIGURE 9.7: Matrix of Yearly Curriculum (Ninth and Tenth Grade Yearly Plan)

9th Grade yearly Plan			
Week	*A*	*B*	*C*
1-2	Class Orientation, Rules amd Organization Pre-fitness Test		
3-10	Fitness Unit	Aquatics Unit	Gymnastics
11-18	Team Sports	Fitness Unit	Aquatics Unit
19-26	Gymnastics	Team Sports	Fitness Unit
27-34	Aquatics Unit	Gymnastics	Team Sports
35-27	Closure Unit	Closure Unit	Closure Unit
38	Finals, Grades, Collect Locks, Clean Out Lockers		

10th Grade yearly Plan			
Week	*A*	*B*	*C*
1-2	Class Orientation, Rules amd Organization Pre-fitness Test		
3-10	Self Defense	Analysis of Movement	Indiv./Dual Sports-Outd. Ed
11-18	Dance	Self Defense	Analysis of Movement
19-26	Indiv./Dual Sports-Outd. Ed	Dance	Self Defense
27-34	Analysis of Movement	Indiv./Dual Sports-Outd. Ed	Dance
35-37	Closure Unit	Closure Unit	Closure Unit
38	Finals, Grades, Collect Locks, Clean Out Lockers		

for each semester. Be sure to consider which units are taught according to the time of year and weather. Scheduling should be based on the number of sections by grade level, the facilities, and the number of staff members. Once the yearly plan is in place, the department chair is ready to make staff assignments. The grade levels that are to be taught are discussed with each staff member.

In order to strengthen our curriculum and to keep it flexible, we have learned to teach every course at each grade level. All assignments are based on school enrollment. These numbers are provided by our two feeder middle schools, and they determine the number of ninth grade sections that will be needed. Our department has worked very hard with the administration to have coeducational classes by grade levels, so the sections are balanced by the computer.

Speaking of computers, I highly recommend that as department chair you learn how to use a computer. It will make your job so much easier. For example, I use a spreadsheet for supervision assignments. I create column headings for period, locker room, gate area, and week (see Figure 9.8). I then make

FIGURE 9.8: Data Base (Supervision Schedule)

First Semester Supervision Schedule				
1st Period		**1st 6 Wks**	**2nd 6 Wks**	**3rd 6 Wks**
West Gare		MacAuley	Oseguera	Smith
Boys Lk Rm		McCurdy	Smith	Oseguera
Boys Lk Rm		Oseguera	McCurdy	MacAuley
Boys Lk Rm		Smith	MacAuley	McCurdy
East Gate		Brenes	Brenes	Brenes
Girls W Lk Rm		Sauceda	Sauceda	Sauceda
Girls E Lk Rm		Bogdanoff	Bogdanoff	Bogdanoff
2nd Period		**1st 6 Wks**	**2nd 6 Wks**	**3rd 6 Wks**
West Gare		Oseguera	Brenes	McCurdy
Boys Lk Rm		Smith	MacAuley	Brenes
Boys Lk Rm		McCurdy	Smith	MacAuley
Boys Lk Rm		Brenes	Oseguera	Smith
East Gate		Bogdanoff	Thompson	Bogdanoff
Girls W Lk Rm		Sauceda	Sauceda	Sauceda
Girls E Lk Rm				
3rd Period		**1st 6 Wks**	**2nd 6 Wks**	**3rd 6 Wks**
West Gare		Smith	Oseguera	ManAuley
Boys Lk Rm		MacAuley	McCurdy	Smith
Boys Lk Rm		McCurdy	MacAuley	Brenes
Boys Lk Rm		Brenes	Smith	Oseguera
East Gate		Bogdanoff	Thompson	Bogdanoff
Girls W Lk Rm		Sauceda	Sauceda	Sauceda
Girls E Lk Rm		Thompson	Bogdanoff	Thompson
4th Period		**1st 6 Wks**	**2nd 6 Wks**	**3rd 6 Wks**
West Gare		LaCommare	Smith	McCurdy
Boys Lk Rm		Oseguera	LaCommare	MacAuley
Boys Lk Rm		Smith	Brenes	LaCommare
Boys Lk Rm		McCurdy	MacAuley	Oseguera
East Gate		Thompson	Iverson	Sauceda
Girls W Lk Rm		Iverson	Sauceda	Iverson
Girls E Lk Rm		Bogdanoff	Thompson	Thompson
5th Period		**1st 6 Wks**	**2nd 6 Wks**	**3rd 6 Wks**
West Gare		McCurdy	LaCommare	Oseguera
Boys Lk Rm		LaCommare	MacAuley	Smith
Boys Lk Rm		Brenes	Oseguera	McCurdy
Boys Lk Rm		Smith	Brenes	LaCommare
East Gate		Iverson	Sauceda	Reed
Girls W Lk Rm		Reed	Iverson	Sauceda
Girls E Lk Rm		Thompson	Bogdanoff	Thompson
6th Period		**1st 6 Wks**	**2nd 6 Wks**	**3rd 6 Wks**
Boys Lk Rm		FB Coaches	FB Coaches	BKB Coaches
Var Lk Rm		FB Coaches	FB Coaches	FB Coaches

staffing assignments. When using a computer, be sure to back up everything on another disk. It is possible to lose files on the hard drive. A good resource for learning to use the computer in physical education is *Using Technology in Physical Education, 2nd Edition* (Mohnsen 1998). This book will get you up and running with ease.

To keep yourself and the department abreast of current trends, make sure you are a member of the American Alliance for Health, Physical Education, Recreation and Dance and the state organization. These organizations will provide you with current professional literature, including *JOPERD, Strategies*, and/or *Research Quarterly*. I also read my state journal and the NASPE Newsletter, along with magazines that focus on wellness and physical activity.

The most exciting resource, of course, is the Internet. Learn how to infuse the Internet into your lessons. There are many wonderful physical education sites to visit. Be progressive and stay up with the times!

Inservices, workshops, conferences, and convention attendance become even more important to you as the department chairperson. You gather information not only for yourself, but also for other department members. And, you may need to arrange for professional development seminars on topics ranging from the use of technology in physical education to curriculum writing, assessment, teaching styles, and interdisciplinary instruction. Take pride in being the instructional leader for your department, and when possible lead the professional development yourself. Provide time for all your department members to share their knowledge on professional development days and during department meetings. Teacher/leaders encourage their colleagues to learn more and try new ideas.

As a new leader, you also will need professional development related to leadership skills, including listening, paraphrasing, negotiating, and collaborating. Remember also that knowledge is power. And be sure to stay abreast of current research, future trends (both within and outside physical education), and professional issues.

Consensus building is a key process skill required of department chairpersons. When department issues arise and the situation becomes uneasy, lead your department through these steps:

1. State the issue. Let everyone in the group express his or her own opinion without interruptions from others.

2. List the recommendations.

3. Chart the pros and cons related to each recommendation.

4. Tally individual preferences.

5. Discuss the language of the primary recommendation.

6. Ask each person in the group if he or she can live with the recommendation.

7. If someone still has a problem with the recommendation, identify what changes need to be made, and let the group discuss it one more time or until consensus is reached.

This process is healthy and friendly, and it allows the department chairperson to remain neutral in the role of the recorder. All department members get to practice good listening and communication skills during this process.

Another sensitive issue is the handling of financial requests. The physical education budget is handled through the general fund. Department members submit equipment requests, which are given to the department chair. The district submits bids for approved equipment. As the department chairperson, you must know what funds are available and how to find alternative sources of funding. Grants can provide additional revenue, and there may be pockets of money in the business community.

I was able to apply for three grants (see Figure 9.9 for an example) and I received funding for two of them during the first couple months of the school year. I urge you to apply for every grant available. Be aware that the smaller grant applications are easier to write, especially if you have no experience.

Be forward thinking in your requests for money. The business community likes to see schools address the future in relation to the upcoming work force and the roles students play in the community. If you can answer who, what, where, when, why, and how, you can write a grant. Enjoy the journey, and don't be discouraged if your first proposal is not accepted. Tweak it a little, adjust the weaknesses, rename it, and apply again with another organization.

Participate in School-Site Leadership

What does it mean for a physical educator to be a site leader? What additional skills are necessary to a school site leader? In this section, we will look at being the chair of a site committee and the presenter for schoolwide inservices.

It is not unusual for physical education chairpersons to be leaders at the site level. They already possess the ability to organize, schedule, speak, and influence others. Actually, this is the next step in the leadership continuum, to a new forum from which physical education can speak.

My first leadership role within the school community was chairing a committee on assessing student work. The questions that needed to be addressed included, How do we know it is outstanding? What are the criteria? Who designs the rubric to measure the expectation of performance?

Student work was assessed by different teachers, which made for wonderful discussions. For example, the special education teachers saw one student's work as great. Other teachers were very impressed with the student's ability to express himself so clearly. The college prep teachers felt the student's work was poor. This wide range of analysis lead to further discussions of teacher expectations in the classroom. As the discussion group leader, I used physical education as an analogy. The range of skill abilities in one class spans both ends of the learning spectrum. In order to meet the learning needs of all students in the same lesson, we use a teaching strategy called inclusion.

The skill being mastered (the lay-up) is set up in a variety of challenges, so the student may choose the level of difficulty. The concept of the lesson is stressed at each level and at all stations. The students are challenged to demonstrate the skill at a pace where control is demonstrated and successfully achieved. The teacher observes the performances of the students and moves them to different levels according to the skill ability observed. The learning expectation is stated up front. The rubric is on the worksheet, which allows the students to know what is expected.

The goal is to be able to outwit your opponent in a one-on-one situation in basketball, maintain position of the ball, and drive for the basket to execute a lay-up during a game situation.

My analogy allowed others to see physical education in a positive light, and the leadership opportunity allowed me to illustrate my understanding of assessment.

To present materials out of your area of expertise is a real challenge. I moved from a committee chair to being a school-wide presenter. When you do presentations, be sure to have a beginning, a middle, and an end. Start with a cartoon or something that relates to the topic, but with a chuckle, and then discuss the intended outcomes of the session. Present the facts in a timely manner, and include some interaction with the audience. Ask for feedback and relate the discussion to the next portion of the presentation.

Coaches also are seen as site leaders. Most coaches are members of the physical education department. These individuals may be great coaches and average teachers, or great teachers and average coaches. It is the coach who gets involved in the business of the school who is looked upon as a site leader. This unique individual is great at teaching, coaching, and leading because of his or her ability to set and meet goals.

Like many teacher/leaders, my goal setting experiences also are a byproduct of athletics. The process includes weekly team meetings with the athletes. These meetings teach the students how to set personal goals, practice goals, game goals, team goals, and seasonal goals. For example, my field hockey team set the following seasonal goal: "The team will score from a defensive clear."

In order to meet a goal, the skills must be practiced. So every day, hockey practice would end with the goalie clearing the ball to the sweep. The sweep scooped the ball to the right halfback, who swung the play to the other side of the field to the left wing. The left wing drove the ball to the center, the center passed the ball to right inner who rushed for score. This continued all season. The students looked forward to executing the drill. And sure enough, what you practice does occur. During the game with our cross town rival, the opportunity arose for the goalie to clear the ball. The rest went like clockwork. Everyone was off the bench to witness the goal. The team went crazy. They met their season goal.

The game was lost, but the team won the intrinsic award of meeting their seasonal goal. The students learned the value of goal setting. They learned about pride, dedication, hard work, and team work. These qualities stay with a person for a lifetime. I would like to believe that many of my students are leaders in one way or another because they possess the ability to set goals and achieve them.

Initiate School-to-School Leadership

The next step as you develop into a leader is to initiate school-to-school leadership. This section will discuss how to initiate contact with other schools, use professional associations as contacts, and work together with other schools.

How does a teacher/leader initiate contact with other high school physical educators in the district? First of all, there needs to be a purpose, such as developing quality physical education curricula and programs in the district. In order for this to happen

FIGURE 9.9: Sample Grant

Project Title: Wellness in the Twenty-First Century
Submitted to: Montebello Unified School District
Medi-Cal Collaboration

1. Project Description

I propose to keep America healthy. The Surgeon General's Report clearly states, "physical inactivity is hazardous to your health." About 25 percent of adults report no physical activity at all in their leisure time. Only about one-half of U.S. young people (ages 12–21 years) regularly participate in vigorous physical activity. One-fourth report no vigorous physical activity. The CDC (Centers for Disease Control and Prevention) has produced a document, "Guidelines for School and Community Programs to Promote Lifelong Physical Activity Among Young People." This document supports the role of physical activity for all age levels. This proposal strives to improve the quality of life for the students, staff, and community members by encouraging life long practice of physical activity. Our students will work and live in the twenty-first century, maybe! It is up to schools and community programs to keep our kids fit. There is no greater service to humanity than to increase the longevity of one's life. In order to educate and motivate people to be concerned about their health and fitness, I would like to use a high-tech fitness and wellness system called Health First "TriFIT." This state-of-the art technology will provide the student with valuable data about his or her personal well being. The fitness assessment, health risk appraisal, nutrition and exercise, and meal planning software guides the student toward a complete fitness program.

After long negotiations, curriculum planning and facility preparation, a shop class at Bell Gardens High School was renovated last summer into a Wellness Center. The room is furnished with used exercise equipment. The facility has a caged area to secure our modest collection of other technology devices such as heart monitors, VCR, monitor, blood pressure monitor, spirometer, computer, and textbooks. The physical education staff would like to educate and motivate the students, staff, and community on the value of personal fitness using this "state of the art" equipment. The TriFIT 520 System informs the users as to what is going on inside their bodies during physical activity and produces charts, graphs, and personal assessment feedback summaries. This pertinent information is used to make appropriate change and help the individual achieve his or her healthy zone for each fitness assessment. Students, staff, and community members will be able to design their own exercise programs using the TriFIT System. They will learn about the principles of training and the five components of health-related fitness.

The Wellness Center will be open to the public in the mornings two to three times a week before school. Interest will determine future times that the center may be open. The Wellness Center will be used during the day by the students at Bell Gardens High School. Our state framework requires a unit on fitness at the ninth grade level. We have designed a fitness curriculum using the textbook, Personal Fitness: Looking Good, Feeling Good to meet the framework's expectations.

The community will benefit not only in the use of the facility as a Wellness Center, but it will gain fit and knowledgeable citizens in the work force. The health services field is the second largest employer in this nation, with more than 280 job titles. By the year 2000 there will be 3.1 million new jobs created in the health field. These jobs will offer flexible scheduling for employees with a range of education from high school to advanced university degrees. The use of this technology system will prepare students for employment in the health career field focusing on biome-

chanics, exercise physiology, sports medicine/athletic injuries, strength and conditioning, physical therapy, and athletic training. The students at the upper division level will explore these careers and gain insight into the value and practices of how to help others to achieve a healthy lifestyle.

2. Project Budget:

Indicate as specifically as possible the amount of money requested and how it would be spent.

The high tech TriFIT Fitness and Wellness Systems is by Health First Corporation
6811 Academy Parkway East
Albuquerque, NM 87109-4403
800-841-8333

Materials Needed	Cost
The Health First TriFIT 520	$7,000

- Medical grade rolling cart
- IBM compatible 486 computer, 520 MB hard drive
- 3.5" floppy drive
- Super VGA color graphics
- Retractable blood pressure shelf
- Hewlett Packard DeskJet printer
- Health First TriFIT System software plus
  —Fitness assessment and exercise planning software

On-Line Physiological System
- Blood pressure and heart rate
- Skinfold caliper
- Wireless heart rate monitor
- Isometric strength/body weight platform
- Modified sit and reach station
- Bike ergometer

Bike ergometer	$1000
TriFIT Software	$ 935

- Health risk appraisal software
- Fitness assessment
- Exercise planning

Additional Software

• Meal planning	$590
Freight and Handling	$1,430
Sales Tax	
Total	$10,955

Bell Gardens High School will be able to offer its students, staff, parents, and community members a free fitness center with a high quality assessment program that is used by other professionals in Health/Fitness Clubs, Rehab Centers, Corporate Wellness, Hospitals, Insurance Companies, Government/Military installations, and College/ Universities. The physical education program can explore quality assessment procedures. TriFIT™ is the future. It is an affordable cutting edge system. Everyone knows they should exercise, but how do we motivate them to do so? I believe self-analysis is the key. The students will be challenged to explore further the human body in motion and then become the change agents for the future wellness of America.

there needs to be leadership at each of the schools. I suggest you contact your district or county coordinator of physical education. Express your interest in working with other high school physical educators in the district. If no leadership group exists and this is not already stated as a priority, request your coordinator's assistance in helping you create the consortium. If there is no physical education coordinator, the time has come for you to take the lead and initiate leadership for physical education.

Your next step is to identify leadership interest. This can be done by sending out a memo to hand-selected high school physical educators inviting them to meet and exchange program ideas. Suggest a variety of times to meet (mornings, after school, or early evenings). Once you have two or more hand-selected teacher/leaders interested, you can begin to meet regularly to initiate and improve school-to-school leadership. Share your current leadership roles. Encourage one another to represent high school physical education on their site committees. Teach one another leadership strategies such as time management, organizational skills, planning, presentation skills, curriculum development, teaching to standards, and using authentic assessment.

In my situation, our schools are clustered according to their location in the district. There are two feeder schools that articulate with the high school. We recently held our first cluster meeting. The morning session had break-out sessions with 15 participants from pre-K to adult education teachers in each group. The task was to share outstanding student work. The afternoon session had articulation by content area. The physical educators met and discussed the agenda seen in Figure 9.10.

Another strategy is to contact the president of the local unit of your professional association. Ask if he or she can provide an avenue for initiating contact between schools through the local meetings. Seek out the secondary level "movers and shakers." Get involved in their high energy brainstorming sessions. Become progressive and futuristic in your vision for secondary level physical education.

Schools can work together on professional development. They can even perform their own inservices at one another's school sites. Possible areas for inservice include activities, teaching strategies, assessment strategies, technology, and ways to articulate programs. Pursue grant opportunities. Connect with a feeder school and write a grant together for supporting academic and physical development. Take the initiative in reaching out to other schools.

Broaden Your Impact: District Level Leadership

In this section we will look at the kinds of things you can accomplish at the district level. These include curriculum development, staff development, an effective equipment exchange, and districtwide monitoring of physical fitness testing.

School physical education programs are most effective when the goals and expectations match those of the State Department of Education, district curriculum, and the school community. If your district does not have a coordinator for high school physical education, then a teacher/leader needs to assume that responsibility and be the voice for physical education in the district. Ask the assistant superintendent of instruction if you can chair a physical education curriculum committee to create a curriculum or revise the current curriculum.

If you are in charge of writing a district curriculum, be sure to follow the principles outlined in Chapter 3, which deals with curriculum. Begin by writing a letter to the principal at each school in the district asking him or her to nominate one physical educator to be a member of the curriculum committee. And, make sure that the committee consists of elementary teachers, middle school teachers, high school teachers, and adapted physical educators.

During the first meeting, the committee should brainstorm the characteristics of a physically educated person. This is a wonderful activity for educating the committee about the role of physical education in the twenty-first century and the curriculum development process. I also suggest using *The Curriculum Process in Physical Education* (Jewett, Bain, & Ennis 1995). It will guide your progress as you work to develop district standards for physical education.

It is important to link the district's mission statement to the physical education standards to show how physical education supports the entire learning experience of the students. The rest of the process consists of developing grade level standards based on each exit standard. This is a year-long process in itself, and will require meetings at least every other month. The development of the yearly plan, unit plans, and lesson plans can be an additional year or two of work. The final step is to submit the curriculum to the board of education for approval.

The next phase involves implementing the curriculum and inservicing all of the physical educators in the district. The who, when, and how of implementation needs to be addressed by the district office, but it also involves another possible role for a teacher/leader at the high school level. For example, my district is at the step of implementation. I am working with the director of Instructional Division on the plan shown in Figure 9.11.

The plan will need to be repeated for both the middle school and the elementary schools after the high school plan is completed. The best of all situations is to have three physical education mentors who can assist the teacher/leader on special assignment in the curriculum implementation process. Whatever plan is used, however, the district decision will be based on money and time.

The teacher/leader should be assertive in promoting the plan the committee has sent forward. Use the current research from *Physical Activity and Health, A Report of the Surgeon General Executive Summary* (Centers for Disease Control 1996) and *Guidelines for School and Community Programs to Promote Lifelong Physical Activity Among Young People* (Centers for Disease Control 1997). Both of these documents have very clear expectations of the schools' role in promoting life long physical activity using a comprehensive curriculum.

What is the district's vision of physical education? Without a coordinator at the helm, changes will occur slowly. What programs would you like to see in place if you could coordinate physical education in the district? As a high school teacher/leader, you can create a few programs that would be beneficial to physical education in your district. We have already discussed curriculum, but what about staff development? Many physical educators do not attend the local, district, state, or national conventions.

FIGURE 9.10: Cluster Meeting Agenda

1. **Introduction of staff members**
   Have each person state his or her name, number of years of teaching, and extracurricular responsibilities including leadership roles.

2. **Grade level curriculum**
   What is being taught at each grade level and does it alignm with the state framework and the district physical education curriculum guide.

3. **Skill ability of students**
   Discuss the skill level of the students and how it can be sequential from K–12.

4. **Inservice the administrators**
   Design a presentation to educate the administrators about the new physical education program (comprehensive) on your campus. Use the principals forum at the district level.

5. Discuss the passing on of students' physical fitness scores. Discuss the strategy of having the students' fitness scores posted in their transcripts. Stickers can be generated by the district's Information Systems Department.

6. Discuss the intrinsic rewards of physical activity. Fit to achieve, positive self-esteem, low stress, good health. What are some ways for students to inherently be physically active?

7. Share instructional strategies. Command, practice, reciprocal, self-check, and inclusion. Cooperative groups and teaching stations.

8. Share assessment strategies. Dip Stick Quiz (five questions at the start of the lesson); note pad size paper and golf score card pencils. Worksheets, homework, presentations, projects, written tests, demonstrations, skill applications, skill analysis, design a game, create a routine.

9. Discuss the use of technology in physical education. Devices: heart rate monitors, pulse monitors, pedometers, Futrex body composition analyzer, spirometer, sphygmomanometer, and pulse stick. Computer: personal use, instructional use with fitness software, instructional software and Internet, multi-media projects using Hypercard, Hyperstudio, or Powerpoint. CDs: understanding exercise physiology, skill development in sports. Video cameras: Sharp video camera with a three to four-inch view finder for immediate feedback, movement analysis, movement patterns skill development. Digital camera: Multimedia projects to demonstrate student understanding of concepts.

10. Schedule visitations between sites. Visit one another's programs. Develop mentor partnerships to assist one another in teaching and assessment.

FIGURE 9.11: Implementation Plan

Plan 1: Three-year plan addressing introductions and four standards a year for grades 9, 10, 11, and 12 at all three high schools inservicing a trainer of trainer program.

Plan 2: Four-year plan addressing introductions and three standards a year for grades 9, 10, 11, and 12 at all three high schools inservicing a trainer of trainer program.

Plan 3: Hire a teacher/leader-on-special assignment for a year. Inservice the whole staff at each school site on three different days, covering the introduction and four standards for grades 9, 10, 11, and 12.

Plan 4: Hire a teacher/leader on special assignment for a year. Inservice the whole staff at each school site on four different days, covering the introduction and three standards for grades 9, 10, 11, and 12.

Plan 5: District-wide inservice for physical education once a year for four years, addressing the introduction and three standards a year for grades 9, 10, 11, and 12.

Plan 6: District-wide inservice for physical education once a year for three years, addressing the introduction and four standards a year for grades 9, 10, 11, and 12.

Inservices can be provided to demonstrate model lessons, teaching styles, and how to use technology in physical education. They also can show how to create career paths and learn the in's and out's of the accreditation process. Another great project would be to develop an effective equipment exchange program for your district. Such an exchange could include portable climbing walls, portable pools, roller blades, snorkeling/skin diving equipment, canoes, etc. I'm sure you will be able to add to the list according to the climate and geography of your district. Be sure to stretch your imagination and reach out to business partners to assist in developing the program.

After working with the district office in a variety of capacities, you become known as the resource person for physical education!

Assume a Leadership Role in Your Professional Organization

The journey through the leadership continuum will hone your skills and challenge your abilities. As the secondary level teacher/leader, you are well read in current issues in the profession, and an authority on quality physical education. Now, it is time to become active and visible in your professional organization. This section will describe the progression from student member, to professional member, to local unit leader, to local unit president, to state committee member, to state officer. It also will touch on recognition and writing for professional journals.

Student membership is the key to the future. The profession

will be shaped by new visions and progressive leaders in NASPE/AAHPERD. Every college and university teacher should encourage students to join their local majors club. Actually, student membership in the state AHPERD organization is often a requirement of many majors. A good faculty adviser will take the time to mentor student leaders through well planned leadership activities. Master teachers can attend conferences with their student teachers to guide their learning processes to enhance curriculum outcomes, and the student teachers can observe leadership traits in the master teachers.

As a new professional, you pay tribute to your college professors by joining the ranks of quality physical educators in NASPE/AAHPERD and state AHPERD. The members of these professional organization are dedicated to shaping the future of health, physical education, recreation, and dance. You can have an immediate impact in your professional organization because you have a voice in the direction it takes. As a dedicated volunteer, you will learn even more about leadership opportunities. There are offices, committees, task forces, councils, projects, sponsors, partnerships, and programs that all need volunteers. Which one will you choose?

The state organizations usually have local or district associations. Contact your state AHPERD office to find out who the unit/district president is. Communicate by phone or letter to express your interest in attending meetings. Meetings at this level usually address the issues of the local teachers, and put into action the requests of the state association.

You can represent the high school perspective by attending monthly meetings, chairing a few committees, contributing an article for the newsletter, taking on projects, becoming a part of the public speaking group, writing a letter to a legislator, raising funds with the American Heart Association, or organizing the district conference.

At this point, you are confident, knowledgeable, and responsible. The next position at the local level is unit/district president. The tasks remain the same: You bring a secondary level perspective, but now you are the leader. You get to put your ideas into action and bring a different perspective to the unit/district activities. Time seems to be an issue for high school teacher/leaders. Coaching one season rather than three seasons can help in resolving the time constraint.

After a few years of experience at the local level as an officer and now as president, your new responsibility is to attend meetings held four times a year. You are a regional representative to the state association. The state leadership is called the executive board. The association uses a variety of standing committees to accomplish its work and meet its membership needs.

Experienced professionals mentor new leaders and encourage them to become more involved with committee work. The standing committees include awards, budget/treasurer, constitution/bylaws, editorial board, governance and structure, investments, Jump Rope/Hoops for Heart, legislative, long-range planning, membership, nominations, office, publications, public relations, resolutions, scholarships, foundations, liaisons, and conference. These committees review information and make recommendations to the association. There are many choices, so start with your passion and let your voice be heard!

The committee chair keeps the committee on task and the

discussions on course. Agendas need to be planned and followed. Sidebars need to be points of interest for the next agenda. It is important that each meeting is productive. Know ahead of time what you want to accomplish by when and by whom. Assign tasks to committee members and let them know you expect a report at the next meeting. Good leadership at the committee level prepares you to be a state officer.

State offices are elected positions. The state officers discuss finances and policy and take their recommendations to the executive committee. These state leaders are the shakers and the movers in the profession. These are the dedicated and committed folks who serve for the love of teaching and the profession.

Recognition by the association is a celebration of excellence. There are a variety of teacher recognition levels. At the local level, there are unit/district recognition or honors banquets. Honorees at the local level are nominated by their units for state awards, which are given out at the state conference luncheons. State and district award honorees are nominated by their state association for district/national awards. Recognition by your peers in the profession is the highest honor that can be bestowed on a teacher.

Teachers helping teachers helping students learn—isn't that what we do best? Why not share this expertise in another forum—writing. One of the greatest contributions a teacher can give to the profession is to share what works in his or her class. Think for a moment about a program, a teaching strategy, or a practice plan that you created that worked for kids. This is what you need to write about. Try your hand at writing articles for your state journal. When you feel more confident, I suggest you write for NASPE/AAHPERD's journal, *Strategies, A Journal for Physical Education and Sport Educators*.

Chapter Summary

In this chapter I have discussed seven topics that provide a logical progression of growth for the high school teacher/leader. Effective teaching emphasizes the use of varied styles to empower student learning and encourage learning through problem solving. Relationships with all involved—from students to school board members—build the teacher/leader's trust, credibility, patience, dedication, loyalty, and ability to work with others. Department leadership keeps the crew rowing in the same direction and toward the same goal. Participation in school site leadership allows the school community to witness the vital contributions that physical education makes to the school curriculum. Initiating school-to-school leadership contributes to the total development of individuals and programs from school to school.

Broadening your impact with a district level leadership role will facilitate curriculum development, staff development, and any other idea that you are able to set in motion. And finally, your willingness to become involved in your professional organization by taking a leadership role will strengthen your character.

Learn to be a task master, a risk taker, a decision maker, an organizer, a planner, an energizer, an initiator, and a performer so you can fulfill the responsibilities undertaken and still maintain the integrity of a quality educator. You, too, shall learn how to influence others in a meaningful way.

We need good leaders now. The times are changing. It does not have to take 30 years to become a leader. Be a progressive leader and act as a mentor, a trainer, and a coach to develop other leaders. Great leaders have a caring approach. They are able to persuade others, articulate their views, and use a vision to empower others to get the job done. They lead by example and show loyalty, accountability, and respect for all parties involved.

The leadership continuum begins with the teacher, then to the teacher/leader, and goes on through the administrative phase. Where are you on the leadership continuum? Identify your current location and begin to plan how to enhance your leadership skills. Who you are does make a difference! I challenge you to seek responsibility and look out for the welfare of our profession. Leadership for the new millennium began yesterday. Enjoy the journey and empower others to do the same.

I leave you with a quote by Joel Baker:

Vision without action is merely a dream.

Action without vision just passes time.

Vision with action can change the world.

References

California Department of Education. (1986). *Handbook for physical education: Framework for developing a curriculum for California public schools, kindergarten through grade twelve.* Sacramento, CA: Author.

Glover, D. R., & Midura, D. W. (1992). *Team building through physical challenges.* Champaign, IL: Human Kinetics.

Hennessy, B. (1996). *Physical education sourcebook.* Champaign, IL: Human Kinetics.

Jewett, A. E., Bain, L. L., & Ennis, C. D. (1995). *The curriculum process in physical education.* Dubuque, IA: Brown.

Mohnsen, B. S. (1984). *A comparison of most and least effective graduate teaching assistants.* Unpublished doctoral dissertation, University of Southern California, Los Angeles.

Mohnsen, B. S. (1998). *Using technology in physical education* (2nd ed.).Cerritos, CA: Bonnie's Fitware.

Mosston, M., & Ashworth, S. (1994). *Teaching physical education* (4th ed). New York: Macmillan.

National Association for Sport and Physical Education. (1994). *Sport and physical education advocacy kit.* Reston, VA: Author.

National Association for Sport and Physical Education. (1995). *Moving into the future, national standards for physical education. A guide to content and assessment.* St. Louis, MO: Mosby.

Region 9. (1994). *Region 9 sample physical education curriculum.* San Diego, CA: San Diego Office of Education.

Rohnke, K. (1989). *Cowstails and cobras II.* Hamilton, MA: Project Adventure.

Rohnke, K. (1984). *Silver bullets.* Dubuque, IA: Kendall/Hunt.

Spindt G. B., Monti, W. H., & Hennessy, B. (1991). *Moving for life, essentials of physical education.* Dubuque, IA: Kendall/Hunt.

U.S. Department of Health and Human Services. (1997). *Promoting lifelong physical activity among young people: Centers for Disease Control and Prevention's guidelines for school and community.* Atlanta, GA: Author.

U. S. Department of Health and Human Services. (1996). *Physical activity and health: A report of the Surgeon General.* Atlanta, GA: Author.

Weider, J., & Weider, B. (1994). Fitness grows up. *Shape, 14* (2), 16

Wuest, D. E. & Lombardo, B. (1994). *Curriculum and instruction–The secondary school physical education experience.* St. Louis, MO: Mosby.

Resources

Analysis of Movement Unit Plans: Bonnie's Fitware, Cerritos, CA.

DINE Healthy: DINE Systems, Inc., Amherst, NY.

Futrex Body Composition Analyzer: Futrex Inc. Gaithersburg, MD.

Health Related Fitness Tutorial and Portfolio: Bonnie's Fitware, Cerritos, CA.

Tanita's Body Fat Monitor/Scales: Tanita Corporation of America Inc. Arlington Heights, IL.

CHAPTER 10

District leadership

Bonnie Mohnsen

A district leadership position—such as physical education coordinator, director, or supervisor—is the threshold to what has traditionally been thought of as the official administrative position for physical education. The individual who holds such a position is responsible for the physical education program and reports to the board of education. Typically, individuals applying for this type of position must have some sort of leadership or administrative credential as well as credentialing and experience as a physical educator.

The district coordinator can provide leadership for more than 500,000 students (as in the case of the Los Angeles Unified School District), or as few as 30 students housed in one school. I worked as the physical education coordinator for the Montebello Unified School District, which included 27 schools (17 elementary schools, 6 middle schools, 3 high schools, and 1 alternative school) and represented more than 30,000 students. I was responsible not only for the physical education program but also for the high school athletic program, the middle school intramural/extramural program, the elementary recreation program, the K-12 health education program, and a number of drug education and nutrition education grants. This is quite common; district coordinators for physical education often are responsible for programs such as technology, driver education, and safety programs along with their physical education responsibilities.

A typical list of duties for a district level physical education administrator might include the following:

- Coordinates the implementation of all federal, state, and board of education laws and policies regarding physical education
- Coordinates the preparation of all required reports for staff, board of education, county and state departments of education
- Coordinates all district efforts in development of student and staff health and well being
- Coordinates the administration of all required testing in the area of physical education, including supervision and interpretation of data collection and analysis
- Coordinates the development and revision of the physical education curriculum and adoption of textbooks to meet needs identified in physical fitness assessment

- Organizes and conducts staff development activities in physical education instruction and physical fitness assessment
- Prepares and administers the annual physical education budget
- Assists and advises in the selection process of equipment and supplies used in the physical education program
- Coordinates the adapted physical education program for the district, including management of the budget and scheduling of teachers
- Represents the district and provides necessary liaison in the area of physical education in contacts outside the district
- Supervises mentor teachers in physical education.

Frequently, the physical education coordinator in a district will have other responsibilities as well. These might include:

- Prepares and administers the annual elementary recreation budget
- Coordinates the selection and assignment of all personnel employed in the recreation program
- Directs the supervisory personnel assigned to the recreation program
- Coordinates the use of school property permits for the athletic facilities of the district
- Supervises the high school athletic program
- Supervises the middle school intramural program.

Typical employment opportunity flyers note the following requirements for district leadership:

- Minimum qualifications
  - Possession of a valid administrative or supervisory credential issued by the state authorizing service in grades K-12
  - Successful teaching/supervisory experience at the elementary/secondary level in the area of physical education
- Desirable qualifications
  - A college major in physical education

– Ability to work effectively in a multi-ethnic community
– Knowledge or experience in physical education curriculum development, inservice, and instructional methodologies related to learning theory.

The seven major points associated with district leadership include:

1. Involve All Stakeholders
2. Establish Policies and Procedures
3. Develop a Curriculum for Assessment and Accountability
4. Provide Professional Development
5. Maximize Resources
6. Implement New Programs
7. Use Time Effectively and Efficiently.

Involve All Stakeholders

Although it has been acknowledged that the person in the physical education leadership position is the key to the success of the physical education program (Evaul 1995), that person cannot and should not take responsibility for the entire program by him or herself. It is important for the individual in this position to develop and maintain quality relationships with all stakeholders (anyone with a vested interest in the program). In terms of district leadership, these stakeholders include teachers, students, coordinators in neighboring districts, personnel at institutes of higher education, leaders of professional organizations, site administrators, district office administrators (including the superintendent), community members (including parents), and the local board of education. Each of these individuals can play an important role in developing a quality physical education program. Let's take a look at enhancing the relationship between the district leader and several of these groups.

Relationship with Physical Educators

The foundation for the relationship between the coordinator and the physical education teachers depends on whether the coordinator arrived at the position from within or outside the district. Each scenario provides its own set of advantages and challenges that must be addressed by the new leader.

An "in-house" appointment brings with it all previous relationships between the current leader and the physical educators in the district. These relationships were based on a peer situation where both individuals were teachers sharing common concerns and perceptions. However, once one of the individuals in the relationship becomes an administrator, the relationship is bound to change to some extent. The advantage of this situation is that the individual in the leadership or administrative role may continue to be perceived as a friend or colleague who will serve as an advocate for physical education and physical educators within his or her new role as an administrator. The challenge is that the leader may continue to be thought of as "one of us," with little or no power allocated to his or her new role.

Certainly there are other power bases besides positional power, and it is important for the "in-house appointee" to garner as much power as possible from these other bases. These include skill/expertise power, reward power, popularity power,

respect power, and coercive power. Power does not simply mean the ability to tell others what to do; rather, it refers to the ability to gather support and involvement from others. Many sources of power are available for the taking, and leadership is certainly what you make of it.

Individuals coming from outside the district have the advantage of positional power along with the mystique of being an unknown entity. This can be advantageous to the leader, since it starts the leader off with the ability to establish new relationships using the type of leadership style that he or she prefers. The challenge is getting past being seen as an outsider who does not know the history of the district, has not paid his or her dues within the current organization, does not have an in-house network of established relationships, and has not worked his or her way through the system. This necessitates the leader getting to know as much as possible about the organization and its people as quickly as possible. One-on-one conversations with as many different individuals in the organization as possible is time consuming but well worth the effort.

Regardless of which way the leader enters the system, there is typically a honeymoon period of several months when the leader is granted a great deal of leeway in terms of making decisions and establishing procedures. This is the ideal time to learn one's position and, if necessary, getting to know the organization's history. The two best ways to accomplish these tasks are by reading everything currently in the files that relates to physical education, and by meeting individually with every physical educator in the organization to begin to establish a relationship and to solicit ideas for the physical education program. In larger districts, leaders should at least try to meet with the department chairperson/team leader from each site or have small-group meetings by level or cluster.

As time goes on, an operational system should be established that allows all interested physical educators the opportunity to continue to influence the direction the district takes in terms of physical education. The best strategy for this is to set up a district physical education advisory committee. Ideally, there should be at least one representative from each school or building. However, it is equally important that anyone who wishes to join the committee feels welcome.

The purpose of the committee is to share information, determine the future of physical education in the district, and develop wish lists. This committee should meet approximately once a month, and should have a specific agenda so that the members feel a real need to attend. The members of the committee should be privy to information that is not typically sent to all physical educators. Members should be encouraged to share this information with their colleagues to keep them informed and to encourage their involvement.

It is important for the physical education advisory committee members to convey the information they hear back to their schools and solicit input from their colleagues for the next meeting. However, it also is important for the leader to have some type of direct contact with all physical educators. In small districts, this can be one-on-one discussions with visits to the physical educator's class. In larger districts, these type of discussions and visits may be prohibitive or at the very least rare. I have found a newsletter and other direct mailings effective for getting the message out to all. (Granted, not everyone will read the information, but at least everyone has equal access to it!) In order for this technique to be effective, however, the mailing must be sent to each physical educator rather than sending a single copy to the entire physical education department in hopes that it will reach all.

There also will be opportunities for oral presentations to all physical educators. It is important that these opportunities be viewed as an important way to establish relationships with the physical educators and to share the district's and the advisory committee's vision for physical education in the district. Such sharing of information and vision provides everyone with the opportunity to "buy in," ask questions, and contribute ideas. As technology advances and every site is connected to the Internet, a web site or listserv also can be a very effective form of communication.

An effective district leader also is one who takes the time to support each physical educator in his or her effort to be a professional. Providing membership applications for local professional associations and distributing flyers about local conferences and workshops can help teachers take their initial steps toward professional involvement. In addition, professional associations often provide the vehicle for recognizing exemplary teachers. The district leader can play an important role in nominating deserving teachers for various awards, such as outstanding teaching and service to the profession.

Relationships with Other Physical Education Professionals

Relationships with other physical education professionals include those between the district leader and coordinators in neighboring districts, personnel at institutes of higher education, and leaders of professional organizations. For each of these groups, collaborative projects promote the opportunity to contribute to and affect the implementation of quality physical education programs.

A consortium of district leaders can work together to create a common curriculum, a newsletter, or assessment tools. This collaboration results in a product that can be shared by all districts. Collaborative professional development opportunities also can be effective as long as there is sufficient room in the inservice for all interested parties. If the collaboration results in only a handful of educators from each district attending the inservice, then it may be better to plan and organize workshops only for one district.

Collaborative projects with personnel at institutes of higher education can include teacher action research projects where the university provides research expertise while the district provides the students and teachers for the research project. Other joint projects include membership on the district's advisory committee, presentations to teachers based on current research, preparation of student teachers, assistance with writing/revising curriculum, and development of proposals for grant funds.

Collaborative projects with members/leaders of the professional organizations also can prove to be mutually beneficial. I have personally found it effective to invite the professional organization in to handle all potentially political issues. For example, if the physical education advisory committee wants smaller class size, then the professional organization leaders are brought together to discuss the plan, leaving the issue outside the educational structure of the district.

Relationship with Site Administrators

Historically, the district leader for physical education carried the title of supervisor. Associated with this title was the responsibility for hiring and evaluating teachers. Over time and with the increased interest in site-based management, these responsibilities have typically shifted to the principal and the site-based decision-making council. As a result, the district leader for physical education must assume a new role with the site administrator.

Essentially, the leader becomes the staff person or consultant responsible for working with the physical education program. As such, the leader must constantly keep the site administrator up-to-date on physical education programs, concerns, and needs. This is important, since it is the site leader who will actually implement and oversee the programs. There is definitely a fine line between encouraging site administrators to implement the necessary programs to improve physical education and leaving enough room for the site administrator to make the final decisions. I have found that regularly scheduled meetings with site administrators (principals and assistant principals) as a group is an effective strategy for keeping them informed and letting them discuss projects. Also, depending on the size of the district, it is important to meet with the site administrator individually at least once a year to discuss ideas and concerns.

Relationship with District Office Administrators

The primary purpose of a strong relationship with other district office administrators (other subject area coordinators, directors, and assistant superintendents), including the superintendent, is to ensure equal funding and respect for physical education as compared to other subject areas. One of the first strategies is to get other district office administrators to refer to physical education as "physical education" and not "P.E.", "gym", or "athletics". Once the linguistics are in place, the second step is to educate colleagues on the purpose and features of a quality physical education program. The more they become aware of what physical education is, the more they can help to promote quality programs and begin collaborative programs that are inclusive of physical education.

A sure sign that the relationship between the district leader for physical education and the other district office administrators is weak is when there are projects going on in the district (e.g., professional development days, presentations to the board of education, interdisciplinary teams) that exclude physical education. A sure sign that the relationship is strong is when district administrators seek out physical education coordinators when questions/issues/opportunities in relationship to physical education and physical activity arise. It is important to note that the education of district office colleagues on the importance of quality physical education is never ending.

Relationship with Community Members

The relationship one develops with members of the community is typically related to the amount of public relations initiated by the district leader and other physical educators in the district. NASPE has published an outstanding document, Sport and Physical Education Advocacy Kit (1994), which provides a wealth of information on initiating and sustaining good relations with the community, including community organizations, business people, the press, legislators, and parents. Generally, any attempt at public relations should be based on a long-term public relations plan. One-shot or once-a-year programs don't provide the necessary sustained effort to effect a change in public opinion. If one-shot efforts did work, we wouldn't see the same commercial over and over again, or new commercials on the same product year after year. The folks in marketing know that they must keep their message constantly in view of the public.

The foundation for such a public relations plan is an excellent physical education program. The plan itself must be based on the truth, and the premise that the public has a right to be informed about the programs. All avenues of communication (e.g., newsletters, public presentations, mall events, newspaper, radio, television, web sites, cable) should be included. The message should be that physical education is no longer a "throw out the ball" program. Community members must be informed that physical education promotes physical fitness, health, motor skills, and psychosocial growth of their children. The following three steps help to ensure that your message is heard (Mohnsen 1997, p. 32):

1. Determine your message, including information on your current program and your future needs.
2. Use a variety of methods—print, video, audio, and displays—to present your message.
3. Don't give up—no matter what does or doesn't happen. Keep delivering your message.

Relationship with Board of Education

The district leader for physical education is in a very unique position to influence the district's board of education. Often the coordinator is allowed to officially address the board once a year to inform members of new programs, goals, successes, and challenges related to physical education. In order to increase this contact time, district leaders also can ask to make special presentations. These might include presenting the results of a district wide assessment (i.e., physical fitness testing), honoring a teacher or program for an outstanding performance, asking the board to acknowledge National Physical Education Week with a resolution, accepting a grant or donation from outside the district, or providing an update on an innovative program. The district leader also should encourage physical educators to get on the board of education's agenda to share information about their physical education programs.

There also are informal opportunities to affect the attitudes of board members. Social events that provide opportunities for conversations with individual board members can offer some of the most beneficial opportunities for change. For example, sharing stories of successful physical education programs and their effect on individual students can generate interest in the physical education program.

I was fortunate as a district leader in the Montebello Unified School District, because each coordinator was given the opportunity to influence the board members by decorating their office and meeting room once or twice a year. The selection of

student work, articles on quality programs, pictures of actual programs in the district, and results from program assessments all provided a silent avenue for educating the board on the features and importance of a quality physical education program. Offer to decorate the offices of your school board members!

If you are assuming from the length of this section that relationships form a significant portion of the leader's time in a district position, you are correct. For this position, and many other leadership positions, relationships are everything. This does not preclude the need for hard work, but hard work without relationships results in great programs that are rarely implemented.

Establish Policies and Procedures

How much do you pay teachers for extra duties? Can teachers borrow instructional materials from the district office? If yes, for how long? Must all physical educators be trained in CPR and First Aid? Are teachers paid for their time if they attend conferences on weekends?

Established policies and procedures will make these and other decisions easier. They also will help to establish consistency, so that there is equity in the treatment of all personnel. In fact, one study of the effectiveness of policies and procedures concluded that they pay for themselves in the long run by making the organization work (Horine 1991).

Policies are statements that guide decision making. They are based on truths, facts, and expert opinions. Procedures are methods or techniques for conducting activities. They describe the manner in which an activity must be accomplished. Although district administrators often write policies, they must be approved by the board of education. However, district administrators typically have the sole discretion to select procedures to carry out policies.

The first step in creating policies and procedures is to brainstorm a list of all areas that need consistency during the decision-making process. Then, review all current policies and procedures, looking for omissions and inconsistencies. Next, propose, in conjunction with the physical education advisory committee, new policies or procedures. Finally, have teachers and administrators—and in some cases legal counsel—review the new policies and procedures for additional input.

After board of education approval, the policies and procedures are then placed inside a policy handbook and distributed to the appropriate personnel. One copy per school is a minimum. Figure 10.1 provides a skeleton outline of policies and procedures for a district physical education program.

Develop a Curriculum for Assessment and Accountability

It is typically the legal responsibility of the local district to create and implement curricula. Nonetheless, there are numerous districts across the United States that either have no physical education curriculum or haven't reviewed it since the 1960s. This is a detriment to our profession, and district leaders must take the initiative to pursue the creation of a physical education curriculum for both student assessment and program accountability.

As noted in Chapter 3, there are National Standards and

FIGURE 10.1: Sample Outline for Policies and Procedures

I. **Equipment and supplies**
  A. Definition of equipment and supplies
  B. Centralized purchases
  C. Individual school purchases
  D. Maintenance and care
  E. Sharing of equipment and supplies

II. **Instruction materials**
  A. Approval for use in class
  B. Sharing of instructional materials

III. **Health and safety**
  A. Accident forms
  B. Treatment for injuries
  C. Certification of teachers in cardiopulmonary resuscitation and first aid

IV. **Additional duties**
  A. Salary for extra duties
  B. Compensation for attending professional development opportunities

V. **Interaction with teachers**
  A. Summative evaluation of teachers
  B. Formative evaluation of teachers

VI. **Data retention**
  A. Type of data for retention
  B. Length of retention

VII. **Transportation**
  A. Driver
  B. Supervision
  C. Guardian permission

VIII. **Office**
  A. Personnel
  B. Operation

IX. **Facilities**
  A. Maintenance
  B. Permits for use
  C. Fees
  D. Safety

numerous models and samples of curriculum to assist the district leader with this task. These resources should be used to assist with the process and eliminate redundancy while still allowing for local needs and buy-in from the physical educators.

As difficult as the creation of a physical education curriculum may be, the implementation of that curriculum is far more difficult. The first step is the selection of the curriculum committee. If the committee consists only of individuals who are new to the district or who hold a particular philosophy, then implementation will be even more difficult. It is the responsibility of the local leader to ensure that all schools, grade levels, and points of view are represented on the committee. This will certainly contribute to more lively discussions than if everyone were of one mind, but it also will help to ensure the acceptance of the new curriculum by all involved. It should be noted that committee members have the responsibility for sharing their discussions and work with other members of their departments and soliciting their ideas throughout the curriculum development process.

Once the curriculum is completed and adopted by the local board of education, the task still is not complete. Three steps remain. First, a timeline must be created showing the implementation cycle. Will the entire curriculum be implemented at once? Will the curriculum be implemented at certain grade levels first? Will certain parts of the curriculum be implemented at each grade level?

Second, there must be an assessment piece that holds the physical educators accountable for implementation. How will you know if your physical educators are following the curriculum? Will you be asking for facility assignments? Will you be asking for unit or lesson plans? Will you want to see evidence of implementation, such as samples of student work?

Third, the local leader must provide professional development opportunities for the physical educators to assist them with the implementation of the curriculum. Will you simply ask your physical educators to sink or swim, or will you have a systematic plan for professional development that addresses all components of the new curriculum? Will you provide a variety of pathways for physical educators to secure the new information related to the curriculum?

Provide Professional Development

Professional development helps physical educators implement a new curriculum, and it helps them between curriculum rewrites to constantly upgrade their skills and to stay abreast of new ideas and research. Again, it is not uncommon to visit districts where there has been no professional development specifically for physical educators in years. District leaders have a fundamental responsibility for ensuring that continual professional development occurs in their district that meets the needs of the physical educators.

Chapter 4 does an excellent job describing the important elements of professional development; therefore, this section will focus on the points important to the district leader. It is especially important at the district level for the professional development model to include guest speakers, opportunities for physical educators to discuss issues and share ideas, and optional opportunities for learning, which include making contributions to the profession, visiting other schools, and developing personal plans for life long learning.

Guest speakers—especially at the start of the school year—can bring a more global perspective of physical education to the audience. An effective guest speaker provides both motivation and content. The content, objectives, and long-range plan for the district's physical education program, along with state and local laws and politics should be articulated by the district leader, so that the guest speaker can focus on the specific needs of the physical educators.

Guest speakers should be planned for well in advance, so that there is time to complete all paperwork and arrangements. All verbal arrangements with the speaker should be followed by formal approval from the local board of education and written verification to the speaker. Often, speakers will arrange for their own air transportation, but local transportation and lodging should be arranged by the district. Compensation will vary from speaker to speaker, and needs to be negotiated up front. Typically the speaker's fee does not include expenses, so the speaker must submit receipts at the conclusion of the trip along with an invoice for payment.

Some sporting goods manufacturers (e.g., Sportime, US Games, Polar) will assist with the compensation and/or transportation expenses for speakers. Simply keep in mind that the manufacturers support speakers who promote their products. This may or may not be in keeping with your district's needs or long-range professional development plans.

Staff development days during the year provide another opportunity for physical educators to learn and apply new ideas and teaching strategies. It can be especially effective if all schools or groups of schools in the district share common staff development days. This provides additional opportunities for guest speakers and for collaboration among physical educators who can learn much from their colleagues.

Whatever the focus of these days, it is important to stay with an ongoing topic, such as teaching strategies, assessment, or technology rather than jumping from topic to topic. Sometimes, you will also be faced with educators returning late from lunch or not returning at all, or leaving early. As the district leader, you can set the professional tone for the meeting by letting the physical educators know what is expected of them for the day, including the agenda, signing in and out procedures, and new learning. In addition, prior arrangements should be made so that athletic contests and practices do not occur on the these days. Finally, at each staff development I like to give away equipment, books, and materials randomly. However, I distribute the tickets for the drawings immediately following lunch.

Ongoing professional development opportunities also can be provided after school, on weekends, during the evenings, and during the school day. Although—with appropriate funding— substitutes can be provided for school day inservices, the question is how to compensate teachers for attending after school, weekend, and evening events. Some districts have special compensation packages (i.e., $25 per hour) written into the teacher's contract. Another strategy involves working with a local institute of higher education so that college credit is provided for attendance at inservices. A third strategy is to provide instructional materials to teachers who attend workshops. It is important, whichever strategy is selected, to have it spelled out in the district policy/procedure manual.

Contributing to professional activities is another way to increase your teachers' learning while simultaneously having them give something back to the profession. Many professionals have found that contributing to the profession renews their own excitement about the role they play in the lives of the students. It also provides opportunities for contact with other professionals who can validate instructional strategies, ideas, and feelings. Involvement with one's professional association as an officer or committee member, participating on a schoolwide committee, supervising a student teacher, and making presentations to colleagues or community groups are all opportunities for giving and receiving.

"A picture is worth a thousand words" certainly holds true for implementing a new teaching idea or strategy. Providing opportunities for your teachers to see the actual strategy in action with students often convinces them that the technique is valuable and worth trying. In addition, visits to other schools provide opportunities for discussions with other teachers. Visitations, whenever possible, should be done in teams, or at least in pairs. The dialogue that results between two or more participants can be much more valuable than the single thoughts of one individual. It also is important to provide teachers with specific questions to ask and points to observe, so that they are ready to benefit from the experience.

Just like school-aged students, adults learn in different ways. It is important to encourage teachers to develop their own personal plans for life long learning. Reading, listening, and discussing are all effective strategies for pursuing new information. In addition to local inservices, there also are numerous conferences and conventions, not to mention graduate school and online courses (see Chapter 11). However, it is important that the learning plan be written ahead of time, so that the goals—along with the process and product of the learning—are documented.

Maximize Resources

Often, the district's general fund provides district leaders with a physical education instructional budget for professional development and sometimes even for instructional materials. Typically this budget is minimal and allows for only a few activities per year. However, many district leaders also have budgets for various grants, especially if they are in charge of health education or health service programs. District coordinators also may have access to additional funds due to their relationship with the technology, recreation, or interdisciplinary budgets. It is important to always be on the lookout for additional sources of revenue and to ensure that each expenditure represents the best use of the allocated funds. In addition, district leaders need to provide guidance, and perhaps centralized purchasing, so that all physical educators in the district get the greatest purchasing power from their budgets.

Each year, the previous year's budget is analyzed, and a new budget request is prepared. Often referred to as "zero based" budgeting, each year's request for funds starts from ground zero. Each budget area request for funds, even if it is the same amount as the previous year, needs to be justified in terms of student learning. For example, an inservice on effective instructional software and textbooks is linked to increased student learning, since it provides additional instructional strategies for student learning. The district's physical education long-range plan and an inventory of any holdings will help with preparation. Once the budget is constructed and the justification pieces in place, the budget is presented to your administrator and, eventually, to the board of education for approval before any expenditures can be made.

Once the budget is approved, each expenditure must still be approved by the district's board of education. Often, leaders believe that as long as they have money in their budgets, they can purchase whatever they want. This is not the case. Each purchase must be justified, as was the original budget.

Centralized purchasing of physical education supplies and equipment, whether the money comes from the district's budget or each school's budget, reduces the overall cost to the district. As the district leader for physical education, it is your responsibility to write up the specifications for equipment and supplies, so that the district's purchasing department can initiate the bidding process.

During the bidding process, vendors submit quotes for the cost of each item. The items must meet the specifications you developed in order to be considered. Therefore, it is important to be very specific. If you simply request volleyballs, the lowest bid may be for a rubber ball that deflates easily.

I use a supply/equipment selection committee to assist with the writing of the specifications, and a feedback form for physical educators to report any deficiencies to me. I have found that even though mass (centralized) purchasing clearly reduces the cost of the materials, it is also important to leave some room for innovative purchases and creativity on the part of individual teachers.

Most, if not all, districts have accounting departments that monitor expenses. However, the accounting is often several weeks or months behind actual expenses. So, with the current availability of computers, it is a good idea to keep your own accounting of expenditures. This provides you with up-to-the-minute information on how much money is left in the budget for emergencies or special purchases.

So far, we have been discussing the day-to-day operation budget available in most districts. However, it is equally important to maintain a prioritized wish list. Simply imagine if $1,000, $10,000, or $100,000 were given to you tomorrow. What would you spend it on? This becomes your wish list. As much as this may sound like wishful thinking, it is not. There are times when grants or grant opportunities actually come along, and it is those individuals who are prepared who get the funds.

The creation of the wish list often provides the impetus for the district leader to look for additional funding. This can be in the form of fundraising, grant writing, and the use of alternative funds in creative ways. Chapter 5 does an excellent job covering fundraising and grant writing. As a district leader, however, it is important to be on the lookout for any and all alternative funding sources. A request for proposals was once sent out from our state department of education for using technology across the curriculum—specifically those subject areas with state frameworks were listed. Physical education, as is often the case, was omitted from the list. But, since a framework was in the process of being developed, we applied for the grant anyway. We not only received the funding for using technology to teach analysis of movement to our high school students, we also were

awarded one of the largest grants in the state.

One unique area for securing additional funds is by tapping into other grants and programs that have similar outcomes to physical education and utilizing some of that money for physical education programs. I have found the Federal Drug Free Schools money to be a great resource for funding fitness equipment for adult wellness centers and project adventure ropes courses. The connection for the ropes courses is the research on the use of ropes courses in drug withdrawal programs. The connection with fitness equipment for adult wellness centers is the modeling of healthy behaviors by the teachers, administrators, and community members. Of course, the low ropes course and fitness equipment also are used during physical education.

In California, we have tobacco prevention education money, and we have found this to be a great source of revenue for heart monitors. The legislation states that tobacco money must be used to educate students on heart/lung physiology, and what better way than to put the student in touch with their own physiology. One last example deals with a recreation budget that was quite extensive in one district. At each site, the recreation personnel were required to collect data and submit monthly reports. This provided the opening for the purchase of computers for the recreation personnel, who also happened to be the physical educators. This allowed for a computer to be placed in each physical education office at every middle school in the district. Again, it was used for the recreation program, but also for the physical education program.

Although funds are typically not allocated to the district physical education leader to maintain and construct new facilities, should rehab funds or new construction funds find their way to a district, it is the physical education leader who will be asked for input on the plans. It is certainly beyond the scope of this book to get into specifics on facility planning; however, there are a number of good books, such as Play for All Guidelines (Moore, et al. 1987), Facility Planning for Physical Education, Recreation, and Athletics (Flynn 1993), and Points About Playgrounds (Christiansen 1995) that will provide you with the necessary information should the time arrive.

Implement New Programs

Conducting a good physical education program means more than maintaining the status quo. It means pushing the envelope, trying new ideas, and implementing new programs. It means being proactive or anticipative rather than reactive.

As a district leader, you no doubt will have a number of new ideas that you will want to implement. But, it also is important to find out what your teachers want to try, and to encourage them and support their creativity. The district's physical education advisory committee is typically the best place for teachers to share creative ideas and set goals and priorities.

At the district level, I found it beneficial to not only bring together the physical educators, but also the health educators, nurses, counselors/psychologists, nutritionists, risk managers, and facilities directors. Collectively, this committee was known as the Healthy Kids Advisory Committee, and it was based on the coordinated school health model. Its purpose was to share programs, ideas, and concerns, and to create a collective vision of where the school district needed to go in terms of student health and wellness. This committee also served as the advisory committee for several drug prevention and tobacco prevention grants. Thus, we had input from a variety of programs in terms of how best to spend the money. As noted earlier, some benefits of this collaboration for physical education included low ropes courses, heart monitors, and fitness centers.

In other districts where I have visited, the district leader and physical educators have focused their energy on bringing technology into physical education programs; creating authentic assessment tools, including samples for each rubric level; inservicing the entire staff on social initiatives; and increasing the activity offerings through inservices throughout the year on new activities. Regardless of the thrust, the most effective programs are those that gain the support of everyone involved.

Use Time Efficiently and Effectively

It is important to use time efficiently and effectively in order to get more accomplished each day; however, it is equally important to prevent stress and burnout. The role of middle management is literally that—in the middle. Forever feeling the expectations of the superintendent and board of education, along with empathy for the realities experienced by the teachers in the field, as middle management you will no doubt experience constant role conflict. This role conflict, along with the other pressures of the job, can quickly lead to stress. So, what can you do?

Some people are more comfortable working around clutter, while others require a neat office; regardless, there needs to be some order to your office. You must be able to quickly find requested items and pieces of information. How many times have you looked for the same information? How much time did this require?

In addition to a neat office, I have found that the creation of information packets covering common questions and requests for information (i.e., coeducational physical education, class size, research on quality physical education) saves me an incredible amount of time, since I can quickly send the requester the appropriate packet.

Equally important to having the items you need is discarding the materials that you no longer require. Each piece of paper should only be touched once before taking action on it. Look at it and read it, and then either file it, deal with it, or throw it away. It may take time to clean your office, but like many organizational tasks, the rewards are worth the effort. Take time each June, or whichever month is best for you, and throw out files and papers that are no longer needed. Update and backup important electronic files, and delete those that are no longer necessary. A neatly organized office will reduce your stress and allow you to work more effectively.

The most important relationship is the one you establish with your secretary. The time invested in describing projects and programs along with specific details for each assigned task will reap dividends in time saved. The better informed your secretary, the more he or she will be able to handle questions for you and lighten some of your work load. In addition, the more prepared your secretary is, the more you will be able to delegate.

Communication—by mail, phone, e-mail, or visits—can fill up your day and prevent you from accomplishing important long-term projects. This, in turn, leads to greater stress and burnout. Managing your communications is a key to staying efficient and effective. The first rule is to group the various types of correspondence and then allocate a specific amount of time to this necessary task each day. It is important to stay on top of these tasks, otherwise they will become unmanageable. Some folks like to address them first thing in the morning; others like to do them in the afternoon when their energy level starts to drop. Regardless of when you assign time to do it, do it once a day and then focus on your major projects.

Efforts to communicate by mail, phone, or one-on-one conversations take a great deal of time, but I find that meetings take even more time. Before calling a meeting, answer a few but important questions:

- Can I accomplish the purpose of this meeting without actually having a meeting (i.e., can the information be sent out for reading, or will a conference call suffice)?
- Who really needs to be at the meeting?
- How much time needs to be allocated for the meeting?
- What is the precise agenda for the meeting? (Send it out ahead of time so people come prepared.)

Once the decision is made to go forth with the meeting, be sure to start and stop on time. Ask if there are any additional items for the agenda, and then follow the agenda. Respect the time of the attendees by limiting off-task conversations that prevent the agenda from moving along. In the same vein, only attend meetings where the purpose, goals, agenda, and time frames are defined and relevant to you. Prepare ahead of time by reading the agenda and collecting the necessary materials to fully participate in the discussions.

If you are having difficulty managing your time or finding the time to complete important projects, begin to monitor how you spend your time. Look for items that can be grouped together for more efficient use of time, and look for items that can be eliminated or delegated. Also, ask yourself the hard question, "Am I procrastinating?" Often, we procrastinate out of fear—we want to perform the job perfectly, and out of fear of failure, we tend to put important long-range projects on the back burner.

Another common deterrent to completing tasks is constantly preparing for activities (i.e., professional development, meetings) at the last minute. This tends to create crisis situations that in turn take up more of your time. Instead, take a long-range (one year) view of what you plan to accomplish, and then break it down into monthly, weekly, and daily tasks. Commit yourself to finishing the piece assigned to each day. Prioritize your day so that you can follow through on your commitments. You will find that you end up with more time, because you are not constantly putting out fires.

Above all else, the answer to relieving stress and burnout is to have a life outside the office. Often, leadership positions can become all encompassing. Early morning tasks, major projects to work on throughout the day, meetings in the late afternoons when teachers are free, and evening/weekend activities can quickly overtake your life. It is important to learn to say "no" once your plate is full. Inasmuch as you schedule time for meetings and workshops, also schedule time for working on projects, so you don't have to take them home. Also, schedule time during the day to take a walk and simply reflect. Remember, we are in the business of physical education, and we know the importance of physical activity for health and wellness. You find that you come back refreshed and can actually accomplish more.

Chapter Summary

District leadership positions are changing and, in some cases, declining as we move into the new millennium. Those currently in district leadership positions must strive toward promoting quality physical education programs within their district, and they must encourage others districts to enlist the services of a physical education leader. The question really comes down to (depending on the size of the district): Is it worth having a district leader if it means that each physical educator in the district must increase his or her class size by one student? If we look at the research, the answer is an overwhelming "yes".

It is the district leader who develops and maintains relationships with all stakeholders; establishes policies and procedures; ensures the development of a curriculum; makes creative use of funds, including the solicitation of new funds; ensures that professional development opportunities meet the needs of the physical educators; and infuses the district with innovative and creative programs.

While much is asked of teachers, even more is asked of leaders. A final responsibility of a leader is to maintain his or her own physical and mental health by utilizing time effectively and efficiently including a sufficient amount of "me time" to maintain balance in his or her own life.

References

Bucher, C. A. (1997). *Management of physical education and sport* (11th ed.). DuBuque, IA: WCB/MCGraw-Hill.

Christiansen, M. L. (1995). *Points about playgrounds.* Arlington, VA: National Recreation and Park Association.

Evaul, T. (1995). *Characteristics of quality physical education programs.* Paper presented at the AAHPERD National Convention, Portland, OR.

Flynn, R. B. (1993). *Facility planning for physical education, recreation, and athletics.* Reston, VA: AAHPERD.

Horine, L. (1991). *Administration of physical education and sport programs* (2nd ed.). Dubuque, IA: Wm. C. Brown.

Jensen, C. R. (1988). *Administrative management of physical education and athletic programs* (2nd ed.). Philadelphia, PA: Lea and Febiger.

Mohnsen, B. S. (1997). *Teaching middle school physical education: A blueprint for developing an exemplary program.* Champaign, IL: Human Kinetics.

Moore, R. C., Goltsman, S. M., & Iacofano, D. S. (1987). *Play for all guidelines.* Berkeley, CA: MIG Communications.

National Association for Sport & Physical Education. (1994). *Sport and physical education advocacy kit.* Reston, VA: Author.

Pestolesi, R. A., & Sinclair, W. A. (1978). *Creative administration in physical education and athletics.* Englewood Cliffs, NJ: Prentice-Hall.

Railey, J. H., & Railey-Tschauner, P. (1993). *Managing physical education, fitness, and sports programs* (2nd ed.). Mountain View, CA: Mayfield.

Tillman, K., Voltmer, E. F., Esslinger, A. A., & McCue, B. (1996). *The administration of physical education, sport, and leisure programs* (6th ed.). Needham Heights, MA: Allyn & Bacon.

The New Leadership Paradigm for Physical Education

CHAPTER 11

Regional Leadership

Bonnie Mohnsen

Regional leadership refers to any leadership position where the leader is responsible for more than one school district. This can be a formal position with a county office (California) or area educational agency (Iowa), an informal position as the designated leader for a consortium of several school districts as described in the previous chapter, or a private consultant for several districts in a local area.

For example, I work for the Orange County (California) Department of Education, which oversees 27 school districts representing more than 400,000 students. My job is different from a state leader who oversees all schools in one state, and it is different from a district leader who is only responsible for the schools within one district. Regional leaders assist physical educators who work for different superintendents and boards of education with separate mission statements, curricula, and yearly agendas. One of the greatest challenges for a regional leader is guiding the different school systems in a coordinated effort toward quality physical education.

A typical list of duties for a regional level physical education administrator includes the following:

- Plan, prioritize, assign, review, and participate in the work of staff responsible for the coordination and implementation of the state physical education framework.

- Recommend and assist in the implementation of goals and objectives, establish schedules and methods for providing physical education instructional programs, implement policies and procedures.

- Organize, schedule, and implement a variety of training programs and workshops dealing with the physical education curriculum; provide consultation and technical assistance to all school districts in the area of physical education.

- Promote and coordinate activities relating to the implementation of the physical education curriculum; prepare program event materials, including news releases, flyers, schedules of events, pamphlets, and brochures.

- Oversee, monitor, and supervise the development of program curricula and instructional strategies and activities; coordinate the development, selection, and procurement of instructional materials and equipment.

- Maintain awareness of developments in the physical education instructional fields, incorporate developments into programs as appropriate.

- Coordinate and support the cooperation of agencies involved with physical education, prepare presentations on program goals and objectives.

- Participate in the preparation and administration of the program's budget, submit budget recommendations and monitor expenditures.

Typical employment opportunity flyers note the following requirements for regional leadership:

- Knowledge of:
  - Physical education curricula
  - Community-based organizations and educational agencies that support physical education
  - Basic operations, services, and activities of the instructional area
  - Basic procedures, methods, and techniques of budget preparation and control
  - Evaluation and assessment techniques used in determining proper teaching and instructional methods
  - Recent developments, current literature, and sources of information related to instructional methods
  - Modern office equipment, including computers
  - Education codes and the policies, rules, and regulations of the governing agency
  - Pertinent federal, state, and local laws, codes, and regulations.

- Skill to:
  - Coordinate, direct, and implement instructional programs suited to the needs of the community
  - Recommend and implement goals, objectives, and practices for providing effective and efficient instructional programs
  - Direct staff development programs on various subject areas
  - Plan, direct, and coordinate various programs

- Elicit community and organizational support for instructional programs
- Make public presentations
- Understand and interpret pertinent state education and administrative codes, policies, and procedures
- Maintain mental capacity that allows the capability of making sound decisions and demonstrating intellectual capabilities
- Communicate effectively in the English language both in oral and written form
- Create and maintain strong cooperative relationships with community agencies, school personnel, and professional individuals
- Develop and deliver presentations to a variety of audiences.

Given these responsibilities, the seven selected major points for this chapter are:

1. Be a Visionary
2. Create an Advisory Committee
3. Communicate the Vision to all Stakeholders
4. Create Models
5. Provide Inclusive Professional Development
6. Be Creative with Funding Issues
7. Groom a Replacement.

Be a Visionary

In the current world, the only constant is change. Therefore, a leader must be adaptable to change. But more importantly, a leader must initiate many of the changes as they relate to his or her areas of responsibilities.

Before someone assumes the job of regional leader, he or she needs to ask, "Why do I really want this job?" If the answer relates to getting out of the classroom, having more power, or increasing one's status, the individual may want to reconsider. However, if the reason is due to a burning desire to improve physical education or, better yet, a compelling vision of how to improve physical education, the agency has found the right person for the job.

All new jobs offer the employee a "honeymoon period" during the first several weeks of employment. This is the one period when a leader may have free time. This honeymoon period is an ideal time to accomplish two tasks in particular. The first is reading everything possible related to the job. Often, employees leave a set of files when they leave their positions. Take this time to go through the files page by page, taking notes and recording ideas as they come to mind. Familiarize yourself with all local, state, and federal policies, procedures, and legal codes. Being aware of constraints and requirements is not only beneficial in terms of questions you will be asked but also in terms of setting up the parameters for your vision of quality physical education.

The second task is to record your personal vision for quality physical education in the region. The vision should include what the programs in various districts will look like at the end of your first year of tenure; what the programs in various

districts will look like at the end of your third year of tenure; and what the program in various districts will look like at the end of your fifth year of tenure. These thoughts should be posted somewhere in your office, so that you can refer to them often and note the extent to which you implement them. Then, you should write down ways to reach each part of the vision. These become your intermediate goals, and they should be prioritized. It is important that your vision and your intermediate goals are specific and attainable.

Although the honeymoon period is an ideal time to record your personal vision, it may not all come to you in one sitting, in a few weeks, or even in the first year. Therefore, I make it a point to never be without a notepad or computer on which to record my thoughts. Unique ideas and brilliant solutions do not arrive on a predetermined schedule. As leaders, we must be prepared to accept these insights whenever they appear and record them so that they don't become fleeting thoughts.

Colleagues, leaders in charge of other programs in your region, and leaders with similar responsibilities in neighboring regional systems can provide additional impetus for the creation of new visions. Discussing projects, ideas, and concerns can lead to new goals for the following year. Finally, discussions with these individuals can lead to collaborative projects that support both your vision and that of your colleagues.

Create an Advisory Committee

It is important to know one's own beliefs and to have a personal vision for quality physical education. However, in order to implement change, the vision must be broader than one individual. The creation of an advisory committee can institutionalize the vision for physical education, assist with implementation of the vision, and help to address issues as they arise.

The Orange County physical education advisory committee is open to any administrator, elementary teacher (both elementary teachers and physical education teachers teach K-6 physical education), middle school physical educator, high school physical educator, and community member in the area. However, we also work very hard to encourage every district to send at least one representative. We meet three times a year, with subcommittee meetings occurring more frequently.

The first task of the advisory committee is to create its vision. This vision must be broader than the one created for each district, since it must encompass the needs and desires of various school systems. This process alone can take up to a year (three meetings), especially if committee members have never before created a vision. Initially, advisory committee members brainstorm their visionary ideas. Then, committee members select one vision to work on in-depth. For each vision statement, committee members write activities for year one, year two, and year three. Figure 11.1 shows the three-year plan that the Orange County physical education advisory committee developed. Note the inclusion of an evaluation piece to ensure implementation of both the activities and the ultimate vision.

During each year of implementation, subcommittees are formed to work on areas of emphasis. For example, in year one of the Orange County plan, the following subcommittees were created: adopt-a-playground/fitness center, family involvement, public relations, and staff wellness. For year two, public relations, family involvement, and assessment subcommittees were formed. For year three, interdisciplinary and leadership subcommittees were formed.

Typical agendas for advisory committee meetings include introductions and sharing by committee members, coordinator update, discussion of common issues, and subcommittee work (three-year plan). It is the subcommittee work and the constant movement toward the three-year vision that provides committee members with a very concrete reason for staying actively involved. I find that it also is very important to offer these folks additional incentives for attending meetings. These include valuable information, sources for free equipment and supplies, and opportunities for professional growth that are unavailable to other educators in the region.

Communicate the Vision to All Stakeholders

Having a vision is great, but sharing the vision with everyone involved makes it a reality. In the last chapter, the stakeholders for a district were defined; at the regional level the stakeholders include all those stakeholders from each district. Therefore, the number of possible relationships for the leader increases at an exponential rate. As the regional leader for physical education, you become a spokesperson for the profession. Effective leaders are, above all, good storytellers. All interactions provide potential opportunities for promoting physical education. Often, it is the personal relationships we create that result in tremendous leaps and bounds in the promotion of physical education.

I have made it a point to advocate for physical education during all interactions with my colleagues at the Orange County Department of Education. I have taught each and every person to say "physical education" instead of "P.E." In addition, I have made it a point to include physical education in every regional project (e.g., technology plan, interdisciplinary models, administrative training programs, video development).

Recently, I mentioned to a colleague in charge of our academic decathlon (knowledge competition for high school students) that physical education was still not part of this activity. She replied that as soon as I wrote a test (50 questions), she would include it. The next week, I walked into her office and handed her the test. I believe that the number one reason for the inclusion of physical education in the academic decathlon was my personal relationship with this colleague. The second reason was that I didn't procrastinate in developing the test.

Because we in regional leadership are accountable to various educational agencies in our geographic area, we must maintain communication with the boards of education, superintendents, administrative staff, and teachers in each and every district. I have found the distribution of an elementary and a secondary physical education newsletter a must in maintaining open communication with the 20,000-plus educators in my region. The newsletter is published three times per year (September, January, and April). It always contains a listing of workshops, a calendar of events, and a coordinator update. In addition, timely news articles are included, along with in-depth coverage of a specific topic (e.g., curriculum development, assessment, playground equipment and safety, lesson plans). The newsletter also is used to introduce new physical education products that have been developed by the Orange County Department of Education.

A collaborative relationship with the local professional organization is a must. Often, an educational agency cannot become politically involved in issues; however, professional organizations can and should take political stands on issues that affect their membership. A mutually beneficial relationship with a professional organization can serve the profession well. For example, in my region, we are currently in the process of establishing a foundation for physical education as one of our subcommittee public relations projects. Although I have the time and expertise to do the paper work and leg work required to establish the foundation, the professional organization is in a much better position to oversee the foundation.

Institutes of higher education (IHE) also are important entities with which to establish open communication. A positive, collaborative relationship with these institutes can result in better qualified new teachers. I am often invited by our local IHE to speak to their students about projects and inservices available throughout the region. In turn, I invite a representative from each IHE to attend our regional advisory committee meetings. Because more and more grants are requiring collaboration, a positive working relationship with your local IHEs can result in additional funds for both programs. Finally, a strong relationship with the IHE can provide academic credit for your professional development learning opportunities.

Create Models

If I divided my time between the 27 school districts, 400 schools, 600 physical educators, and 20,000 teachers/administrators in Orange County, I would accomplish very little. However, the development of models, including curriculum standards, unit plans/lesson plans, instructional materials, and assessment tools, along with the process for replicating and using these tools goes a long way toward assisting many teachers and administrators in the region.

In 1994, our first official state physical education framework was published. Many of the districts in the region had either never written a physical education curriculum, or the curriculum was 20 to 30 years old. Our framework, which is similar to the National Standards for Physical Education, is based on a conceptual curriculum model; however, most of the administrators and educators in the region were familiar with an activity model. Each of these facts pointed to the need for sample physical education exit and grade level standards.

Although each of the 27 school districts in Orange County have or are in the process of developing their own physical education standards, the region's model standards have served as an example of what is necessary in order to align with the framework. In addition, the process that the sample curriculum committee piloted has served as a model for the districts as they worked on their curricula. It is interesting to note that, even though each district has created a physical education curriculum committee and worked through the process themselves, the standards across the school districts are very similar. This fact has facilitated the creation of unit/lesson plan models and instructional materials along with sample assessment tools.

Once most of the districts finished their curriculum standards, they began to ask about model physical education lesson

FIGURE 11.1: Orange County Department of Education Three-Year Plan for Physical Education

Vision 1

Expectancy

All students have equal access to appropriate and sufficient equipment, supplies, and technology

Activities/Timelines

- *First Year:*

Identify and support one elementary, middle school, and high school in the use of technology in physical education

Provide workshops on the use of technology in physical education

Describe the use of technology in physical education in the spring newsletter

Publish in the winter newsletter a comprehensive list of equipment and supplies (noting the availability of free equipment and supplies) that support the framework

- *Second Year:*

Identify and support one elementary, middle school, and high school in the use of technology in physical education

Provide workshops on the use of technology in physical education

Continue to identify free and inexpensive resources for physical education equipment and supplies, along with a suggested budgetary figure for physical education equipment

Create an "Adopt-a-Playground" program

Create an "Adopt-a-Fitness Center" program

- *Third Year:*

Identify and support one elementary, middle school, and high school in each district in the use of technology in physical education

Provide workshops on technology in physical education

Continue to identify free and inexpensive resources for physical education equipment and supplies

Implement an "Adopt-a-Playground" program

Implement an "Adopt-a-Fitness Center" program

Costs

- *First Year:*

Technology hardware/software funds for identified schools

- *Second Year:*

Technology hardware/software funds for identified schools

- *Third Year:*

Sponsorship for "Adopt-a-Playground"

Sponsorship for "Adopt-a-Fitness Center"

Technology hardware/software funds for identified schools

Evaluation

Survey schools to determine status of technology equipment

Survey schools to determine status of equipment and supplies

Survey schools to determine status of "Adopt-a-Playground" program

Survey schools to determine status of "Adopt-a-Fitness Center" program

Vision 2

Expectancy

All students, teachers, and families participate in life long wellness and physical activities

Activities/Timelines

- *First Year:*

Create a staff wellness plan

Create a fit family program (age-appropriate activities that parents can do with their children); this became "Families in Training" and is sponsored by Pacific Mutual

- *Second Year:*

Inservice physical educators on staff wellness plan

Implement "Families in Training" at 15 elementary schools

- *Third Year:*

Implement staff wellness program in one school in each district

Implement "Families in Training" at 30 elementary schools

Costs

- *Second Year:*

Funding for fit family ("Families in Training") program

- *Third Year:*

Personnel for wellness program

Funding for fit family ("Families in Training") program

Evaluation

Survey schools to determine status of staff wellness programs

Survey schools to determine status of fit family ("Families in Training") program

Vision 3

Expectancy

All students succeed in the physical education curriculum

Activities/Timelines

- *First Year:*

Each district identifies one lead teacher to attend Orange County Department of Education workshops and communicate information back to district

Provide district level workshops on the framework, including setting a positive environment

Each district creates a K-12 physical education curriculum based on the framework

Provide countywide workshops on developing unit and lesson plans along with effective instructional strategies (after school, week-long summer institute)

Create an elementary physical education certification program

Write the script for a video on sheltered instruction in physical education

- *Second Year:*

Each district and secondary school identifies one lead teacher to attend Orange County Department of Education workshops and communicate information back to district and school

Each district creates a K-12 physical education curriculum based on the framework

Develop daily lesson plans for K-5

Provide countywide workshop on teaching elementary lesson plans

Develop unit plans for one-third of the instructional units for grades 6-10

Provide countywide workshops on teaching middle school and high school units

Provide countywide leadership series for physical educators

Get approval for elementary physical education certification program

Produce video on sheltered instruction in physical education

Develop K-12 sample physical education portfolio

- *Third Year:*

Each district and school identifies one lead teacher to attend Orange County Department of Education workshops and communicate information back to district and school

Each district creates or implements a

K-12 physical education curriculum based on the framework, and adjusts it as necessary

Provide countywide workshop on teaching elementary lesson plans

Develop unit plans for one-third of the instructional units for grades 6-10

Provide countywide workshops on teaching middle school and high school units

Provide countywide physical education leadership academy to selected group of physical educators

Implement elementary physical education certification program

Distribute video on sheltered instruction in physical education

Develop K-12 sample physical education portfolio

■ **Costs**
   – *All Years:*
District stipends or substitute time for professional development activities

■ **Evaluation**
Check sign-in sheets for attendance at professional development activities

Survey schools for documentation on school level workshops

Survey schools on implementation of curriculum and unit/lesson plans (possible visitations)

Survey elementary certification participants as to quality and effectiveness of program

Completion of products (portfolio, video)

Vision 4
■ **Expectancy**
Physical education is viewed by all as an equal and integrated component of the education system

■ **Activities/Timelines**
   – *First Year:*
Create and distribute information on the importance of physical educators being members of schoolwide committees

Work on sample interdisciplinary models that include physical education content

Create sample inservices on wellness and social initiatives that physical education teachers can present to other staff members

   – *Second Year:*
At least one schoolwide committee at

each secondary school has a physical education teacher member

Distribute sample interdisciplinary models that include physical education content on request

Create additional sample interdisciplinary models that include physical education content.

Provide countywide inservices on how to present wellness and social initiatives to staff members

Provide countywide inservice on interdisciplinary models including physical education

Include physical education in academic decathlon program

Distribute press releases to local media

Create a video public service announcement

Create a packet containing research on the importance of quality physical education

   – *Third Year:*
At least two schoolwide committees at each secondary school have a physical education teacher member

Distribute sample interdisciplinary models that include physical education content to all secondary schools

Each middle school and high school physical education staff will provide one presentation (wellness or social initiatives) for their entire staff

Distribute press releases to local media

Distribute video public service announcement

Distribute packet containing research on the importance of quality physical education

■ **Costs**
   – *Second Year:*
Create public service announcement

■ **Evaluation**
Survey schools to determine membership in schoolwide committees

Survey schools to determine how interdisciplinary models are being utilized

Survey schools to determine number of presentations by physical educators to entire staff

Statistics on number of showings of public service announcement

Number of press releases published

Inclusion in academic decathlon program

Distribution and use of quality physical education research packet

Vision 5
■ **Expectancy**
Physical education teachers are viewed as educators by school officials, parents, and community members

■ **Activities/Timelines**
   – *First Year:*
Membership in the California Association for Health, Physical Education, Recreation and Dance is increased by 10 percent

All physical educators attend one workshop, inservice, or conference on physical education

   – *Second Year:*
Membership in the California Association for Health, Physical Education, Recreation and Dance is increased by 10 percent

All physical educators attend one workshop or conference on physical education outside their school district

Create sample presentations for school boards, business leaders, and parent/community groups

Press releases on the progress of "Everyone Can Through Quality Physical Education" are distributed countywide

   – *Third Year:*
Membership in the California Association for Health, Physical Education, Recreation, and Dance is increased by 10 percent

All physical educators attend two workshops or conferences on physical education or a related education area outside their school district

In each district, a presentation is made to the school board, one business group, and one parent/ community group

Brochure created and distributed countywide on quality physical education and the progress of "Everyone Can Through Quality Physical Education"

■ **Costs**
   – *Third Year:*
Creation and printing of brochures

plans—especially for the elementary level, where we have very few physical education specialists. We looked at the various commercial elementary physical education lessons and found that none were based on a conceptual curriculum model. So, we began to create 1,080 K-5 physical education lesson plans that aligned with our K-5 standards. We compensated the grade level writers using the money we had earned from selling our sample curriculum standards outside our immediate area. Each lesson contained lesson standards, teacher directions, learning activities, and closure questions. Each aspect of the lesson contained a reference number that linked it to the grade level standard. In addition, task cards were created for the various learning activities.

We decided to create one-third of the sixth through tenth grade unit/lesson plans each year. Unlike the elementary teachers, the sixth through tenth grade teachers are credentialed physical educators who know how to teach physical education. However, in many cases, these teachers did not know how to incorporate all the new standards into their unit plans. In addition, there were several new instructional activities (e.g., self-defense, Frisbee, rhythms) with which many teachers were unfamiliar. We began writing unit/lessons for the more unique activities (e.g., Medieval Times, tumbling and gymnastics, square dance, orienteering) and moved toward the more common ones. All of the materials were provided at no cost to the districts within our region and sold outside our region in order to fund future projects.

Now that we had our standards and sample unit/lesson plans in place, the question arose as to whether the students were actually meeting the standards. So, the physical education advisory committee decided to focus on assessment. It created a subcommittee to work on a sample K-12 physical education portfolio using the proceeds from the lesson plans. The subcommittee worked for a year and, in October 1997, a copy of the sample K-12 physical education portfolio was sent to each school district in Orange County with permission to adapt or reproduce. We also made the product available for sale.

Provide Inclusive Professional Development

Professional development is typically the number one responsibility of a regional leader. But—unlike a district leader—a regional leader is dealing with a number of different districts, each with its own agenda for professional development. The question, then, is how to provide high-quality professional development, as defined in Chapter 4, to so many different school districts and schools.

One strategy is certainly being on call to respond and assist individual districts and schools with their personal agendas. The difficulty with this approach is that it requires a great deal of time, and depending on the number of districts/schools under your direction, you may or may not be able to address all of their needs. In a time when regional leadership is diminishing, this approach may not be in the best interest of the profession.

The second approach is to have your physical education advisory committee include a professional development focus in its plan. This focus should take into consideration the overall plan to improve physical education. For example, the plan developed by our advisory committee included the following secondary professional development focus:

- Year 1: Physical education framework awareness training, new trends in physical education
- Year 2: Curriculum development process
- Year 3: One-third of the instructional units for grades 6, 7, 8, 9, and 10, and electives
- Year 4: One-third of the instructional units for grades 6, 7, 8, 9, and 10, and electives
- Year 5: One-third of the instructional units for grades 6, 7, 8, 9, and 10, and electives.

The advantage of this approach is that you can focus on a few topics or issues each year rather than offering a variety of topics. It also is possible to offer the sessions on different days and at different times in order to meet the needs of all teachers. For example, Saturday sessions, evening sessions, summer sessions, and weekday sessions provide options for teachers as they develop their own professional development plans.

The weakness with this approach is that there are districts and schools that cannot proceed this quickly and, therefore, get lost in the process. However, taking into consideration the new technology, it is possible to provide the professional development listed in the plan while still bringing along those schools and districts that may be behind.

We have established a system whereby each yearly topic is delivered via the Internet starting in the year following the live delivery. Once the topic is set up for delivery on the Internet, it can continue for several years with very little maintenance. Be aware, however, that the initial development of online inservices is very time consuming.

Developing a quality professional development opportunity via the Internet requires the same commitment as a live professional development opportunity. The first step in learning to deliver a professional development opportunity via the Internet is taking a course using this media. Throughout the learning opportunity, special attention should be paid not only to the content, but to how the content is delivered and is learning structured.

During the 1996-1997 school year, my regional office began to experiment with a combination of learning experiences including Public Broadcast Services (PBS), World Wide Web, e-mail, listserv, and Virtual Auditorium. The specific topics were our new physical education framework, the National Physical Education Standards, and state fitness testing. These initial topics were selected because of the timeliness of the topics—the framework and National Standards were relatively new, and our state had recently adopted a new state fitness test (Fitnessgram); the topics had already been delivered through a traditional (live) model, so many of the instructional resources were already created; and this particular inservice was the first in a series designed to improve the quality of physical education instruction in Orange County.

The course was submitted to one of our local universities as part of its extended education program. It was assigned a course number, and was made available to educators for one unit of college credit. Advertisements were created by both the university and the Orange County Department of Education. The flyers were distributed to physical educators throughout the region as well as to physical educators in neighboring regions.

FIGURE 11.2: Modules

Module 1	Introduction	Signing up for a listserv
Module 2	Reform Movement	Accessing a web site
Module 3	Education Codes	Creating bookmarks
Module 4	Learning Environment	Virtual auditorium
Module 5	Curriculum Development	Accessing web sites
Module 6	Goal 1	Accessing web sites
Module 7	Goal 2	Virtual auditorium
Module 8	Goal 3	Search tools
Module 9	Instructional Strategies	Virtual field trip
Module 10	Instructional Materials	Virtual auditorium-guest Web whacker
Module 11	Assessment Tools	Interactive web pages Audio
Module 12	Portfolios	File transfer
Module 13	History of Fitness Testing	Search tools
Module 14	Fitnessgram Test Battery	Virtual auditorium-guest Video conferencing
Module 15	Cardiorespiratory Endurance	Video
Module 16	Strength, Endurance, and Flexibility	Video Chat software

In addition, articles were written and published in one state professional journal and two national professional journals, so that physical educators from across the United States might participate in this unique learning opportunity.

The only prerequisites for the course required participants to have an e-mail address and Internet access. Participants were informed that there would be 16 learning modules that they could complete any time between October 15, 1996, and May 15, 1997. In total, 50 physical educators signed up to participate in this learning opportunity.

The course began with an e-mail message welcoming each participant to the course and providing an Internet address each person could "click on" to get to the course syllabus. The syllabus provided participants with the objectives, a list of the 16 modules (see Figure 11.2), course assessment information, and textbook references. The participants were asked to read the syllabus and then click on Module 1.

The first module did not provide any physical education

content information. It simply congratulated participants on their web navigating skills, and then listed all participants in the class and their e-mail addresses. The participants were grouped in triads as study teams. They were asked to send an e-mail message to their teammates introducing themselves, along with a copy to the instructor.

Throughout the course, lessons required participants to discuss ideas and concepts with their teammates. To that end, the first module ended with instructions on how to sign up for the class listserv. The listserv allowed participants to address a question or concern to the entire class using one e-mail message. Participants were informed that they could interact with the entire class, their teammates, or the instructor at any time throughout the course when they needed assistance or wanted additional information.

Most modules included an Internet skill as well as physical education content. Both learning activities were taught simultaneously and in support of one another. This strategy provided participants with "real-life" reasons for learning the Internet skill, since in many cases it was required to access the physical education content. Every week or two, a new module was posted and linked to the syllabus. The last module was posted on March 18, 1997. Participants were free to complete each module once it was posted, or at any time before May 15, 1997.

Special events were held several times between October 15, 1996, and March 18, 1997, including three one-hour video broadcasts on the California physical education framework. These were produced by the Educational Telecommunications Network, and broadcast over our local public broadcasting network (KOCE). Participants could watch the broadcast live or tape it for later viewing. Participants not within receiving distance of the broadcast could purchase the video from the Los Angeles County Office of Education.

The other special event included simultaneous online text-based discussions via a Virtual Auditorium provided by Classroom Connect, and videoconferencing. Four Virtual Auditorium experiences were held during the course. The first two involved interaction between participants and the instructor, while the last two included a guest speaker. After the final Virtual Auditorium experience, those participants with the necessary equipment had the opportunity to try a videoconferencing experience using free "Cu-SeeMe" software.

During the Virtual Field Trip, participants visited a web site developed by one school that had implemented many of the new ideas found in the framework and the National Standards. The site contained text-based information as well as pictures of the program. The first guest speaker for the Virtual Auditorium was one of the teachers from this school, who was able to answer questions from the participants. The second guest speaker was a representative from the agency that had developed the fitness testing program.

For regional leaders, this type of professional development is ideal, since we often cover large geographic areas. It solves the problem of having to repeat the professional development opportunity in a number of different locations. In addition, experts can be invited to share their knowledge and understanding right from their homes, located anywhere in the United States or the world.

Be Creative with Funding Issues

Regional coordinators typically make due with very limited budgets; most are even smaller than those of district coordinators. So, financial creativity is the name of the game for initiating those innovative projects that require funding. How often have you wanted to try an alternative professional development idea, provide funds for a particular school that has the potential for being a model for others, or develop new materials for your teachers, but your budget didn't afford you the opportunity?

I have found five successful avenues for securing additional funding for the projects my advisory committee and I wish to conduct: charging for workshops, developing and selling materials, asking for donations or soliciting grants, and creating a foundation.

When I first began to offer professional development opportunities, I offered them for free, and I did the presenting/facilitating so that there would be little or no cost involved. I found that many teachers who signed up for the workshop never showed up, and many teachers who had not signed up did. It appeared that they were not committed to the learning opportunities, since there were no fees involved.

I also noticed that my colleagues (coordinators of other subject areas) were charging nominal fees ($10–$25 per day) for their workshops, and that professional businesses were charging high fees ($150–$300 per day) with very high attendance. So, I started charging $15, and then later $20, for a full-day workshop. I used the money for refreshments and additional speakers when necessary, but more importantly I saved the money for advisory committee projects. The fee didn't seem to prevent anyone from attending the workshops, and typically the school or district paid the fee for the teacher out of their staff development fund.

I also have found that the creation and sale of instructional materials can add quite a few dollars to the budget. I was fortunate enough to request and receive start-up funds from my director of instruction; however, I also could have used revenue from workshop attendance to start the instructional materials development fund. As teachers were brought together to work on the instructional materials, I was able to either pay for their substitute (if during school time) or a stipend (for their personal time). The instructional materials were then given to teachers in our region for free or a nominal fee, and sold outside the region. The revenue from one project provided the funds for the next project.

Donations are often a hit-or-miss proposition. I have one colleague who requested free equipment from 100 companies. Ninety-nine companies turned him down, but one furnished his entire fitness center. I have sent out several letters to the local fitness centers, hospitals, athletic teams, and health spas requesting new or used equipment for our schools. Although I can't say that this has been very successful, I have gotten a few schools some equipment through funds generated by gate receipts from professional athletic competitions. The athletic teams designate one night as School A's night, and both the school and the organization sell tickets. Then, the gate revenue is split between the organization and the school.

As described in Chapter 5, many requests for proposals are distributed annually, and some can be used to fund physical education projects. However, another possibility is becoming a part of a "non-subject-specific" grant written by your regional office. For example, our office recently wrote a National Challenge Grant that provides $1.5 million in technology funds per year for five years. Although the grant targets technology, and specifically math and science, we wrote in several references to physical education as a subject area which, through interdisciplinary instruction, can assist students in their learning of math and science concepts.

Although there are grant funds for physical education, my experience has been that they are few and far between. This lead our physical education advisory committee to create their own Orange County Physical Education Fund under the Orange County Community Foundation, using start-up funds from a grant awarded by USPE. The initial steps for putting the fund into practice included creating brochures, training teachers to give presentations on quality physical education and requesting donations, and associating ourselves with a nonprofit foundation. The brochures and presentations have resulted in grant donations that are placed in the foundation's account. The governing committee for the foundation then decides how to allocate the funds for improving elementary playgrounds, developing middle and high school fitness labs, and creating innovative physical education programs throughout the region.

Groom a Replacement

There is nothing worse for a leader than to create a quality physical education program, change jobs, and see the program decline in terms of both quality and energy. Grooming a replacement is the best protection for the future of your program. Good leaders mentor others through modeling, teaching, and empowering. Setting a good example is not only a terrific learning experience for others, it's part of the process of self-invention for leaders.

Although I named this section, "groom a replacement," it is actually important to groom several replacements. It is dangerous to select only one person and to work exclusively with that person. The potential always exists that the individual you select will not become your replacement. And, even if the person is eventually selected as your replacement, he or she may never be able to truly establish a solid footing as the regional leader since others may look to him or her with envy and resentment.

Typically, the cream rises to the top. So too do quality individuals. As discussed in previous chapters, quality teachers become quality department chairpersons, who become quality mentor teachers, who become quality leaders. Take a careful look at your advisory committee, and identify those individuals who seem to volunteer for most of the projects. Be careful about bringing individuals along too quickly. Provide key individuals with greater and greater responsibility on committees as chairs or co-facilitators/presenters, and involve them in other projects (e.g., creating instructional materials, assessing software, etc.).

We recently began a summer leadership academy to assist with developing leadership potential. This week-long learning opportunity required interested teachers to apply for 20 open slots. The academy focused on physical education, technology, and leadership. Participants were provided with information on using the most current technology along with leadership skills. Each participant then selected a leadership project that he or she would initiate during the academy and finalize throughout the school year. In addition, each participant selected nine secondary schools in the region where he or she would assist and motivate the physical educators throughout the year.

The mentor/mentee relationship can be a mutually satisfying one. The mentor is able to delegate responsibility to other individuals who may not even work for the regional agency. The mentees benefit from the opportunity to work on exciting projects, meet key people, and learn new skills. However, both mentor and mentee must be careful of the emotional dependency that can develop on either side of the relationship. Both also must be aware that through close association, a failure by one can embarrass the other. By maintaining one's individual identity and mentoring several individuals, the mentor/mentee relationship can result in more benefits and fewer liabilities.

Chapter Summary

Regional leadership positions may be on the decline as we move into the twenty-first century; however, it is incumbent upon those currently in such positions to demonstrate the need for them. It takes courage to be a visionary and an advocate for change, but this is imperative if physical education and its respective leadership positions are to survive into the next millennium.

The regional leader must provide opportunities for collaboration between teachers, administrators, community members, districts, institutes of higher education, and professional organizations. In addition, the regional leader must convince the various stakeholders that they are part of a larger mission. The opportunity to meet, address issues, create an overall plan, and implement a common vision provides individuals with a reason to participate in a common cause. Creating models and professional development opportunities and assisting with funding issues also demonstrate that cooperative efforts are worth the time and energy. Finally, it is important to groom a replacement to ensure there will be continuity and programs will continue to advance.

CHAPTER 12

State Leadership

Spencer Sartorius

During the 1998-1999 school year, slightly more than three quarters of the states, along with several territories—including the Virgin Islands, American Samoa, Guam, and Puerto Rico, employed an individual who is responsible for physical education at the state level. Known as the state director, coordinator, specialist, supervisor, education associate, or consultant, this person is charged with providing physical education leadership and direction at the state level.

The name of the agency where this person works also is known by a variety of names: Department of Education, Department of Public Instruction, State Board of Education, Department of Children, Families and Learning, Department of Elementary and Secondary Education, Office of Education, Department of Education and Cultural Affairs, Office of Public Instruction, or Office of the Superintendent of Public Instruction (Council of Chief State School Officers 1997). Whatever they are called in their individual states, and wherever they may work, they are most generally referred to as *state directors*.

The number of states employing a state director has been in flux since directors first emerged in the early 1900s. As state funding goes; as state superintendents, directors, secretaries, or commissioners go; as politics go; as state priorities go; so goes the state director for physical education (AAHPERD 1976). Actually, this has been the case for all subject area state directors over the years.

The national organization for physical education and health education state directors—the Society of State Directors of Health, Physical Education and Recreation (SSDHPER)—works continuously to encourage states to employ state directors (Society of State Directors of Health, Physical Education and Recreation 1985). The SSDHPER coordinates activities with the American Alliance for Health, Physical Education, Recreation and Dance (AAHPERD), and collaborates in a variety of ways, especially with the National Association for Sport and Physical Education (NASPE) and the American Association for Health Education (AAHE). However, the SSDHPER is not a substructure of the Alliance (Society of State Directors of Health, Physical Education and Recreation 1998).

According to the results of the 1994 School Health Policies and Programs Study conducted by the Centers for Disease Control, 76.5 percent of the states and territories had a person responsible for directing or coordinating physical education (Centers for Disease Control and Prevention 1994).

Approximately four out of five of these state directors also had other responsibilities, including serving as the state director for health or driver education, or serving on a school improvement team. Also, a few states had separate directors for elementary and secondary physical education or adapted physical education.

Just as the title of the chief state school officer varies, the name of the department or office varies, and the title of the state director varies, so too does the position description. However, one common thread that seems to run through all of the positions is that the person in this job exercises state leadership and direction for K-12 public school physical education programs. Currently, more than 90 percent of all states require K-12 schools to provide physical education to some extent (American Health Association 1995).

Typical position announcements for state directors would list requirements such as:

1. Advanced degree (doctorate preferred)
2. Skills such as experience in curriculum and assessment development, standards development, professional development including workshop/inservice presentations
3. Experience in grant writing
4. Experience in managing people and working with teams
5. At least three to five years of teaching experience
6. Administrative experience including budgeting, supervision, and the use of technology.

The responsibilities listed in the position description may well include developing and implementing state level curricula, program evaluation plans, student assessment plans, and teacher inservice and articulation with higher education, other state departments, professional organizations, and other agencies. The determination of what constitutes "state leadership," the scope of the "direction," the political constraints of the specific state, and individual priorities are what make each position unique.

While it is true that each position is unique, this chapter will look at several areas in which common elements tend to be associated with the role of the state director of physical education. One should keep in mind, however, that while these elements may be "common," they might not all be found in the role of any one state director. And, how they are realized will be unique to each director and each state.

Each state places certain limitations and restrictions on the state director. These may be internal limits such as budget, travel limits, or availability of support staff. Or, they may be external limits such as giving priority to other subject areas deemed to be "more basic," or limiting access to schools and teachers or to higher education programs and personnel. It also is true that state directors make the position a reflection of themselves, taking into account their views of the role of education, the place of physical education in the curriculum, the role of the teacher, the role of higher education, and the role of the school administrator. Consequently, the position is not only constructed by state requirements, but also by the individual. This makes the hiring process especially important as experience, vision, and personality will all come into play in determining the director's effectiveness.

The role of the state director is discussed here in relation to seven themes that encompass the most widely performed duties:

1. Communicating with the State Board of Education
2. Communicating with Professional Associations
3. Communicating with Higher Education
4. Professional Development
5. Advocacy
6. Setting Standards
7. Change Agent.

Communicating with the State Board of Education

All states except Wisconsin have a "board of education" that is constitutionally or legislatively defined. These boards may be elected by the public or appointed by the governor. Membership may be a full-time responsibility or boards may only meet monthly. Florida is unique in that its board is, in essence, the "state cabinet." It is made up of state-level elected officials, including the governor and lieutenant governor. Usually, if the chief state school officer (state superintendent) is elected, the board is appointed, and vice versa. The duties and powers of the state board vary with each state, but generally the board sets state policy requirements for K-12 education (Montana Office of Public Instruction 1995).

In describing the state board of education to teachers, I sometimes tell them to think of their own local school boards. I then explain that the state board tends to be much the same. It can reflect "the good, the bad, and the ugly" depending on the issue, political pressure, or financial outlook. The other thing I tell teachers is that most state board members are trying to do the best job they can; for the most part they are caring, concerned people who want to do their best for the taxpayer and for students. Board members tend to come to their jobs without a lot of background in education, although they may have served on a local board. And, they don't necessarily have specific program background information or experience in any content area.

Following are the general roles a state director plays with the state board. However, in each role the state director works to educate the board concerning what constitutes quality physical education:

1. Explaining the ramifications of board decisions
2. Explaining what constitutes best practice
3. Providing state of the state reports
4. Making recommendations
5. Serving as a buffer
6. Conducting research.

The state director may explain the ramifications of board decisions to board members.

For example, the director might explain what would happen if the state requirement for physical education were reduced from four years to two, or from two to one. The intent is to prevent poor decisions from being made.

Frequently, state boards conduct some type of hearing prior to making a policy decision such as the one noted in the previous example. In this case, the state director may gather information to present, arrange for educators to make presentations, or coordinate a statewide effort to bring political pressure on the board.

The state director gathers information in numerous ways: contacting other state directors, calling schools, searching the Internet, or contacting national organizations. Some states have resource libraries and technicians available to research various topics. The Montana Office of Public Instruction has resource center staff who gather and store information for program representatives. In the past, staff members have searched the literature on the relationship between physical activity and learning, physical education time requirements in the various states, and state standards for health and physical education.

The state director must know what factors influence the board. For some, it may be large numbers of people for or against a position, while for others it may be the influence of a state official such as the governor. The board in Montana is generally influenced more by a few parents than by a host of teachers (whom they may view as self-serving). Thus, it is generally good strategy to involve parents and students in any lobbying effort.

State directors have input into such decisions as changing the amount of time given to physical education in schools and certifying or endorsing requirements for physical educators or requirements for professional development. They provide supporting information to help board members make informed decisions. Positive change is more likely to occur when supporting information and political pressure come together at the same time.

At times, the state director must provide an explanation of what constitutes "best practice."

A situation where such an explanation would be appropriate would be when a state board considers allowing recess or athletic participation to count toward meeting the state requirement for physical education. Again, the state director's role is to facilitate good decision making.

Like many local school boards, the state board may sometimes be swayed by a vocal minority that wishes to impose its

Sample State of the State Report: Physical Education

Today, there are almost 1,000 schools in our state; there are 600 elementary, 200 middle and 200 high schools. These schools range in size from one teacher and three students to our largest high schools with almost 2,000 students. They are spread across a state roughly the size of Ohio, Pennsylvania, New York, and New Jersey combined! Serving the physical education needs of these students are classroom teachers in our smaller elementary schools and specialists in our larger, with specialists serving all the middle and high schools. State requirements ensure that physical education is provided at the elementary level as well as the middle and high school levels.

Issues:

There are issues that are apparent in our physical education programs that we should study.

1. Elementary classroom teachers with little higher education background in physical education have low confidence in providing physical education.

2. There are no clear, specific state standards for physical education. The current standards are general, vague, and difficult to assess.

3. Student assessment continues to cause problems. Assessment is usually the prerogative of the instructor, with some assessment based on whether or not students shower or whether they have a good attitude.

Strengths:

1. Physical education continues to be taught by teachers who are motivated, and who want to provide the best possible education for their students.

2. The recent change in state requirements that limited class size to a maximum of 30 at the secondary level has resulted in an improvement in the quality of programs offered.

3. Changes in the teacher preparation standards for our units of higher education are providing for more consistency among units, as well as improving the quality of our programs.

Recommendations:

1. Study the teacher preparation programs of elementary teachers to ensure that adequate preparatory courses are available and are required of prospective teachers, who will provide this curriculum to their students.

2. Develop state standards for physical education based on the National Standards now in place.

3. Develop assessment guidelines and materials and ensure professional development opportunities for secondary physical education specialists to encourage appropriate student assessment.

Questions and Answers:

I will be happy to respond to all questions presented by individual Board of Public Education members.

---

will on everyone. This has happened in several states with regard to the previous example. Advocates of this position often argue: "Recess will get my kid moving, so why not count it for P.E?" or, "My kid runs all over during football practice and stays in shape that way, so why can't he skip P.E?" If they do not know the goals and objectives of a quality physical education program, state board members might think these arguments are valid. Thus, the state director must step forward, explain the philosophical differences between athletics and physical education, and explain the needs of all students. Once arguments focus on program goals, objectives, and outcomes, most boards are prone to make the right choices.

Many state directors provide of an annual State of the State report. (See sample above.)

In some instances, they also give annual reports to the board that outline program progress, issues, and future directions. These occasions provide an excellent opportunity to educate the board on the need for quality physical education programs and what they accomplish, as well as future professional development needs. The state director also might use these occasions to relay information from national groups, the state AHPERD, teachers, and higher education. In short, the director serves as a conduit to coordinate communication between various groups and the board.

State directors often make recommendations to the board.

These may take many forms, from recommendations for policy decisions to recommendations for a specific school district or program. In this role, the state director acts as the board's content area expert. The state director may make recommendations relating to a state requirement such as minimum length of time for elementary physical education class, whether or not to allow a district to try a new program that does not conform to state requirements, or whether to accept an unendorsed teacher. It is imperative that the state director remain abreast of cutting edge developments in the state and the nation. Educators, administrators, and school board members all look to the state director to be proactive and to present the best possible information.

Sometimes the state director acts as a buffer for the board.

In this role, the state director defends an action or requirement for a board member, and takes the brunt of criticism. Physical education is seen by some as a frill, and we continue to see attempts to reduce, eliminate, or modify state requirements. Similar to attacks on human sexuality education, values education, art, or music, these attacks appear quickly and are usually orchestrated by a few very vocal, demanding people.

In such a situation, the state director serves as the resource for accurate information, the historian who can explain previous decisions, and the expert on the ramifications of the proposed changes. The state director serves as the board's expert, presenting the case for why things are the way they are. Many times, notice is short as a group pushes for a quick decision before any organized opposition has time to react. The state director can work to slow an agenda or delay a decision while additional information is gathered.

In Montana, a comprehensive review of the accreditation standards for K-12 education resulted in a competition between curricular areas for limited student time. Increasing requirements in mathematics, social studies, and science would have effectively squeezed out programs in physical education, the arts, and vocational education. Without advocates for a well-rounded program—including the state director and state AHPERD—the educational program may well have been narrowed to include only academics. Instead, the board recognized the need and rationale for a comprehensive program (Montana Board of Public Education 1997).

Some state directors conduct research for their boards.

This may range from informal information gathering to conducting formal, state-level studies. The effectiveness of the state director in this role is based on his or her credibility and the quality of the research.

Some boards are not aware that new innovations or ideas in other curricular areas—such as the development of standards and benchmarks or multiple assessment strategies including the use of portfolios—also can play a part in physical education. Some board members would be surprised to hear of the varied uses of technology in physical education, or the culturally sensitive activities that can be included in programs, or how physical education can work with children who have diverse needs or limited English proficiency. The emotional and social benefits derived from physical education often surprise board members.

Communicating with Professional Associations

The state director serves an important role in communicating with professional associations by:

1. Providing technical information and guidance

2. Acting as a conduit for communication

3. Providing recommendations and advance warning

4. Providing encouragement for "best practice."

In most states, the state director has very close ties with the state AHPERD. In fact, the state director often serves in some capacity on the state AHPERD's executive board. While the closest ties may well be with the state AHPERD, there are other professional associations with which the state director may interact. These include the state teacher associations (NEA, AFT), recreation association, health association, Governor's Council on Physical Fitness and Sports, and the state chapters of a variety of other national coalitions and organizations. In addition, the state director often has close ties with the national organizations with which these groups are affiliated.

The key to success in this role is developing and nurturing a good working relationship with leaders in these organizations.

This role involves many of the following elements.

The state director provides technical information and guidance.

Professional associations need information, direction, and suggestions for how to go about influencing change. This can take many forms, from simply responding to questions at board meetings to suggesting approaches to the state board of education, state superintendent, regents, or legislature. It also can involve offering suggestions on how the association can best advocate for the profession: who to target, how to approach them, and who has the influence.

The guiding principles for approaching the state board or advocating are the same. First, don't assume that people outside the profession have the same zeal for the program that we do. Don't assume they have the same information. Don't assume they are familiar with what is happening in quality programs. I always tell our association that the people we are trying to influence are the product of our programs—20 years ago! Consequently, putting together concise information on the health status of children, including physical fitness and activity, is a good idea. Program descriptions, including information about health benefits, are effective. It is also a good idea to enlist the support of leaders, parents, and students who can verbalize the benefits of a program and be seen as "neutrals."

Professional associations also are active in developing products such as curriculum guidelines, assessment models, or state standards. Many also provide staff development opportunities such as inservice programs or workshops. The state director assists with these efforts. This assistance might be in the form of promotion, gathering resources, or advocating models.

The state director acts as a conduit for communication.

State directors serve their state AHPERD by ensuring that information from national agencies or organizations, state agencies, and other educational units gets to the field. They coordinate what happens to that information, getting it into the appropriate hands. Some information is more appropriate in the hands of K-12 principals, some in the hands of superintendents, while other information is more appropriate for the deans of colleges of education. The state director acts as a mail sorter and deliverer, as well as a reference and advocate. In this capacity, the state director helps the AAHPERD in its communication role and provides reinforcement for national initiatives.

Sometimes, getting information into the right hands is a shared responsibility. The state director might provide address labels or envelopes, and the state AHPERD might do the mailing. In another example, the state AHPERD might get information to its membership and the state director might make sure that it gets to non-members.

In Montana, I provide the MAHPERD executive board with relevant new information from federal or national sources such as *Physical Activity and Health; A Report of the Surgeon General* (Centers for Disease Control 1996), or the *Guidelines for School and Community Programs to Promote Lifelong Physical Activity Among Young People* (Centers for Disease Control 1997), which followed the Surgeon General's report. The expectation is that board members will then pass that information on to the membership. On the other hand, board members ensure that any information coming from AAHPERD also gets to me. The key is that we jointly determine the best routes to ensure broad coverage.

Many state directors provide guidance, recommendations, and advance warning.

Probably one of the most familiar roles of the state director is that of keeping state organizations and professional associations abreast of impending change and offering advice on what to do about it. This includes keeping the association informed regarding a potential change in the state requirements for physical education, providing information on the status of the Surgeon General's report on Physical Activity, or monitoring a move by a state legislature to count extracurricular activities in meeting the requirement for physical education. Or, it may be of a positive nature: providing planning support for a physical activity day, planning for the development of state-wide standards, or working to reduce the maximum number of students in a single physical education class.

In 1989, a bill was introduced in the Montana legislature that would have eliminated the requirement for the state supervisor's position (Montana Office of Public Instruction 1991). The state supervisor notified the Montana AHPERD, and representatives appeared and provided testimony at a legislative hearing. Had the state supervisor not sounded the alarm, no one would have spoken in defense of a mandated position.

State directors provide encouragement for "best practice."

This important role is shared by AAHPERD, higher education, national organizations and agencies—as well as with the state director. National and state organizations and agencies see the state director as the single most important person in the state to provide with information they want shared with local teachers.

State directors also share information and materials with each other on a routine basis. At the annual meeting of the Society of State Directors of Health, Physical Education and Recreation, presentations are made by representatives of national agencies and organizations, representatives of AAHPERD, and state directors. These presentations involve new initiatives, changes, coming materials/events/issues, and anything else that could have national implications.

State directors also provide annual state reports that are consolidated and distributed to the SSDHPER membership. These reports describe the latest state projects and trends and detail innovative ideas. Examples in Montana are the summer "master teacher" program, correlation of the Montana and National Standards (Montana Office of Public Instruction & Montana Association for Health, Physical Education, Recreation and Dance 1996), and curriculum framework (Montana Office of Public Instruction 1995) and assessment development (Montana Office of Public Instruction 1993a, 1993b, 1993c, 1993d, & 1993e).

The master teacher program brings together 25 teachers annually for an intense two-week training involving curriculum development, standards, assessment, diversity, technology and program integration. These teachers then serve as resources to their local school districts and regions on curriculum and

program development. Montana, in a joint project between the state AHPERD and the state director, conducted and published a correlation of Montana standards to the National Standards. Work is now in progress on the next step: a revision of the Montana standards to incorporate National Standard thinking. This will again be a joint undertaking. Efforts in many states are now centered around standards development, assessment, and technology.

Communicating with Higher Education

The role the state director plays in higher education varies widely from state to state. However, several important areas seem to be common to this role:

1. Providing information from the K-12 system
2. Participating in higher education program reviews
3. Facilitating cooperative efforts.

The state director is a source of information from K-12 education.

Higher education must be responsive to the needs of K-12 education in the development of teacher preparation programs. While many higher education institutions have mechanisms in place to obtain information from other colleges and universities and national organizations, most do not have any effective means of collecting information from the K-12 schools for which they develop teachers.

The state director is in constant communication with K-12 board members, administrators, and teachers. In state agencies, communication is a never ending process; letters are constantly going out, newsletters and other publications are developed and distributed, presentations are made, and workshops are conducted. The reverse is also true. There are letters and phone calls, and now e-mail. There are numerous requests to attend meetings, do trainings, and conduct workshops. Because of this activity, state directors have their fingers on the pulse of physical education in the state.

Many directors hear comments like: "I wish my teachers had a better background in dealing with inclusion issues." "I wish I had more coursework in basic movement patterns." "The one thing missing in my undergraduate program was student assessment."

These are important pieces of information for institutions of higher education to have prior to program modification. Again, the state director serves as the conduit of information, not only from the top down, but from the bottom up.

Some state directors serve on formal boards or committees that link them with higher education institutions. This provides an excellent avenue for the exchange of information. Most state directors also talk to physical education students about K-12 education. This provides information not only to the students, but to the instructor as well.

State directors participate in teacher preparation program reviews.

Many state departments of education are involved in ensuring the quality and consistency of teacher preparation programs. Some state departments of education have developed standards for teacher preparation programs in their states. Others use guidelines developed by the National Council for the Accreditation of Teacher Education (NCATE). Still others have cooperative arrangements with NCATE to accept the reviews conducted by one another to avoid unnecessary duplication. The state director may play some role in this process, from the development of state standards to on-site review team participation (Montana Board of Public Education 1994).

In Montana, the state director coordinates the development of the committee that reviews the teacher preparation standards. This committee eliminates, adds, or modifies current standards on a five-year cycle. It includes representatives from higher education and K-12 education. The state director also has participated on numerous higher education reviews that have resulted in programs being modified to meet national and NCATE standards.

State directors facilitate cooperative efforts.

Many higher education institutions have missions that include "service" and "research," and the state director has job responsibilities that depend on this type of assistance. State departments of education are involved in numerous activities that require volunteer assistance: state curriculum guidelines, assessment models, teacher preparation standards, or state physical education standards. Most often, state directors chair these efforts for the department and are dependent on the resources found at institutions of higher education.

This typically fits into the "service" mission of such organizations. Other activities, such as presenting at state AHPERD conventions and providing inservice programs for local districts and regional/state workshops also fit into this mission. Many times the state director serves as the coordinator for these kinds of activities. The state director also may assist in research efforts—as a participant or by securing school/teacher/administrator participation, mailing information, or creating promotional materials.

Professional Development

Probably the most familiar role the state director assumes is that of provider of services related to professional development. This role includes:

1. Providing inservice and preservice programs
2. Conducting workshops
3. Developing and disseminating materials
4. Serving as a facilitator.

A normal year for the state director may include single-day inservice programs at a dozen schools, quarterly regional workshops of two to three days duration, and two or three statewide summer programs of three to five days duration. The scope of this role is limited by resources, time, and personnel; however, all state directors do this in some fashion. Sometimes a state director overcomes the barriers by working creatively with higher education institutions or the state AHPERD to combine resources, expertise, or administrative and support capacity.

Examples of this are the master teacher program cited earlier, and training of trainers programs. Both efforts prepare addi-

tional experts who can serve as resources to their own as well as other schools. These programs are especially effective as they usually result in greater participation and generally are learning experiences for both participants and program providers.

State directors provide inservice and preservice education.

Many state directors are available almost "on call" to provide inservice and preservice programs to school districts and institutions of higher education. Another common role of state directors is providing technical assistance to local districts and higher education institutions. Technical assistance is any help a program needs to make it more effective at what it is trying to accomplish.

A common form of assistance is providing inservice and preservice programs. K-12 topics include curriculum process coordination, curriculum content, National Standards, program evaluation, student assessment, and inclusion. In higher education, assistance might take the form of guest lecturing on curriculum development for graduate classes, general K-12 education information for undergraduates, or a State of the State address to prospective elementary classroom teachers.

State directors provide workshops for K-12 teachers.

In this role, the director must assess the needs in the field and the desires of teachers and administrators in order to develop meaningful workshop programs. Needs are determined through program observation, discussions with state AHPERD officers, school administrators, and higher education faculty, or even through the use of a survey.

The state director continuously monitors the needs of the state in the area of physical education, the desires of teachers and administrators, and national trends and develops programs and workshops to meet these needs. Workshops can last from a single day to more than a week and this effort often involves coordinating a complex program, logistics, and multiple speakers.

The state director collaborates with other groups and develops an annual plan to ensure that programs do not overlap, that classes are disrupted as little as possible, and that the needs of all concerned are met. Annual plans vary greatly in number and length of workshops; however, all successful plans involve the active input of various groups including the state AHPERD and higher education institutions. (See sample plan on next page.)

State directors develop and disseminate written and electronic materials.

When developing materials, the state director must determine the needs and decide how to meet those needs and how to best disseminate the information. In the past, that meant writing curriculum frameworks, statewide standards, evaluation and assessment outlines, as well as guidelines on a variety of topics. Now, it also involves making materials available electronically.

The widespread use of the computer, state and national networks, and the Internet have resulted in state home pages that include listings for a variety of materials. Teachers can now access materials and download those materials they wish to retain. In fact, many directors have provided inservice, workshops, or materials on the use of technology.

Physical education materials currently available electronically through the Montana system (http://www.metnet.mt.gov)

Montana Plan for Standards Development in Physical Education

ACTIVITY	TIMELINE
1. Correlation project	12/96
2. Develop plan for standards	6/97
3. Office approval of plan	7/97
4. Budget secured	8/97
5. Meeting to develop standards	11/97
Two or three-day meeting including:	
– State AHPERD	
– K-12 teacher	
– Higher education	
– School administrators	
– Public	
6. Compiling, printing, and distributing draft	1/98
7. Input from first draft and revision	4/98
8. Revision and submission to state board	6/98
9. Distribution of state standards	9/98

include model curriculum guides, program evaluation materials, booklets on student assessment, and a "shareboard" where educators can share ideas, concerns, or program information.

State directors serve a facilitating role in professional development.

Professional development is a shared responsibility with school administrators, state education agencies, units of higher education, and other agencies and organizations. Most units of higher education view professional development as a part of their "service" mission. Many state AHPERD associations consider professional development an important role, especially in the use of Jump Rope for Heart dollars. Many times the best thing a state director can do is to channel services and programs to fit the needs of the K-12 schools and their teachers. They can ensure that the "right" program gets to the "right" place, and that it is delivered by the "right" people to the "right" audience.

Of course, this involves the never ending needs assessment process for the state that has been mentioned previously. This "brokering of services" role helps both units of higher education and the state AHPERD deliver services to schools with a minimum of problem, as the state director provides the critical element—access.

Advocacy

The state director for physical education has, at various times, been known as the "point of the spear" when issues involving advocacy arise. When it is necessary to make the case for physical education, most agencies, groups, and organizations turn to the state director for leadership.

Advocacy takes many forms, and requires a variety of

approaches. The state director must be aware not only of the facts surrounding the issue, but also of the politics involved. Advocacy can take place at several levels:

1. At the local level
2. At the state level
3. At the national level.

The state director is an advocate at the local level.

This usually involves supporting local programs with school administrators, boards, and parents. A common role for the state director involves talking to school district administrators and boards about physical education programs. The state director serves as the "outside expert" in such situations, helping district staff make the case for quality programs. Sometimes this role includes making presentations at school board or community meetings.

The state director must be aware of current research and effective programs and trends, yet he or she also must be sensitive to the political climate of the district. Two things have worked well for me during the past 20 years. First, I have taken course work in general school administration—school law, school finance, and evaluation—so that I can talk to administrators and boards about general school district problems and issues, and about how physical education fits into the picture. If you don't understand administrative issues, how can you effectively fit physical education into the picture? Second, I talk to boards and administrators in straight-forward language; I don't try to intimidate or suggest that I have the one and only answer. I try to help them reach informed decisions on their own.

Finally, I try to remember that board members and administrators have all gone through our programs as students; and that they are making decisions based on their experiences. I admit that some of these experiences were not good. I don't defend programs that were in place 20 years ago, but rather talk about the needs of kids and the changes that have taken place. I describe what our programs look like and try to accomplish today.

The state director is an advocate at the state level.

The state director organizes efforts to advocate for effective physical education programs. The state director is usually one of the first people to become aware of issues in physical education programming at the state level. He or she generally is the initial advocate for effective programs with the state board of education, state legislature, state parent/student/teacher organization, or other statewide group.

It is especially important for the state director to advocate for quality physical education programs within their own agency! While this may sound easy, it is very time consuming. It means going to staff meetings and making sure physical education is included in considerations that tend to revolve more around other "core" programs. It means making sure that top management personnel—including the superintendent or commissioner—have relevant, timely information. And, it means developing a rapport and establishing credibility with the office decision makers. It means including these management people and the superintendent in meetings, conferences, and programs, as well as in decisions concerning physical education. Without such advocacy, many state departments might develop programs and initiatives—including standards, curricula, time requirements for programs, teacher certification and endorsement plans, or restructuring plans—that do not include physical education.

The state director is an advocate at the national level.

The state director is usually one of the first people to become aware of national concerns, and therefore must serve as an advocate for the needs of the state. The state director knows the roles national agencies and organizations play in the development of effective programs within the states. He or she articulates state needs to Congress, the President's Council on Physical Fitness and Sport, the Departments of Education and Health and Human Services, AAHPERD, and other national groups and organizations. The state director is usually the only person with a state perspective on the needs of physical education programs and teachers, including the needs of large and small schools, wealthy and poor schools, and rural and urban schools. Effectiveness at the national level is usually the result of two things: activity, and longevity. The more active and involved state directors are, the more well-known they will be, and the more often they will be called upon for advice.

Setting Standards

Standards are being developed, or have been developed, in a variety of curricular areas and at a variety of levels. Most standards go beyond a simple requirement for physical education and deal with the quality of the program provided. The state director, in many instances, is involved in the development of standards. This may involve:

1. Establishing standards at the local level

2. Establishing standards at the state level

3. Establishing standards at the national level.

The state director may assist in setting standards at the local level.

Many state directors are involved in local school district curriculum development processes, including the development of standards, performance indicators, benchmarks, and evaluation procedures. In states with regional or district coordinators, this role may focus more on lending technical assistance. The state director usually relies on national and state standards as "guiding principles" for developing appropriate local standards. This might include interpreting the intent of national and state standards.

State directors also may be involved in helping districts solicit local involvement. Many school districts use the state specialist on physical education as the drawing card for a communitywide meeting designed to start a project moving. It is common to have not only teachers and administrators at this type of meeting, but also parents, health club instructors, and health and medical care personnel. These tend to be the people who are most interested in the topic, and those who are willing to get involved.

The state director is involved in helping set standards at the state level.

When state standards are being considered by the state board of education, legislature, or state superintendent, the person charged with leading the process is usually the state director. He or she determines a process, selects representatives from the field, secures input, determines what the format will look like, secures support, and presents the results to the education or political community. These standards vary from state guidelines for physical education to state curricula, to learner outcomes at various grade levels, to specific program content. Standards also may involve certification requirements, class size, assessment requirements, statewide fitness testing, and class time requirements.

In Montana, since 1980, the state board of public education has asked the state director to determine the process to review the Montana Teacher Preparation Standards. This includes developing a process, securing input, and presenting results to the board for approval. In addition, during the last statewide review of the Montana accreditation standards, the state director served as the committee's resource person and as the spokesman to the board once the process was completed.

The state director helps set standards at the national level.

The recent development of National Standards in a variety of curricular areas, including the National Standards for Physical Education released in 1996 (NASPE 1995), involved broad input and broad support from the field. State directors played a variety of roles in this area—from direct involvement in the development, to national diffusion efforts, and finally to diffusion and implementation efforts within individual states. The state director and state AHPERD worked closely in providing inservice, programs, and support for standards development.

Change Agent

Everything that has been said thus far in this chapter reflects the role of state directors as change agents. This role includes everything from the development or improvement of requirements at the state level to initiation or improvement of programs at the local level. Whatever the "state of the state" of physical education, the state director works to facilitate changes that will result in even higher quality programs for teachers and students. These changes may be seen at the legislative or state board level, at the department of education level, in higher education programs, or at the local level.

In more than 20 years as a state director, I have been directly involved in changes that are now reflected in the accreditation standards for K-12 schools, as well as the teacher preparation standards for our colleges and universities. I have served as a registered lobbyist to the legislature, providing input and suggestions for changes to bills. I have provided input for curriculum development processes at the district level, and I have spoken to school boards and administrative groups, parent groups, and a variety of organizations. I mention these because they are typical of what state directors are doing nationwide.

To facilitate change at the local level, state directors must understand people: teachers, administrators, parents, and community members. They also must understand the politics of the community and of the state. If they are to avoid high levels of frustration, they must understand that change in education is a slow process.

I couch discussions about change in terms of what it will mean to students, what it will mean to teachers, and what it will mean to the credibility and prestige of the school program. Of course, each teacher is motivated differently; however, most teachers believe their state directors are credible. They believe in the credibility of their professional associations and their National Standards. They sincerely want quality programs for their students. Once teachers believe in the value of change, some will change and that will lead others to change. The key for the state director is to initiate the process.

Chapter Summary

State directors fill a variety of leadership roles. They represent not only the state's physical education teachers but also the state superintendent's office, state department of education, parents, administrators, and—of course—the state's students. State directors assume leadership roles in activities at the national, state, and local levels. A wide variety of people, agencies, and organizations depend on the effective leadership of the state director.

Communication, professional development, development of standards, and serving as a change agent for effective education require a variety of skills and experiences. Most people see state directors in the limited framework in which they know them: teachers think they serve as a curriculum/development resource, others may see them as program writers at the state-level, and still others may view them in a monitoring role. However, the state director has a varied, unique position, one that is vital to the implementation and success of physical education programs for all students.

In the end, those states with a state director for physical education will have more effective physical education programs. Those states should appreciate the assistance and make use of the resource available to them. Those states that do not have a state director should consider forming a statewide coalition of interested individuals and organizations and begin work toward achieving that goal. A state director for physical education will enhance professional development, communication, involvement, preservice education, standards development, and advocacy. And this adds up to better, more effective programs for our youth.

I believe there are two things that tend to make state directors even more effective. The first is length of time on the job. It is almost a given that with experience comes credibility. Experience also means you know how to get the job done, you know who the power brokers are, and you know how to effectively move things along. Experience in the state as a teacher and/or school administrator also is an advantage. The second thing that makes a successful state director is support. The more support and active involvement from teachers, the state AHPERD, other organizations and higher education units, the more that can be done.

The way I articulate this message to people is by telling them that by working cooperatively together, we can create a whole that is greater than the sum of its individual parts. And that's a winner for all of us!

References

AAHPERD. (1976). 50 years of leadership: The Society of State Directors of Health, Physical Education and Recreation 1926-1976. *Journal of Physical Education and Recreation.*

American Health Association. (1995). School physical education. *Journal of School Health (65)* 8.

Centers for Disease Control and Prevention, Division of Adolescent and School Health. (1994). *1994 school health policies and program study.* Atlanta, GA: Author.

Centers for Disease Control and Prevention. (1996). *Physical activity and health: A report of the surgeon general.* Atlanta, GA: Author.

Council of Chief State School Officers . (1997). *Comprehensive school health program staff in state education agencies directory.* Washington, DC: Author.

Guidelines for school and community programs to promote life-long physical activity among young people. (Morbidity and Mortality Weekly Report No. RR-6, March 7, 1997). Atlanta, GA: Centers for Disease Control and Prevention.

Montana Board of Public Education. (1994). *Montana teacher education program standards.* Helena, MT: Author.

Montana Board of Public Education. (1997). *Montana school accreditation: Standards and procedures manual.* Helena, MT: Author.

Montana Office of Public Instruction & Montana Association for Health, Physical Education, Recreation and Dance. (1996). *Health enhancement: Montana and national standards.* Helena, MT: Author.

Montana Office of Public Instruction. (1991). *School laws of Montana 1989 and 1991.* Helena, MT: Author.

Montana Office of Public Instruction. (1993a). *Montana assessment for health enhancement.* Helena, MT: Author.

Montana Office of Public Instruction. (1993b). *Montana health enhancement…an expanded concept: Assessment and planning.* Helena, MT: Author.

Montana Office of Public Instruction. (1993c). *Program assessment: a six-step process to curriculum improvement.* Helena, MT: Author.

Montana Office of Public Instruction. (1993d). *Assessment planning: a process guide with three design options.* Helena, MT: Author.

Montana Office of Public Instruction. (1993e). *Student assessment: keys to improving student success.* Helena, MT: Author.

Montana Office of Public Instruction. (1995). *Montana model curriculum for health enhancement, grades K-6 and 7-12.* Helena, MT: Author.

Montana Office of Public Instruction. (1995). *School laws of Montana, 1995.* Helena, MT: Author.

National Association for Sport and Physical Education. (1995). *Moving into the future: National Standards for physical education.* Reston, VA: Author.

The Society of State Directors of Health, Physical Education and Recreation. (1985). *A statement of basic beliefs.* Reston, VA: Author.

The Society of State Directors of Health, Physical Education and Recreation. (1998). *Strengthening leadership capacity in health, physical education and recreation in a time of change.* Reston, VA: Author.

Part 4. Where To Go Next

Grant me the self-awareness to know honestly what I am, what I can do, and what I cannot;

Grant me the judgment to channel my energies into those avenues which best utilize my abilities and do not require talents which I do not possess;

Grant me the wisdom to cheerfully admit error and learn from my experiences, that I may grow and develop and avoid repetition of mistakes;

Grant me the courage to make decisions whenever they are necessary and to avoid rashness when they are not;

Grant me the consideration to recognize the worth of each individual, and to respect all those with whom I have contact, neither stifling their development nor exalting myself at their expense;

Grant me the insight to develop a personal philosophy, that my life may have more meaning and satisfaction and that I may avoid capricious action under pressures of expediency;

—R. Saltonstall, *Human Relations in Administration*

CHAPTER 13

The Impact of Future Trends on Physical Education and the Role of Leadership

Bonnie Mohnsen

The first social revolution—the Agricultural Revolution—began after 10 million years of hunting and gathering food. From 8000 BC to the late 1600s AD, humans grew their own food. With the coming of machines came the second revolution—the Industrial Revolution. This revolution brought many new job opportunities, but it also caused some people to lose jobs to the machines. These people fought hard against the new technology. Since the middle 1900s AD, the human race has been involved with the third revolution—the Information Revolution. The development of computers and improvements in telecommunications brought us into the Information Age.

Social revolutions bring about changes in the way people work and live. Americans today start working two years later and retire five years sooner than they did in 1950. The number of paid holidays has doubled, and vacation days are up by 63 percent. Life expectancy is up nearly six years from what it was in 1970. Today there are cellular phones, computers small enough to be held in the palm of the hand, and immediate access to more information than one could possibly absorb in an entire lifetime.

As we enter the new millennium, even more changes are occurring at an ever accelerating pace, and education and learning are not immune. It is predicted that within the next decade, education will change more than it has since the modern education system was created more than 300 years ago. Education will no longer be the private domain of the school system. Every employing institution will become a learning center in order to keep its employees abreast of current technology and information.

Coupled with these educational changes is the prediction that 40 percent of the United States public school teachers will retire or otherwise leave the profession by the 2003–04 school year. This, combined with dramatic enrollment increases due to immigrant children and second generation baby boomers, will create a demand for new teachers. Efforts in states such as California to reduce class size will mean even more hiring.

Changes in education affect physical education and the role that leadership plays in promoting quality physical education programs. This chapter examines several future trends and their possible impact on both physical education and its leadership.

The seven major points for this chapter include:

1. New Theories on Learning

2. Increases in Information

3. Advances in Technology

4. Increases in Home Schooling

5. The Need for Life Long Learning

6. Increases in Longevity

7. Increases in Violence

New Theories on Learning

New theories of learning are emerging, along with adequate research to support their claims. Some of the new learning principles based on brain-research (Caine, Caine, & Crowell 1994) include:

- People learn and retain information only when the knowledge has relevance and meaning for them

- Emotions are critical and at the heart of learning

- The brain processes parts and wholes simultaneously

- Learning involves both focused attention and peripheral perception

- The brain downshifts under perceived threats and learns optimally when appropriately challenged

- Enriched learning experiences (inclusion of all senses) are retained longer

- Learning engages the entire physiology.

The last principle is the most intriguing in terms of the role of physical education in learning. Brain researchers now believe that what happens in the body can affect the brain, and what

> ### Brain-Based Learning Resources
> *(see Chapter 13 References)*
>
> Inside the Brain: Revolutionary Discoveries of How the Mind Works (Ronald Kotulak)
>
> The Learning Brain (Eric Jensen)
>
> Making Connections: Teaching and the Human Brain (Geoffrey Caine & Renate Nummela Caine)
>
> Mindshifts (Geoffrey Caine, Renate Nummela Caine, & Sam Crowell)
>
> Smart Moves: Why Learning Is Not All in Your Head (Carla Hannaford)

happens in the brain can affect the body. Hope, purpose, and determination are not merely mental states. They have electro-chemical connections that play a large part in the workings of the immune system and, indeed, in the entire economy of the total human organism. Neuron growth, nourishment, and inter-actions are integral to the perception and interpretation of expe-riences. Strenuous activity has been shown to improve oxygenated blood flow to the brain and thus increase learning (Kotulak 1996).

It is imperative that schools of education include the new developments in neuroscience, systems theories, cognitive psychology, learning and motivation, and human development in their teacher education programs. A better understanding of all these principles by the entire education community will not only improve student learning but also will heighten the respect for physical education and the role that physical activity plays in the human experience.

Many of the "brain-based" learning principles have been the impetus for new educational trends such as block scheduling, interdisciplinary instruction, and inclusion. Physical educators must stay abreast of these and other new approaches to learning—both in terms of cognitive information and motor skill acquisition. Understanding and applying these theories will increase student understanding and ability to demonstrate new learning. In addition, the ability of physical educators to carry on conversations about learning with other educators will improve their standing in the educational community. Finally, it will provide physical educators with a platform for defending programs and improving the quality and status of their field. Leaders can ensure that physical educators understand new learning principles by providing learning opportunities related to this emerging area of information.

Increases in Information

The amount of information we have is currently doubling every year, and between the years 2010 and 2020, information experts predict that knowledge will double every 70 days. Eight-five percent of the information in the National Institute of Health computers is upgraded every five years. Skills and knowledge are becoming obsolete faster than ever. For example, the half-life of an engineer's knowledge is as little as three years in some fields.

As information increases, so too will information related to the discipline of physical education and its associated subdisci-plines of biomechanics, exercise physiology, social-psychology, motor learning, historical perspectives, aesthetics, and motor development. Physical educators and leaders alike must stay abreast of current research. Researchers must continue to publish in practitioner journals, translating research into usable pieces of knowledge. In turn, physical educators must select the most pertinent information from the body of knowledge to pass on to the K-12 student. The increase in information certainly makes a case for focusing on a few significant areas of informa-tion as opposed to trying to learn a little bit about everything. It also makes a case for identifying those key standards that students need to know in order to be educated—or in the case of our subject area—physically educated.

FIGURE 13.1: Technological Advances and their Effect on Physical Education

Large flat-panel monitors with brightness of a standard CRT display ➤ model "life-size" demonstrations of motor skill

Interpretative telephony (language translation) ➤ ability to communicate with every child in the class

Smart machine ➤ individualized skill analysis and feedback for student

Holograms ➤ demonstrations of sport strategies

Electronic notepads ➤ data collection by students on the field

Digital interactive television ➤ demonstrations of current professional athletes

Virtual reality ➤ rock climbing simulations

Palm technology ➤ handheld roll books

Computers worn as part of clothing ➤ access to computers in the gymnasium, on the field, and during activity

Desktop videoconferencing ➤ sharing of instructional strategies between physical education teachers

Advances in Technology

The most rapid advances occurring today are in the area of technology. The power of technology is doubling every 18 months, and there is no end in sight. The technology of the future will include an all-in-one box that contains a television, a telephone, and a computer. Figure 13.1 shows but a few of the new technologies on the horizon and their possible applications in physical education. It will be incumbent upon physical education leaders to stay abreast of the latest technological advancements so that these devices are used to promote and provide quality physical education experiences.

One of the most significant technological advances on the horizon is interactivity on the Internet. The early dominant language, HTML, did not lend itself to highly interactive activi-ties. But newer languages will improve this situation. Interactivity on the Internet will provide new learning experi-ences for students in physical education. The ability of teachers and students to be online for extended periods may mean that content will be covered more rapidly and in greater depth than ever before. Students will be able to complete homework assignments with the assistance of experts and software accessed on the Internet.

Computer software also will come of age in the next decade. New software programs will be dramatically enhanced by multi-media, interactivity, simulations, virtual reality, and other new tools. Imagine being able to interact with holograms of famous athletes/coaches/physical educators (living and dead), and to expe-rience through virtual reality a wide variety of physical activities typically unavailable to the user. Students from inner cities will participate in outdoor education experiences. Students living in desert environments will participate in downhill and cross-country skiing. Students living in mountain areas will participate in surfing and SCUBA activities. Not only will students experience the activity, but the software will provide relevant feedback, allowing them to improve their technique and accomplishment.

Distance learning—the use of telecommunications equipment such telephone, television, fiber optics, cable broadcast, and satellites to send instructional programming to learners—will become even more commonplace. Teleconferencing via satellite links and other technologies will bring two-way interactive videoconferencing into every classroom.

As a result, teaching may become more centralized, with a few "star teachers" providing instruction for classes located across the United States. A hand full of physical educators delivering instruction through distance learning could replace 40,000 local teachers. Students would use the Internet as a way of participating in follow-up activities.

Increases in Home Schooling

Today, more than half a million children are home schooled by their parents in the United States—up from 10,000 just two decades ago. That's only about one percent of all K-12 students, but the number is increasing rapidly, according to Patricia Lines, senior research analyst at the United States Department of Education. More students will be learning at home, using computers and advanced educational software, as we approach the millennium. Home schoolers are already the leading users of educational technology in the United States.

There are interactive courses available on CD-ROM to assist parents with home schooling. These courses interact with the student in the student's own language. They determine and store information about the student's learning weaknesses and use this information during the instructional process. This approach combines learning and assessment into one cyclical process where assessment is constantly used to determine what learning material is to be presented next.

Online courses are popping up all over the Internet. Currently, many high school students are enrolled in online advanced placement and college level courses. Students can take courses at their own pace and get credit whenever they have mastered the material. Assistance from course facilitators and other leaders is available online. And, incredible information resources are available for students who are conducting research.

With or without physical education, home schoolers are progressing through their K-12 education. We can either hide our heads in the sand and pretend that we are not responsible for these students who are outside the traditional school setting, or we can ensure that all students become physically educated. Online K-12 physical education courses will become a reality. The only question is, "what kind of reality?"

Will these courses simply encourage participation in any readily available activity, or will these courses produce physically educated adults? Leaders in the field physical education must take a proactive approach to this situation and become involved in the creation and distribution of K-12 online physical education learning materials.

The Need for Life Long Learning

As the information base explodes, the work performed also changes. It is predicted that future workers will need to prepare for two or three career changes during their lifetimes. Jobs will

Update 2005: Home Schooling and Physical Education - Juan Chan, a home-schooled child of 12, begins his school work with a 20-minute aerobic workout wearing a heart monitor. At the end of the workout, Juan transfers the data from the heart monitor to his computer, analyzes the graph depicting his heart rate during the workout, and stores it as one piece of evidence that he participates in aerobic activity within his target heart rate range at least three times a week.

Next, Juan, noting that his golf game has been off lately, decides to practice his golf swing. Using electronic mail, he sends messages to three of his friends asking if they would like to play golf later in the day. He then searches the Internet looking for access to one of the best golf instructors in the world. After verifying the instructor's credentials, Juan e-mails the instructor a video clip of his golf swing with his own self-analysis. Within minutes, the golf instructor responds in agreement with Juan's analysis and noting a few additional points that Juan should consider. In addition, the instructor sends along a hologram of a professional golfer. Juan runs the hologram program and practices along with the professional. Juan then sends another video clip of his performance to the golf instructor in order to verify that he has in fact corrected several of the errors in his performance.

become more specialized, and the skills and knowledge required to perform the jobs will become obsolete faster than ever. These changes will necessitate education for adults as well as children.

The need for adult education will be met through online/on-demand training courses available through global universities. Such universities will emerge to provide training through computer networks, satellite television, and other advances. Access to adult learning also will be available at local schools, which will be open from early morning to late at night to meet the needs of an ever increasing learning community. Finally, businesses will need to create and implement on-the-job training strategies that will develop highly skilled workers who will continuously upgrade their skills and retrain in response to new global markets and technologies.

Without the influence of physical education leaders, life long learning will be defined exclusive of physical education. However, there are rapid increases in the expanding knowledge based related to physical education and its related subdisciplines as well. Physical education leaders must make this known to the educational community and create adult learning opportunities inclusive of physical education. Similar to home-schooling for K-12 students, we must create and distribute home learning opportunities for adult learners related to physical education and physical activity experiences.

Increases in Longevity

Life expectancy has steadily increased during the last century. In the United States, life expectancy is now 77 years, and the number of Americans living to 100 is increasing

Update 2008: Life Long Learning and Physical Education -
The school of the 21st century has become a mecca for life long learning. Individuals from birth to old age participate in learning activities such as discussion groups, lectures, and "hands-on" investigations related to health, physical activity, and wellness issues. Numerous resources are available, from Internet access to computer software. Especially important are devices that, while too expensive for the average home, provide participants with significant learning experiences in arenas of physical activity. Wall climbing simulations, wellness centers equipped with the latest in fitness devices, numerous virtual reality stations for practicing motor skills (i.e., skiing, fencing, golfing), and virtual caves for participation in team sports with virtual players are available 24 hours a day with supervised instructors available for one-on-one and small-group assistance.

We certainly learned throughout the 20th century the importance of allocating resources to prevention through education (including kinesthetic learning) instead of the more expensive intervention measures necessary when individuals are not encouraged to reach their full potential.

weekly. It is anticipated that the quality of health care will continue to improve as well as life expectancy with the advent of medical advances such as "micromachines." These small, ultra-thin machines will travel through human blood vessels to repair damaged areas.

Businesses are already recognizing the impact that increases in longevity will have on their organizations, especially in terms of health concerns. Wellness programs are becoming increasing popular as one alternative to rising health care costs (Popcorn 1992). Companies such as Ford Motor Company, Chrysler Corporation, and Campbell Soup have instituted companywide wellness programs.

Sentry Life Insurance has an on-site fitness center with a 25 meter pool, a gymnasium, racquetball and handball courts, an indoor golf driving range, and a weight training room. The program focuses on individualized fitness goals for employees and their families. In addition, Sentry offers early glaucoma screening, lower back clinics, hypertension screening, a program on dental health, and classes on healthful cooking. Sentry employs health professionals for weight control and nutritional counseling, and fitness experts to teach skiing, slimnastics, first aid, self-defense, and cardiovascular fitness.

Naisbitt and Aburdene (1985) reported the following benefits from companywide wellness programs:

- New York Telephone Company saves at least $2.7 million annually in reduced absenteeism and insurance costs

- Toronto's Canada Life Insurance recouped $37,000 in direct savings, $231,000 in decreased turnovers, and 22 percent in reduced absenteeism

- Lockheed estimates $1 million annual savings on life insurance premiums directly related to employee participation in its wellness program.

The government is also alert to the changes in longevity and the potential impact on health care costs. The Surgeon General's report (1996) concluded that people of all ages, both male and female, can substantially improve their health and quality of life by including moderate (30 or more minutes of physical activity most, if not all, days of the week) amounts of physical activity in their daily lives. These recommendations increase the public's awareness of the importance of physical activity and fitness.

The Surgeon General's report also recommends that "every effort should to be made to encourage schools to require daily physical education in each grade and to promote physical activities that can be enjoyed throughout life" (p. 6). This recommendation is based on research that shows favorable attitudes toward physical education and perceived benefits derived from physical activity being positively related with adolescent participation in physical activity (Ferguson et al. 1989; Zakarian et al. 1994; Tappe, Duda, & Menges-Ehrnwald 1990).

Increases in human longevity have great implications for physical education. Even though health care is improving, it will be difficult to sustain the health care costs as more and more older adults require constant attention. Exercise has been shown to improve strength and speed in older people (Fiatarone et al. 1994) and strengthen bones (Nelson et al. 1991). The need for self-health care will continue to grow, as will the importance of physical activity, physical education, and health programs. Physical education leaders need to capitalize on the recent efforts supported by the Surgeon General's report and the future needs of an aging society. Advocacy efforts should be increased in order to take advantage of this timely support. Continued efforts in the areas of adult physical activity and learning programs also will sustain this effort.

Increases in Violence

The Federal Bureau of Investigation estimates that 1.8 million people in the United States are victims of violence each year, including 400 children each month who die from gun violence. In 1993, more than one million substantiated cases of child abuse were reported. People 12 to 24 years old have the highest risk of nonfatal assault of any age in the United States. Violence is the leading cause of death among male and female African-Americans, age 15 to 31.

During every school day in 1992, at least 100,000 students carried guns to school, 160,000 students skipped class due to fear of physical harm, 40 students were hurt or killed by firearms, 6,250 teachers were threatened with bodily injury, and 260 teachers were physically assaulted (Burrus 1993, Prothrow-Stith & Quaday 1995). Yes, there is violence in our society and in our schools, and as our society becomes more diverse it will continue to exist.

As Prothrow-Stith and Quaday (1995) explain, "Twenty years ago, we thought children were safe in their homes. Then we learned about physical and sexual abuse visited upon some children in their homes. Abuse that was hidden for years. We thought children were safe in their neighborhoods, particularly the suburbs and rural areas. But slowly violence has crept into the suburbs and into rural areas across America. Violence knows no social, racial, ethnic, gender or age restrictions. Directly or

Update 2010: Violence in the United States Is on a Rapid Decline - Thanks to the 2005 interagency agreement between educational, social, and recreational institutions to combine resources in order to provide safe environments 24 hours a day in all communities, allowing youngsters and adults alike to participate in physical activity and other recreational pursuits, today we see a tremendous decline in the number of violent episodes across the United States.

In addition to meeting the leisure needs of our society, these institutions have provided day care for many children while their parents work. And, a number of new jobs have opened up, lowering the unemployment rate. This has been a win-win-win project!

indirectly, we are all victims of the violence that is sweeping across the nation" (p. 2). This violence is leaving physical wounds as well as much deeper scars, hidden in the hearts and minds of our children, schools, and communities.

The task of curbing violence is a multifaceted one that requires many dedicated professionals from a variety of fields working within their individual disciplines and as part of an interdisciplinary team to create a range of intervention strategies. The school stands as a logical center for the coalition committed to violence prevention. Physical education and phys-

ical activity can help with this significant social issue.

Leaders in physical education must continue to promote and provide physical alternatives to involvement with gang activity and violence. After-school recreation and intramural programs offer all students a safe alternative to the streets. In addition, stressing the development of prosocial skills, conflict resolution, self-esteem, and personal defense in physical education will do much to sustain the role of physical education in our school systems— as long as we inform the public of our activities and their benefits. Therefore, it continues to be very important that physical education leaders address advocacy issues as we enter the new millennium.

Chapter Summary

Change begets more change. As physical education leaders, we must constantly be in tune with changes in society, technology, education, and physical education. These changes will and do affect the roles we play in promoting quality physical education programs. Being visionary leaders requires us to keep one eye on the future and the other on day-to-day operations.

Margaret Mead once said, "Never doubt that a small group of thoughtful, committed citizens can change the world; indeed, it's the only thing that ever has." The authors of this book have shared with you their knowledge, skills, and experiences. It is their hope that you will take this information and lead others in the quest for quality physical education into and beyond the twenty-first century.

References

Bruder, I. (1991). Distance learning. *Electronic Learning, 11*(3), 20-28.

Burrus, D., & Gittines, R. (1993). *Technotrends: How to use technology to go beyond your competition.* New York: HarperBusiness.

Caine, G., & Caine, R. N. (1991). *Making connections: Teaching and the human brain.* Alexandria, VA: Association for Supervision and Curriculum Development.

Caine, G., Caine, R. N., & Crowell, S. (1994). *Mindshifts.* Tucson, AZ: Zephyr Press.

Centers for Disease Control and Prevention. (1996). *Physical activity and health: A report of the surgeon general.* Atlanta, GA: Author.

Cornish, E. (1996). *Outlook '97.* Bethesda, MD: World Future Society.

Davis, S., & Botkin, J. (1994). *The monster under the bed.* New York: Simon and Schuster.

Ferguson, K. J., Yesalis, C. E., Pomreh, P. R., & Kirkpatrick, M. B. (1989). Attitudes, knowledge and beliefs as predictors of exercise intent and behavior in school children. *Journal of School Health, 59*, 112-115.

Fiatarone, M. O., O'Neill, E. F., Ryan, N. D., Clements, K. M., Solares, G. R., & Nelson, M. E. (1994). Exercise training and nutritional supplementation for physical frailty in very elderly people. *New England Journal of Medicine, 330*, 1769–1775.

Gathany, N. C., & Stehr-Green, J. K. (1994). Putting life into computer-based training: The creation of an epidemiologic case study. *Educational Technology, 34*(6), 44-47.

Hannaford, C. (1995). *Smart moves: Why learning is not all in your head.* Arlington, VA: Great Ocean Publishers.

Hargadon, T. (1992). Communications medium. *New Media, 2*(11), 29.

Jensen, E. (1994). *The learning brain.* Del Mar, CA: Turning Point for Teachers.

Kotulak, R. (1996). *Inside the brain: Revolutionary discoveries of how the mind works.* Kansas City, KS: Andrews and McMeel.

Mohnsen, B. S. (1997). *Teaching middle school physical education: A blueprint for developing an exemplary program.* Champaign, IL: Human Kinetics.

Naisbitt, J. (1984). *Megatrends: Ten new directions transforming our lives.* New York: Warner Books.

Naisbitt, J., & Aburdene, P. (1985). *Re-inventing the corporation.* New York: Warner Books.

Nelson, M. E., Fisher, E. C., Dilmanian, F. A., Dallal, G. E., & Evans, W. J. (1991). A one-year walking program and increased dietary calcium in postmenopausal women: Effects on bone. *American Journal of Clinical Nutrition, 53*, 1304–1311.

Popcorn, F. (1992). *The Popcorn report on the future of your company, your world, your life.* New York: HarperCollins.

Pritchett, P. (1996). *MindShift: The employee handbook for understanding the changing world of work.* Dallas, TX: Pritchett and Associates, Inc.

Prothrow-Stith, D., & Quaday, S. (1995). *Hidden casualties: The relationship between violence and learning.* Washington, DC: National Consortium for African American Children, Inc. and the National Health and Education Consortium.

Rockman, S., & Lillenthal, K. (1992). *Today's distance learning. Inventing Tomorrow's Schools, 2*(1), 5-6.

Tappe, M. K., Duda, J. L., & Menges-Ehrnwald, P. (1990). Personal investment predictors of adolescent motivation orientation toward exercise. *Canadian Journal of Sport Sciences, 15*, 185-192.

Zakarian, J. M., Hovell, M. F., Hofstetter, C. R., Sallis, J. F., & Keating, K. J. (1994). Correlates of vigorous exercise in a predominantly low SES and minority high school population. *Preventive Medicine, 23*, 314-321.

Mohnsen, B. S. (Ed.). (1998). *Concepts of physical education: What every student needs to know.* Reston, VA: NASPE/AAHPERD.

NASPE/AAHPERD. (1995). *Moving into the future: National physical education standards: A guide to content and assessment.* Reston, VA: Author.

NASPE/AAHPERD. (1995). *National standards for beginning physical education teachers.* Reston, VA: Author.

NASPE/AAHPERD. (1995). *Developmentally appropriate practice in movement programs for young children: Ages 3-5.* Reston, VA: Author.

NASPE/AAHPERD. (1992). *Developmentally appropriate physical education practices for children.* Reston, VA: Author.

NASPE/AAHPERD. (1995). *Appropriate practices for middle school physical education.* Reston, VA: Author.

NASPE/AAHPERD. (1998). *Appropriate practices for high school physical education.* Reston, VA: Author.

NASPE/AAHPERD. (1998). *Physical education program improvement and self study guides: Middle school.* Reston, VA: Author.

NASPE/AAHPERD. (1998). *Physical education program improvement and self study guides: High school.* Reston, VA: Author.

NASPE/AAHPERD. (1994). *Physical education program improvement and appraisal checklist for elementary school.* Reston, VA: Author.

NASPE/AAHPERD. (1995). *Including students with disabilities in regular physical education.* Reston, VA: Author.

NASPE/AAHPERD. (1998). *Shape of the nation.* Reston, VA: Author.

Call 1-800-321-0789 to order.

Editor

Bonnie Mohnsen Dr. Bonnie Mohnsen is the Physical Education and Integrated Technology Coordinator for the Orange County Department of Education. Bonnie was a physical education teacher in the Los Angeles Unified School District for 13 years. She has worked as a physical education consultant for both the Los Angeles County Office of Education and the Montebello Unified School District. Bonnie received her Ph.D. in 1984 from the University of Southern California in Physical Education and Educational Administration with computer programming as her foreign language. Since 1984, Bonnie has presented at over 250 workshops/inservices on topics ranging from Curriculum Development and Instructional Strategies to Technology. Bonnie is one of the contributing authors for the Physical Education Sourcebook, the author of Using Technology in Physical Education, Building a Quality Physical Education Program (Grades 6-12), and Middle School Physical Education, and is the editor of NASPE's Concepts of Physical Education: What Every Student Needs to Know, an important follow up document to the National Standards for Physical Education. Bonnie was a member of the California Physical Education Framework Writing Committee, the California Model Curriculum Standards Vignette Writing Committee and the California Program Quality Review Writing Committee for Physical Education. Most recently, Bonnie was named the 1997 California, Southwest District, and National Physical Education Administrator of the Year.

Authors

Jayne D. Greenberg Dr. Jayne Greenberg is the Physical Education Supervisor for Miami-Dade County Public Schools, Miami, Florida and an adjunct Professor in the Sports Administration Department at St. Thomas University. Over the past several years, Dr. Greenberg has secured over $570,000 in awarded grants and approximately $100,000 in Corporate Sponsorship. In addition, Dr. Greenberg has been a national consultant, assisting school systems in setting up FIT-TECH; an international consultant, coordinating Olympic education programs in Canada and developing the Sport Science program in Malaysia; has published numerous articles; and has been a speaker at several state and national conferences.

Bobbie Harris Bobbie Harris is the Project Director of Physical Dimensions, the Kansas High School Physical Activity and Health/Wellness Curriculum. She was the Physical Education Coordinator, PreK-12, for the Wichita Public Schools after working as a high school physical education teacher and coach for 20 years. Bobbie earned a Master of Education in Physical Education degree, and an Administrative Certificate.

Bobbie has participated in the Kansas Association for Health,

Physical Education, Recreation and Dance (KAHPERD) in the positions of Secondary Chair, High School Chair, Middle School Chair, Convention Chair, convention speaker and Journal contributor. In 1986, she received the Kansas NASPE Outstanding Secondary Teacher of the Year, in 1987, the 6-A Kansas Girls Tennis Coach of the Year, and in 1996, she received the American Alliance of Health, Physical Education, Recreation and Dance (AAHPERD) Council of School Leadership in Physical Education (CSLPE) Honor Award for her work in curriculum writing and assessment development. Bobbie and other Wichita teachers have had many opportunities to travel around the country and share the Wichita Curriculum and Assessment Project. She has helped create the Wichita Youth Alliance which serves the youth of Wichita and has been recognized as one of the three programs that helped Wichita become a finalist for the All American City Award.

Dorri Hawkes Dorri Hawkes is a highly acclaimed teacher, presenter, curriculum writer and facilitator of adult learning. Dorri has the experience of working both as a classroom teacher grades K-12 and a Physical Education teacher, grades K-12. She served as a mentor teacher for five years, chaired curriculum writing committees for health and physical education, organized a myriad of school and district wide events, and inserviced staff throughout the district on numerous teaching/learning strategies. Ms Hawkes has a Bachelor of Education Degree from Calgary, Canada, and a Masters Degree in Education Administration. She is a Senior Associate of the California Academy of Physical Education, a trainer for The California School Leadership Academy, a former coach for the Physical Education Middle School Demonstration Program, and an accomplished workshop facilitator sought throughout California. Dorri's depth of knowledge and skill as a teacher, and a lifelong learner as well as her passionate advocacy for children reflect the optimum qualities of a powerful change agent.

Betty F. Hennessy Betty Hennessy, Ph.D., has worked as a physical education consultant in the Los Angeles County Office of Education since 1979. As a specialist in the Division of Curriculum, Instruction and Assessment Services, Betty provides leadership resources and professional development to 104 school districts. From 1986 to 1988, she also served as a visiting physical education consultant to the California State Department of Education. Prior to her consulting work, Dr. Hennessy spent seven years as a physical education teacher. She continues to teach selected courses at universities in the Los Angeles region. In addition to her committee work on assorted state and county documents, Betty is the co-author of the Essentials of Physical Education textbook series and is the editor of the Physical Education Sourcebook. Betty has been a chair of the National Council on Physical Education for Children and is the chair-elect of the National Council for School Leaders in Physical Education. Betty has been recognized by state and national physical education administrator councils and is the recipient of the Honor Award presented by the California Association for Health, Physical Education, Recreation, and Dance (AHPERD) and the Honor Fellow Award presented by the American Alliance for Health, Physical Education, Recreation, and Dance (AAHPERD).

Karen Mendon   Karen Mendon has been employed as a physical educator in the Montebello Unified School District, at the intermediate level, for the past 24 years. During this time, she has been active in leadership roles at her school and at the district level. She has been involved in school leadership by being a member on various school committees and coordinating a physical education grant. She has been involved in service to the district by being a mentor teacher, co-facilitating a physical education curriculum committee, and volunteering for several health committees. Her academic background is extensive and on going with a BA in Physical Education and an MA in Curriculum and Instruction.

Rita Mercier   Rita Mercier is a knowledgeable, dynamic educator, author, and workshop facilitator who has inspired thousands of teachers throughout California and the nation to reevaluate traditional student and adult learning strategies. Rita taught physical education for twelve years, five years as a mentor. She has taught K-12, served as a Magnet School Resource Teacher, President of the San Diego chapter of the California Association for Health, Physical Education, Recreation, and Dance (CAHPERD) and was actively involved in change at the district level. After receiving a Masters Degree in Educational Administration, Ms. Mercier served as the Physical Education/School Safety Coordinator for Riverside and San Bernardino Counties for five years. As a Coordinator, Rita co-authored the California School Leadership Academy Module Physical Education for Lifelong Well Being and was the co-chair of The California Academy for Physical Education, a pilot for the Physical Education and Health Subject Matter Project. Rita is currently a private consultant working with California schools and districts to maximize change efforts designed to ensure success for all students.

Spencer Sartorius   Currently Spencer Sartorius serves in two capacities for the Montana Office of Public Instruction: first, he is the State Supervisor for Health and Physical Education and second, is the Administrator of the Health Enhancement and Safety Division which encompasses more than fifteen separate programs. Spencer has served as President

of the Montana Association for Health, Physical Education, Recreation, and Dance (AHPERD) as well as President of the Society of State Directors of Health, Physical Education and Recreation (SSDHPER). He has received the Honor Award from both associations as well as the Honor Award from the Council of School Administrators of Health and Physical Education, the Director's Award from the Division of Adolescent and School Health, Centers for Disease Control and Prevention, and the 1988 Award of Excellence from Montana State University, Billings.

Carolyn Thompson   Carolyn Thompson has been teaching secondary physical education for 29 years. She received a Bachelor of Arts Degree from California State University, Chico in 1968. Her teaching career began in Northern California where she taught physical education and coached for thirteen years. In 1983, Carolyn transferred to Bell Gardens High School in the Montebello Unified School District. In 1986, she was named Acting Coordinator for Physical Education and Recreation for the Montebello Unified School District. In 1990, she was on special assignment to develop a health curriculum. She is currently teaching physical education in the Health Careers Pathway.

As an active member at the local, district, state and national levels of the American Alliance for Health, Physical Education, Recreation, and Dance (AAHPERD), Carolyn was the 1993 California AHPERD Outstanding Secondary School Physical Educator of the Year and 1994 Southwest District AAHPERD Secondary School Physical Education Teacher of the Year. This honor moved her forward to the national level where she was selected as 1994 National Secondary School Physical Education Teacher of the Year (a National Association for Sport and Physical Education award). She has traveled throughout the United States promoting quality physical education.

Kathy Ermler   Dr. Kathy Ermler is an associate professor in the Division of Health, Physical Education, and Recreation at Emporia State University. She is the lead author of the Physical dimensions curriculum and a member of the original planning team for the project. Dr. Ermler is one of the founders and directors for the TAKE AIM! Summer Physical Education Conference offered each summer at Emporia State University. She is a well-known presenter and has published numerous professional articles and books. She is the editor of the Kansas Association for Health, Physical Education, Recreation, and Dance (AHPERD) Journal.

WITHDRAWN

GOSHEN COLLEGE - GOOD LIBRARY

3 9310 01014010 9

DATE DUE

GAYLORD			PRINTED IN U.S.A.